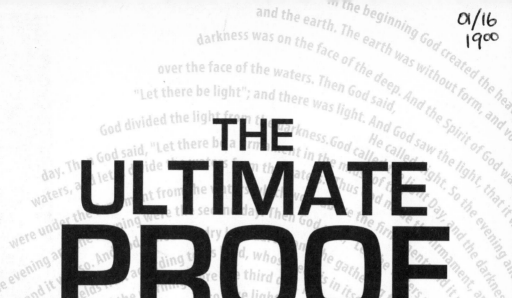

THE ULTIMATE PROOF OF CREATION

resolving the origins debate

Master Books®

First printing: May 2009
Sixth printing: May 2015

ISBN-13: 978-0-89051-568-6
Library of Congress Number: 2009926372

Illustrations are by Dan Lietha
Cover Design by Diana Bogardus

Unless otherwise indicated, Scripture quotations are from the New International Version of the Holy Bible.

Please consider requesting that a copy of this volume be purchased by your local library system.

Printed in the United States of America

Please visit our website for other great titles:
www.masterbooks.com

For information regarding author interviews,
please contact the publicity department at (870) 438-5288.

Master
Books®
A Division of New Leaf Publishing Group
www.masterbooks.com

Withdrawn from Collection

ACKNOWLEDGMENTS

This book would not have been possible without the faithful support and continued friendship of my family, my colleagues at Answers in Genesis, and many others. In particular, I would like to thank Ken Ham, Pastor Jay Lucas, and Dr. Kenneth Gentry for reviewing early drafts of this book and for making many helpful suggestions. I also extend a special thanks to my good friend Dan Lietha for many helpful discussions and for taking the time to illustrate this book.

I particularly wish to acknowledge the late Dr. Greg Bahnsen, whose writings and lectures were the inspiration for this book. Dr. Bahnsen was a brilliant scholar and a faithful Christian. His intelligence went hand in hand with his humility, and his love for the Lord showed in all aspects of his life. Greg was a gifted communicator. His analogies were insightful and very memorable, and I have used a number of them in this book. I regret that I never met Dr. Bahnsen in person. But I pray that this book honors his memory.

Contents

FOREWORD

But sanctify the Lord God in your hearts: and be ready always to give an *answer* to every man that asketh you a reason of the hope that is in you with meekness and fear (1 Pet. 3:15; KJV, emphasis added).

The word "answer" in this passage comes from the Greek word *apologia*. It has nothing to do with apologizing, however. On the contrary, it means:

1. a verbal defense, a speech in defense

2. a reasoned statement or argument

Essentially, 1 Peter 3:15 instructs Christians to always be ready to give a logical, reasoned defense of their faith — to give an answer back.

We live in what is often termed a "scientific age." It is also an era of skepticism in regard to the Bible's claim to be the inerrant Word of God. In particular, the Bible's accounts of creation, the Fall, Noah's Flood, and the Tower of Babel in Genesis chapters 1–11 are widely mocked, for they have been supposedly disproven by "science."

During my more than 30 years' experience in the apologetics ministry now called Answers in Genesis, I can make the following observations:

1. Most Christians cannot give an adequate defense of their faith. Whereas they may know what they believe in regard to the major biblical doctrines, most do not know how to logically deal with a skeptic of the Bible's accuracy. In fact, I have found the majority of Christians have been drawn into a false notion of "neutrality" in such a way that they believe that it's best not to use the Bible in their dealings with skeptics. They are not realizing, however, that in doing so, they have given up ground to their opponent, essentially losing the debate right there and before they even begin their attempted defense of the Christian faith. Most Christians just do not understand the basic, powerful, logical arguments — taken from the Bible itself — that need to be used when dialoguing with a non-Christian (especially at the start of such a dialogue).

   Sadly, the majority of Christians usually end up being put on the defensive by a biblical skeptic. Instead of going on the offensive (which they should be doing when they understand and apply basic, logical reasoning), they are put on the defensive — and the skeptic remains on the offensive.

2. I have noticed that most non-Christians use illogical and fallacious arguments when they dialogue with Christians. These arguments can easily be dealt with if the Christian has learned some basic and easy-to-understand logical arguments that can powerfully defend the Christian faith — ultimately leaving one's opponents with nowhere to go. Most non-Christians have never been confronted with these arguments that Dr. Lisle will present in this book, which can reveal that their position is totally bankrupt!

This much-needed and masterfully done book by Dr. Lisle (PhD researcher with Answers in Genesis) is the result of his intensive and diligent study of the works of some of the greatest apologists of our modern age. Dr. Lisle brilliantly uses what most people might think are technical arguments (that only experts in logic and philosophy might use) and then teaches step by step how the average Christian can become a masterful debater against even the most vehement skeptic — not only hold their ground, but also leave their opponent without excuse concerning the truth of the Bible and the Christian faith.

If every Christian learned and applied the easy-to-understand arguments presented in this book, I believe it wouldn't be long before Christians would be actively seeking out non-Christians to engage in conversation!

Yes, Christians can give a powerful defense of their precious faith and logically defend it. Christians who become equipped can unashamedly be bold (yet polite) in standing on biblical authority, giving a reasoned logical defense of their faith and proclaiming the gospel of Jesus Christ in this increasingly skeptical and anti-Christian world.

You will never think the same way again after reading this masterful book — and you will never dialogue with non-believers in the same way. You will gain a confidence in your faith that you probably have never experienced, and you will become much more emboldened in your Christian faith.

Ken Ham
President/CEO
Answers in Genesis

INTRODUCTION

It's a bold title: *The Ultimate Proof of Creation*. But is there such a thing? There are many books that contain seemingly powerful arguments for biblical creation. And yet not everyone is convinced by such arguments. Evolutionists have their responses to such arguments, just as creationists have their responses to evolutionary arguments. But is there an argument that is so powerful that no refutation is possible? Is there an *ultimate proof* of creation?

If by "ultimate proof" we mean an argument that will *persuade* everyone, then the answer has to be no. The reason is simple: persuasion is subjective. Sometimes people are not persuaded even by a very good argument. Conversely, people are (unfortunately) often persuaded by very bad arguments. Generally speaking, most people are simply not very rational; they are not good, clear thinkers. Of course, this does not mean that people are unintelligent. But most of us are not as rigorously objective as we would like to think. We often believe things for psychological reasons, rather than logical reasons. Many people refuse to accept a very good argument simply because they do not want to believe its conclusion. For these

11

reasons and others, it is impossible to construct an argument that will always persuade everyone.

However, if by an "ultimate proof" we mean an argument that is *conclusive* — one for which no rational refutation is possible — then I am convinced the answer is yes. There is an ultimate proof of creation. There is an argument that demonstrates that the Christian worldview must be true, and thus biblical creation must be true as well since it is foundational to the Christian worldview. There is indeed an argument for creation that is powerful, conclusive, and has no true rebuttal. As such, it is an irrefutable argument — an "ultimate proof" of the Christian worldview.

The proof itself can be stated in a single sentence. Of course, it cannot be explained or fully defended in a single sentence. It can even be stated in many different ways. It can be used to show the truth of biblical creation, the Bible in general, the existence of God, or any foundational aspect of Christianity. However, to understand the argument fully and to anticipate possible comebacks, we need to lay a little groundwork. We must understand the nature of scientific evidence and how it is interpreted. We also must discuss the nature of a worldview, and the relationship between a person's worldview and evidence. We will cover these topics in the next two chapters. Without these concepts, the ultimate proof will not really be very useful. So please read the next chapters very carefully.

The rest of the book will discuss how to apply the ultimate proof in dialogues with evolutionists, and will cover other important concepts as well. These include spotting logical fallacies, using scientific and historic evidence appropriately, biblical examples of defending the faith, and some philosophical concepts as well. This book is intended to give an irrefutable proof of the Christian worldview — emphasizing the defense of the Genesis account of creation.

The Bible teaches that Christians must always be ready to give an answer — a defense of the faith (1 Pet. 3:15). This command is not just for academics — great theologians and scientists. It is for everyone. God expects the average Christian to be able to articulate a logically cogent reason for his or her faith. Sadly, very few Christians can do this well. But the good news is this: if you understand the ultimate proof of creation, you will be able to give an irrefutable defense of the Christian faith. You won't have to know everything about everything. Master the method outlined in the following chapters, and you will be able to defend Christianity against all opposition. If you are a Christian wanting to better defend the faith (and biblical creation in particular), then this book is for you.

However, some reading this book may be skeptical of the Christian position and biblical creation in particular. Perhaps you are wondering if Christianity is rationally defensible. Maybe you believe that evolution has been established beyond doubt and are wondering how anyone could question it. If you are open-minded enough to honestly consider the alternative, you will find one here. Although it may not be the type of argument you've heard before, it is nonetheless a conclusive one. If you are looking for a powerful, irrefutable argument for biblical creation or the Christian worldview in general — whether a Christian or a critic — this book is for you.

The content is intended to be broad-ranging. No previous knowledge of creation or science is required. However, I expect that even experts in creation science and apologetics will benefit from the concepts and techniques introduced within. I have intentionally avoided using excessive technical jargon so that the book can be understood by almost everyone. Of course, some jargon is unavoidable. But when a technical term is essential, it is introduced and clearly explained. Moreover, you will find that the most important concepts are repeated in several chapters and explained in several slightly different ways. This is not an oversight, but a feature that will hopefully aid in retention of the most crucial information.

I expect that people unfamiliar with books on defending the Christian faith may find portions of this book somewhat challenging. Please do not be discouraged by this. Certain concepts will take time to absorb. It's not that the concepts are difficult — I've been able to teach these ideas to teenagers, and even young children. It's just that most people are not used to thinking this way. Most people have not given much thought to some of the most basic, yet important, topics of our existence. So these ideas will be carefully explored and explained in several different ways. Some people learn better by example; they may not fully appreciate an argument until they see it in action. For this reason, there are two appendices that give real-world examples of how to use the ultimate proof of creation.

I have been studying the origins issue for many years now and have given presentations on Genesis at many churches and universities. I have found that the techniques introduced in this book are much more powerful than the arguments that most Christians use. If you can master the ultimate proof, you will not have to read a lot of other books on apologetics, or memorize a lot of scientific information. (Of course, it never hurts to do either of these as well.) Defending the Christian faith is not difficult once we learn how to do it properly. Most of it comes down to good, clear, logical thinking.

Before we delve into the details, a few terms need to be defined in order to prevent misconceptions. In this book, the word "evolution" will be used to indicate the natural method by which life allegedly came about and diversified into all the organisms we see today. According to the idea of evolution, all life forms are related by biological common descent, having evolved over billions of years from an initial single-celled organism, which itself was formed from lifeless chemicals. I realize that the word "evolution" can (in certain contexts) simply mean "change" in a general sense. But since both creationists and evolutionists believe that things change (there is no debate here), only the more specific definition pertaining to origins is of interest in this book.

By "creation," we mean the description of the origin of the universe and life on earth as described in the Book of Genesis and as reinforced and clarified in the other Scriptures. The Bible teaches that God created the universe in six (ordinary) days and that He did so several thousand years ago.[1] God created the initial animals "after their kinds" and made them to be able to reproduce. Animals today are not identical to those God initially created but are still of the same basic kinds. I am well aware that there are other creation stories in existence. However, I have not found any of the non-biblical descriptions of origins (including the big bang, progressive creation, framework hypothesis, or "day-age" creation) to be rationally defensible. Therefore, I can in good conscience only defend the biblical account.

By "unbeliever," I refer to anyone who does not believe what the Bible states — either in whole or in part. So I am including people who believe portions of the Bible, but reject other portions (such as Genesis). I do not claim that those who reject Genesis have necessarily rejected the gospel (which is what is often meant by "unbeliever" in other contexts). Though this book specializes in defending biblical creation, we will find that the techniques can be used to refute absolutely any unbiblical position.

Outline of the Book

We will begin by discussing the nature of evidence. Several common scientific evidences for creation are given in chapter 1. These are good evidences and may be very useful in a debate on origins — if used properly. But they are not the *ultimate proof* of creation. However, it is necessary to understand the kinds of arguments often used in origins debates in order to understand how the ultimate proof is different. In chapter 2 we will explore the concept of a *worldview* and will compare the creation and evolution worldviews. We will discuss the criteria necessary to rationally resolve the origins debate and will find that there is a solution: the ultimate proof.

In chapter 3 we will give three detailed examples of the ultimate proof of creation. In a way, chapter 3 is the "heart" of the book. It will show in detail why the biblical account of creation *must* be true. In chapter 4 we will discuss how to use the ultimate proof of creation in dialogues with an evolutionist. The chapter is not about "tricks," but rather how to answer an opponent in a way that is rational and effective. Several hypothetical examples are provided. In chapter 5 we will develop a general procedure for defending biblical creation and the Christian faith in general. This chapter provides a mental flow chart to aid in dealing with the relevant issues of the debate.

In chapter 6 we will discuss how to correctly use scientific evidence in the origins debate. Scientific evidence can be very effective if it is used properly. Unfortunately, many people use science in an ineffective and fallacious way. When used properly, scientific evidence can expose devastating weaknesses in secular models of origins.

Chapter 7 begins our discussion of logic and logical fallacies, starting with informal fallacies. Logic is a very powerful tool that can help us draw correct conclusions. But it is often misunderstood and misused — especially when people try to defend evolution. Chapter 8 continues with a more in-depth discussion of logic, and formal deductive logic specifically. Chapters 7 and 8 cover not only the basics of spotting logical fallacies, but also provide examples of logical fallacies that are commonly committed by evolutionists. Christians who have been defending creation for some time will recognize many of the examples in these chapters, but may not have previously realized why they are fallacious.

In chapter 9 we will deal with some additional topics that often come up when defending biblical creation. These topics include a discussion of the necessity of an infallible standard, the nature of circular reasoning, the nature of faith, and others. These topics will require an understanding of the material covered in the previous chapters. Chapter 10 deals with biblical issues: what does the Bible have to say about defending the faith? And how did people in the Bible defend the faith? In appendix A we apply the techniques developed in this book to non-natural readings of Genesis, such as "day-age" creationism and theistic evolution. These "compromised" positions will also be found to be rationally defective.

One rather unique aspect of this book is that we get a chance to go beyond mere theory, and we apply the ultimate proof of creation to real-world examples. In appendices B and C, we list a number of actual letters that have been written by critics of biblical creation. We will analyze and respond to these letters using the ultimate proof of creation and the methods developed in this book. Appendix B is the more basic of these two sections and uses primarily the techniques developed in chapters 1 through 5. Appendix C makes use of the additional techniques (such as spotting logical fallacies) covered in the later chapters. These appendices give the reader a chance to learn by example — and to practice defending biblical creation using the procedure developed in this book.

The most important things to know about defending biblical creation are contained in the first five chapters of this book. Chapters 6 through 10 are a bit more advanced than the others, only in the sense that they build on the information covered in the first five chapters. In fact, by design, each chapter in this book builds on the information in the previous chapters. So it is advisable to read the chapters in order if this is your first time reading this book.

Most debates on origins do not deal with the real issue. They are often more autobiographical in nature, with each person explaining why his position seems best to him. The opponents often talk past each other, each interpreting the facts according to his chosen standard. It is time to get to the real heart of the issue and rationally resolve the origins debate. It is time to provide the *ultimate proof of creation*.

Endnotes

1. The exact date of creation is not the topic of this book, and therefore specific chronologies (such as that of Bishop Ussher) will not be defended here. The point is that a natural reading of Genesis indicates that the world is thousands of years old — not millions or billions, and that the first organisms were supernaturally created.

CHAPTER 1

THE NATURE OF EVIDENCE

For this origins debate, I will be using DNA, fossils, and rock layers to support my position," said the evolutionist.

"That's odd," said the creationist. "That's exactly what I was going to use to support my position!"

What is the place of scientific evidence in the debate over origins? Do things like DNA, fossils, and rock layers really support evolution? Do they support creation? Many people (whether creationist or evolutionist) might say that unbiased investigation of scientific evidence is the absolute standard by which the origins debate can be settled. However, such a view does not stand up to careful scrutiny for reasons that we will address in this chapter. Some people take the opposite position; they believe that scientific evidence is utterly irrelevant to the origins debate, the issue being more a matter of faith than reason. However, this too is overly simplistic and will not stand up to rational investigation.

Scientific evidence is very useful when it comes to discussions about the origin of life, the universe, the age of the earth, and so on. Indeed, there are many lines of evidence that confirm that God did create the universe supernaturally several thousand years ago, just as the Bible teaches in Genesis. In fact, the scientific evidence is so compelling that many creationists simply cannot understand how anyone could possibly believe in evolution. Yet, evolutionists who are aware of such evidence remain unconvinced. Apparently, scientific evidence by itself does not conclusively settle the matter. Nonetheless, it is important to be aware of a few of the leading scientific arguments for biblical creation. So, let's begin with some great (but not *ultimate*) lines of evidence that confirm Genesis.[1]

Information Theory

One of the most compelling, commonly used scientific arguments for creation involves the field of information theory. In this technological age, we are inundated with all sorts of information every day, but few people stop to consider what information really is, and where it comes from. Scientifically, we can define information as a coded message containing an expected action and intended purpose. Under this definition, the words of this book qualify as information. They are encoded — the words represent ideas. The expected action is that the reader will read and act upon the words, and the intended purpose is that the reader will become persuaded and better able to defend the Christian faith.[2]

DNA also contains information. DNA (deoxyribonucleic acid) is a long molecule found within living cells and resembles a twisted ladder. The rungs of the ladder form a pattern of base pair triplets that represent amino acid sequences — the building blocks of proteins. DNA contains the "instructions" to build the organism. So different organisms have different DNA patterns. DNA qualifies under the definition of information: it contains an encoded message (the base pair triplets represent amino acids) and has an expected action (the formation of proteins) and an intended purpose (life).

DNA

Whenever we find any sort of information, certain rules or "theorems" apply. Here are two such theorems:

1. There is no known law of nature, no known process, and no known sequence of events that can cause information to originate by itself in matter.[3]

2. When its progress along the chain of transmission events is traced backward, every piece of information leads to a mental source, the mind of the sender.[4]

The first tells us that matter does not spontaneously generate information. The second tells us that only a mental source (a mind) can generate new creative information. In one sense, these theorems are hardly profound; we take for granted that when we read a book it has an author. No one reading this book would conclude that it was generated by a sequence of typos that gradually accumulated over time. Now certainly this book might be a copy of a copy of a copy, but you take it for granted that a mind is ultimately responsible for the information therein (regardless of whether you agree with the information!). The theorems of information science confirm this.

Likewise, these theorems tell us that life cannot have come about as the evolutionists claim. The information in DNA cannot have come about by mutations and natural selection because the laws of information theory tell us that all information comes from a mind. But the information in DNA makes sense in light of biblical creation. It was by the mind of God that the initial information was placed in the DNA of the original organisms on earth. That information has been copied many times, and some of it has been lost. But the information in our DNA ultimately comes from the mind of God, not by a random chance process. The laws of information theory confirm creation.

Sometimes evolutionists will object to this and will point out that mutations occasionally have survival value; they can help the organism survive under certain circumstances. This is true, but it is not relevant to the argument. Mutations have never been observed to add brand-new information, and thus they cannot be the driving mechanism of evolution. Sometimes mutations will cause a section of DNA to get duplicated, but does this really increase the information?

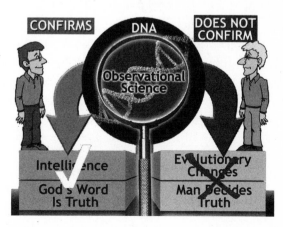

Not at all. By analogy, a copying error in a book may cause a paragraph to get duplicated. But surely it adds no new information. After all, could you learn anything from the duplicated paragraph that you couldn't learn from the original? Creative information cannot spontaneously increase by chance. It is always the result of intelligence. The theorems of information theory tell us this, and our experiences confirm it.

Irreducible Complexity

Another argument that is often waged against evolution concerns the incredible complexity found in living things. Darwin could not possibly have anticipated the astonishing intricacy of even the "simplest" single-celled organism. Every living cell of every organism contains a host of complex biochemical machines, each cooperating with the others to enable the survival of the entire cell. The parts of the cell are interdependent; if any one of them malfunctions, it can lead to the death of the entire cell. In multi-cellular organisms, the cells themselves are specialized, each performing a different task to contribute to the survival of the whole organism. A heart, blood, and blood vessels all work together — without one the others could not survive.

Interdependent parts challenge the idea of particles-to-people evolution. Evolution is supposed to happen in a gradual, stepwise fashion. One by one, mutations are supposed to gradually change one kind of organism into another. So we must ask the question: which evolved first — hearts, blood, or blood vessels? Each is useless without the other two. A stepwise evolutionary process for any interdependent system would seem to be impossible at the outset.

Even within a single living cell, how could the various parts have come about in a gradual fashion? Each part cannot survive without the others. Such a system is said to be "irreducibly complex" because its complexity cannot be reduced without destroying functionality. Any irreducibly complex system cannot have come about by an evolutionary process, since every piece requires all the other pieces at the same time.

Many machines made by human beings are also irreducibly complex. A car does not work unless all of its essential parts are functioning. Since many of the parts of a car are irreducibly complex, it would be logical to conclude that a car is not made by an evolutionary process. It is skillfully planned and made by people who have designed every part to function with all the others. Likewise, living beings have been designed by a Master Planner who has skillfully prepared every part to function together with all the other parts.

Age Indicators

One additional point of conflict between creationists and evolutionists concerns the time scale of origins. Did life take billions of years to come about, or was it created in a short amount of time in the recent past? Many lines of evidence challenge the secular claim that the earth is billions of years old. Many could be listed, and in fact have been listed, on the Answers in Genesis website and in other resources.[5] Here we will examine just a couple to get the flavor.

Many people have heard of carbon dating. However, most laymen are under the mistaken impression that carbon dating is used to show that the earth is millions or billions of years old. This is not the case. Carbon dating always gives ages much less than this, even on things that are allegedly millions or billions of years old. The reason is that the C-14 isotope is short-lived. Here's how it works.

Most carbon is a stable variety called C-12, but a small fraction of carbon is C-14, which is unstable. Unstable means that C-14 is constantly *decaying* — it is continually and spontaneously changing into nitrogen. This happens slowly, one atom at a time. The rate is such that in 5,736 years, half of the C-14 will have decayed into nitrogen. After another 5,736 years, half of the remaining amount will have decayed, leaving only one-fourth of the original, and so on. So by making certain assumptions about the initial amount of C-14 and then measuring the amount of C-14 that remains in an ancient sample, scientists are able to make an estimate of the age.

Since C-14 decays fairly rapidly (at least compared to the secular alleged age of the earth), it would decay to an undetectable amount after 100,000 years. In fact, if the entire mass of the earth were C-14, after one million years not even one atom would be left! So it may come as a shock for those who believe in an old earth to learn that C-14 has been found in allegedly very ancient substances, such as coal and diamonds — coal supposedly formed millions of years ago, in the evolutionary view. And the diamonds in which C-14 has been found are supposed to be over a billion years old in the secular view! The presence of detectable C-14 indicates that the true age of these things is only a few thousand years. Carbon dating certainly challenges the billions-of-years view.

ICR scientists and others have even detected C-14 in dinosaur fossils.[6] In fact, C-14 is found in virtually everything that has carbon in it, even deep down in rock layers that evolutionists believe to be hundreds of millions of years old. Yet, if those rock layers really were so old, they should not have even one atom of C-14 in them. These results are perfectly consistent with biblical creation. According to Genesis, the entire earth is not much more than several thousand years old, so it's hardly surprising to find C-14 in just about everything. This is exactly what the creationist would expect. But carbon-14 is a serious challenge to the evolutionary system with its billions of years.

Such evidences for youth can even be found in outer space. Comets are certainly consistent with the relative youth of the solar system but they pose a problem for the secular view. Comets are made of ice and dirt, and are part of our solar system. They orbit in elliptical paths that occasionally bring them close to the sun. When a comet passes close to the sun, solar radiation heats the comet, causing its icy material to vaporize and disperse into space. This lost material is swept back by solar radiation and solar wind; this is what forms the comet's tail.

Since comets are constantly losing material, they cannot exist forever. It has been estimated that a typical comet can last for a maximum of about 100,000 years before completely running out of material. This is not a problem for the biblical time scale, but it certainly runs against secular thinking. If the solar system were really billions of years old, as evolutionists believe, then why do we still have comets?

Evidence and Rescuing Devices

The scientific evidence certainly confirms biblical creation and appears to defy evolution. Many other examples, too numerous to list, could also have been cited. It may seem that evolution stands refuted. It may seem that we have proved beyond doubt that scientific evidence proves biblical creation and disproves the notion of evolution. But this is not the case.

The above illustrations are very convincing to creationists. But they are not an *ultimate* proof. They do not actually prove biblical creation, nor do they utterly refute evolution or billions of years. The reason is that an evolutionist can always invoke what we might call a "rescuing device." That is, an evolutionist can invent a story to explain away apparently contrary evidence. Let's see how this works in the case of comets as evidence of the solar system's youth.

The secular astronomer believes that the solar system is billions of years old, yet he sees comets within it that supposedly formed billions of years ago. He can observe that comets disintegrate quite rapidly, and he computes that they can only last 100,000 years or so. How is he to resolve this dilemma? "Obviously," says the secular astronomer, "there must be a source that generates new comets to replace the old ones as they disintegrate." So secular astronomers have proposed that there is an "Oort cloud" (named after its inventor, Jan Oort). The Oort cloud is an enormous hypothetical sphere of icy masses surrounding our solar system. It is supposedly far beyond the most distant planets, beyond the range of our most powerful telescopes. Secular astronomers propose that occasionally, objects in the Oort cloud are dislodged from their distant orbit and thrown into the inner solar system to become brand-new comets. Since these new comets continually replace the old ones, the solar system could be billions of years old after all.

> *Rescuing device: a conjecture designed to save a person's view from apparently contrary evidence*

Now keep in mind that no one has ever seen this hypothetical Oort cloud. By construction, it is supposedly much too far away to detect the small objects within it. Currently, there is no observational evidence of any kind for its existence. So, as a creationist, I have no particular reason to think that there is such a thing. As far as I'm concerned, the Oort cloud exists only in the mind of secularists. It's just a rescuing device that "saves" the secularist's view from evidence that would otherwise seem to refute it.

Likewise, the evolutionist could also explain away each of the other arguments above by appealing to a rescuing device. Perhaps there is some kind of unknown mechanism that has contaminated the diamonds and other samples, creating new C-14 in them — in which case such things can be very old after all. Perhaps there is some as-yet-undiscovered mechanism that produces new information in DNA. Perhaps nothing is truly irreducibly complex; it just seems that way due to our inability to imagine the stepwise process. The reason that scientific evidence doesn't ultimately *prove* anything regarding origins is because people can always invoke the *unknown. Any evidence* can be explained away by invoking a rescuing device.

Is a rescuing device unacceptable? Should we criticize the evolutionary astronomers for inventing a mere conjecture to rescue their opinion of vast ages rather than simply accepting the evidence at face value? My response may surprise you. The answer is: no — a rescuing device is not *necessarily* unreasonable. The fact is, we all have rescuing devices. We all have a way of thinking about the world — a worldview. Our worldview contains our most strongly held convictions about how the world works: how it came to be, the nature of reality, the nature of truth, and how we should live. No matter what worldview we have, there will always be some evidence that does not seem to fit it — at least on the surface. And therefore, everyone (whether creationist or evolutionist) must occasionally invoke a rescuing device in order to maintain rationality in his or her worldview.

So I would not necessarily criticize the secular astronomers for inventing an Oort cloud, even though I interpret the data differently. After all, I don't know for certain that there is *not* an Oort cloud either. The fact that we have no evidence for an Oort cloud does not prove that it does not exist. Absence of evidence is not the same as evidence of absence, so we cannot instantly dismiss evolutionary conjectures as necessarily impossible or irrational.

Nonetheless, a conjecture must not be *arbitrary*. If I simply asserted that "the core of Jupiter is made of green cheese" simply because no one has proven otherwise, this would be an unacceptable position. In logical reasoning, no one is allowed to be arbitrary — to just assume something without a good reason. After all, if we're just going to assume something with no reason, then we could equally well assume the exact opposite. Rational debate would be impossible if people simply assumed whatever they wanted and felt no need to provide a reason for their position. Therefore, people must have a reason for their rescuing device if it is to be considered rational.

As an example, consider the "distant starlight problem." This is the argument that the universe must be billions of years old since it apparently takes a very long time for light from the most distant galaxies to reach earth. How would a creationist respond to this claim? Currently, there is no consensus among creation astronomers as to what the solution is. Therefore, creationists must invoke a rescuing device to explain distant starlight. Several good models have been proposed that can potentially solve this difficulty. But since none of them have been conclusively proved, they remain unproven — rescuing devices — at this point in time.

Is this arbitrary? No, the creationist has a good *reason* to believe that there is an answer to distant starlight. First, the creationist has good reasons to believe that the Bible really is what it claims to be: the Word of God. As such, the Bible accurately describes the creation of the universe — that God really did create in six days. Therefore, the Christian has a good reason to think that there really is a rational solution to distant starlight (possibly one of the existing models, or perhaps one that is as yet undiscovered). My reason for my rescuing device is that my worldview insists on one, and I have good reasons to know that my worldview is true.

So a rational person will appeal to his worldview as the *reason* for his rescuing devices. But then, of course, he must have good reasons for his worldview. Evolutionists (and other believers in vast ages) are perfectly justified in believing in an Oort cloud if, and only if, they appeal to their worldview. But appealing to one's worldview is only rational if one's worldview is rational. *The debate over origins therefore must ultimately boil down to a debate over competing worldviews.* As such, we must give some thought to the nature of worldviews and how to judge competing ones.

Worldviews

Most people today have not given much thought to their own worldview. In fact, many people do not even realize they have a worldview. Many people tend to think that all knowledge is acquired by unbiased observation of the evidence around us. This view is called "empiricism" and is itself a kind of worldview. We cannot help but have some beliefs about how the world works, how we attain knowledge, and how we should live. Even if we believe that we have no such beliefs — this is itself a belief. So there's no escaping it. A worldview is inevitable. A rational worldview is not.

Our worldview is a bit like mental glasses. It affects the way we view things. In the same way that a person wearing red glasses sees red everywhere, a person wearing "evolution" glasses sees evolution everywhere. The world is not really red everywhere, nor is there genuine evidence for evolution, but glasses do affect our perception of the world and the conclusions we draw. We

> *Worldview: a network of our most basic beliefs about reality in light of which all observations are interpreted*

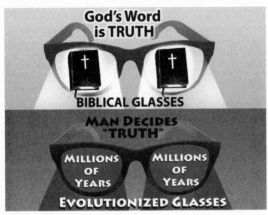

Our worldview controls the way we view the evidence.

will find in this book that the Bible is a bit like corrective lenses. Without "biblical glasses," the world appears fuzzy and unclear. But when our thinking is based on the Bible, the world snaps into focus: it makes sense.

Just as a person wearing red glasses perceives the world differently than a person wearing clear, prescription lenses, so evolutionists "see" the world differently than creationists. We have the same facts. But what we make of those facts is colored by our worldview. Thus, creationists and evolutionists interpret the same facts differently. This point cannot be overstated. Much of the frustration in arguments over origins stems from a failure to recognize that creationists and evolutionists *must* interpret the same data differently due to their different worldviews.

Many people do not want to accept that all evidence must be interpreted in light of prior beliefs — a faith commitment of some kind. Many believe that evidence should be approached in a neutral and unbiased fashion — without any previous beliefs. However, this is impossible. For this view is *itself* a belief about how evidence should be interpreted. Moreover, in order for our observations of evidence to be meaningful, we would have to already believe that our senses are basically reliable. It would do no good to observe some piece of evidence if

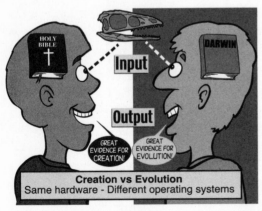

Creationists and evolutionists interpret the same evidence differently because they have different worldviews.

we did not believe our observations are real and reliable.

We cannot avoid wearing "mental glasses" — having a worldview — but it is crucial to wear the right glasses. In the same way that a person wearing red glasses might erroneously conclude that everything in the world is red, so a person with a faulty worldview will draw incorrect conclusions about the universe. But a correct worldview can prevent us from drawing the wrong conclusions and can improve our understanding of the world. For example, when I observe a magician cut a person in half, I conclude that it's a trick — no one was really cut in half, regardless of what I thought I saw. I draw this conclusion not because of the evidence, but because my worldview prevents me from drawing the wrong conclusion.

For example, suppose that your neighbor tells you that she saw a UFO last night.[7] Your worldview will immediately kick in and help you process and interpret this evidence. As your neighbor provides additional details, you will begin forming hypotheses based on your worldview. Perhaps she saw an alien spaceship. Perhaps it was a top secret government experimental aircraft. Maybe she had been drinking again last night. Or perhaps she merely saw the planet Venus. The conclusion you draw will be influenced not only by the evidence, but also by your general understanding of the universe. If you are convinced that extraterrestrial life does not exist, then clearly you will not draw the conclusion that your neighbor saw an alien spacecraft. Your worldview constrains and guides your interpretation of the evidence. This is true of every aspect of life. From UFOs or magic tricks to fossils and DNA,

our worldview tells us what to make of the evidence.

At this point, we have not yet made an argument that Christianity is the correct worldview — that it alone provides the correct way to interpret evidence in regard to origins (or any other issue). But by now it should at least be very clear that everyone interprets evidence in light of his or her worldview. And it is clear that creationists and evolutionists have *different* worldviews, and as a result, they interpret the same evidence differently. For this reason, evidence by itself will not cause a person to reconsider his worldview. Any scientific evidence can be interpreted in such a way as to fit into any given worldview.

A creationist looking at comets concludes that the solar system is young. An evolutionist looking at comets concludes that there must be an Oort cloud. A creationist examining the information in DNA concludes that there is a Creator. An evolutionist looking at the same information concludes that mutations or some unknown mechanism has generated such information. An evolutionist looking at the similarities in the genetic code of various organisms concludes that they must have a common ancestor. A creationist looking at those same similarities concludes that those organisms must have a common Creator. In all cases, the physical, observable evidence is exactly the same for both creationists and evolutionists, yet the conclusions are drastically different.

We all interpret the facts in light of our worldview. Any evidence that seems to challenge our worldview can always be explained by invoking a rescuing device. Many debates on origins are not very effective because the opposing parties do not understand the nature of worldviews, evidence, and rescuing devices. Creationists can be frustrated that evolutionists are not persuaded by the evidence; but evolutionists feel the same way about creationists. Such frustration stems from a failure to consider the real issue: rational people always interpret evidence in a way that is compatible with their worldview. Thus, evidence by itself — without considerations of a worldview — will never settle the debate.

It may seem that we have a "Mexican standoff." It may appear that there is no rational resolution to the issue of origins. After all, no matter how compelling the scientific evidence for creation may seem to creationists, the evolutionists interpret the facts differently. Conversely, the evolutionists are persuaded that the evidence supports their case; but the creationists don't interpret the data in the same way.

Since we always interpret evidence in light of our worldview, and since creationists and evolutionists have different worldviews, is there any way to rationally resolve the debate over origins? In the next chapter, we will see that there is. But the solution can't be to simply discover more scientific evidence. We already have copious amounts of evidence, and yet creationists and evolutionists cannot seem to agree on how to interpret the evidence. The ultimate proof of biblical creation must deal with worldviews. We will find in the next chapter that the biblical creation worldview must be true, because it is the only rational possibility.

Endnotes

1. These *confirm* Genesis in the sense that they are consistent with it; they show agreement. They do not "prove" Genesis in an ultimate sense.
2. Whether or not the recipient of the information does these things is not relevant to the definition. Only an *expected* action and *intended* purpose are required.
3. This is given as Theorem 28 in Dr. Werner Gitt's book *In the Beginning Was Information* (Green Forest, AR: Master Books, 2006), p. 107.
4. This is given as Theorem 15, Gitt, *In the Beginning Was Information*, p. 70 .
5. www.answersingenesis.org; see Don DeYoung, *Thousands not Billions* (Green Forest, AR: Master Books, 2005).
6. ICR is the Institute for Creation Research.
7. Thanks to Jay Lucas for suggesting this illustration.

Chapter 2

Resolving the Origins Debate

I sn't it interesting that two PhD scientists can work side by side with the same physical evidence, and yet draw radically different conclusions about what that evidence means? As I was doing research for my PhD in astrophysics at the University of Colorado, I had the opportunity to dialogue with many of the top minds in astronomy. Most of them believed in the big bang, and a multi-billion-year-old universe. Yet I could see much evidence that the universe was much younger than this. There are other biblical creationist astronomers who are also aware of this evidence. But why were so many at the university unable to see this? And no doubt, many of my colleagues thought it strange that I reject the big bang and the billions-of-years timescale. I suppose they may have thought, *Why does he not see all the evidence for the big bang and the vast age of the universe?*

In the last chapter, we saw that rational people interpret evidence in light of their worldview. Creationists and evolutionists will tend to interpret the same facts in accordance with their differing worldviews. Therefore, scientific evidence *by itself* will not resolve the creation versus evolution debate since

creationists and evolutionists each believe that the evidence is "on their side." In order for the origins debate to be rationally resolved, we must deal with the competing worldviews — not just isolated data. If we are going to rationally resolve which worldview is better than the other, then creationists must learn to understand the worldview of the evolutionist, and evolutionists must learn to understand the worldview of the creationist. Therefore, it is instructive to briefly summarize each position.

The Creation Worldview

The consistent biblical creationist is one whose worldview is based on the Bible; this is his or her ultimate standard.[1] As such, the creationist believes that an all-powerful (Matt. 19:26), all-knowing (Col. 2:3), triune (Isa. 45:5; John 8:18) God created the universe in six ordinary days (Exod. 20:11) thousands, not billions, of years ago (based on genealogies such as Gen. 5:4–32). Today, God upholds the universe by His sustaining power (Heb. 1:3) in a logical and consistent way that we call the "laws of nature" or "laws of science" (Jer. 33:25). The method by which God created the universe is not the same method by which He sustains it; God ended His work of creation by the seventh day (Gen. 2:2).

The world was a paradise when it was first created (Gen. 1:31; Deut. 32:4). The first man (Adam) was given charge over all creation (Gen. 1:28, 2:15). Adam rebelled against the Lord (Gen. 2:16, 3:6). As a result, God cursed His creation (Gene. 3:14–19), which is why we now have death and suffering in the world (Rom. 5:12, 8:21–22). Since all humans today are descended from Adam (Acts 17:26), we all have a sin nature, and we too rebel against God — disobeying His commandments. Like Adam, we deserve death and eternal separation from God. In Christian theology, this is why God became a man (John 1:1,14) and died on a Cross. Jesus took our place as an act of mercy and has offered forgiveness for all who receive Him as Lord (Rom. 10:9–10).

God had created the original animals and plants "after their kind" (Gen. 1:11, 21, 25; NASB), indicating that there are discrete barriers between basic animal and plants kinds, but that there can be variation within. The animals and plants we observe today are all variations of the original kinds (though some kinds have gone extinct). Natural selection happens . . . animals and plants can adapt somewhat to their environment. However, the processes involved never increase the information in the DNA and thus never result in a new kind of organism.

God once flooded the entire earth in response to man's wickedness (Gen. 6:5–7,17) but spared a few people in response to Noah's obedience (Gen. 6:9, 18) and preserved them and the animal kinds by an ark (Gen. 6:19). Creationists believe that most of the fossils found on earth today are a result of this global Flood. This is only a very brief summary of the creationist position. For those unfamiliar with the above concepts, I highly recommend *The New Answers Book* (volumes I–IV).

The Evolution Worldview

Unfortunately, there is no *single* "evolution worldview" to summarize. Different evolutionists hold to slightly different worldviews. However, those worldviews all have certain features in common and are all rationally defective, as we will see. In my scientific career I have had the opportunity to speak with many evolutionists and have read quite a number of evolution-based textbooks. So I will summarize what seems to be the most common position. I again emphasize that not all evolutionists believe everything described below; but in my experience, most evolutionists believe some variation of this.

Evolutionists reject the straightforward record of Genesis. The ultimate standard for an evolutionist varies from person to person, but they all have one — as we will show in chapter 9. Their ultimate standard is often either naturalism[2] (the belief that nature is all that there is) or empiricism (the idea that all knowledge is gained from observations). As a result, evolutionists believe that the universe is billions of years old. It originated in a big bang — a rapid expansion of space, time, and energy from a single infinitesimally small point. Energy cooled and became matter, which condensed into stars and galaxies. Stars made the heavier elements, some of which condensed to become

planets. Our solar system in particular was formed about 4.5 billion years ago from a collapsing gas cloud. The stars, galaxies, and planets are all the result of natural laws working over vast amounts of time.

On earth, certain chemicals came together to form the first self-replicating cell. This cell reproduced others just like it, but occasionally a mutation (a copying mistake) produced a variation. Most of these variations are not as "fit" to their environment, resulting in the death of the organism, and thus the mutation is not passed on. However, some mutations end up benefiting the organism. Such "enhanced" organisms are more able to survive, and end up passing on the mutation to their offspring. In this way, organisms are said to gradually evolve, resulting in the tremendous variety of life forms we observe today. All life is the result of the laws of nature acting over time ("naturalism"). A god is not necessary for the process, though some evolutionists do believe in God or at least *a* god.

According to evolutionists, there has not been a global Flood. Rather, the fossils were supposedly laid down over hundreds of millions of years of mostly gradual processes. Evolutionists tend to hold to the philosophy of *uniformitarianism* (to varying degrees). This is the assumption that present rates and processes are representative of those that have happened in the past: the "present is the key to the past." This is only a brief summary of a typical evolutionist's position. However, since our culture is saturated with evolutionary notions (from television, movies, public education, museums, textbooks, and so on), creationists being uneducated on evolution is generally not as much of a problem as evolutionists being uneducated about creation. This is important to remember when discussing origins; the evolutionist most likely has a number of misconceptions about the creationist position, but the reverse is possible as well.

Secular
Worldview

Biblical
Worldview

At first, it may seem that there is no way to resolve the debate since we have different worldviews.

Is there "neutral ground" in between the secular and biblical worldviews?

Competing Worldviews

We have seen that creationists and evolutionists have a different worldviews — each has a different ultimate standard by which all evidence is interpreted. Once we understand the different worldviews, it is easy to see why people draw different conclusions from the same data. It makes sense that an evolutionist would believe a particular fossil is millions of years old, while a creationist believes that the same fossil dates back to the Flood year. Of course creationists and evolutionists draw different conclusions when observing DNA, comets, or anything in the universe. The evidence does not "speak for itself"; rather, it requires interpretation. And we interpret data in light of our view of the universe and the past. How then can we resolve the debate?

"Neutral ground" is a *secular* concept. It is therefore *not* neutral. Christians who try to debate on "neutral ground" have already lost since they have given up what they are trying to defend.

The Pretended Neutrality Fallacy

When a person first comes to understand that we are dealing with competing worldviews, he or she is often tempted to think that the debate can be settled by "meeting on neutral ground." That is, perhaps there is a position *in between* the evolution and creation worldview — an "intermediate" worldview with things upon which both creationists and evolutionists can agree. Once we agree on the "rules of interpretation," we should then come to agreement on which worldview is better supported by the evidence. On the surface, this certainly seems reasonable.

But upon closer examination, we will find that such an approach cannot possibly work. It is logically flawed, and is unbiblical as well. It is impossible to be neutral with respect to worldviews, and to pretend to be so is fallacious. So we shall call such an attempt the "pretended neutrality fallacy." Everyone must have an unquestionable ultimate standard that forms the basis of his or her worldview. And although I will give a more thorough treatment of this subject in chapter 9, it is useful to show very briefly why the "neutral" approach is fundamentally flawed.

First, it is *logically* flawed. The creationist and evolutionist both have positive worldviews. Each person believes that his or her worldview provides the correct way to interpret evidence. A third (hypothetical) "neutral" worldview will necessarily provide a different interpretation of some evidence than both the creation and evolution worldview would (otherwise, it would essentially *be* one of those worldviews).

If the "neutral" interpretation of some data is *incorrect*, then why should we trust it to reliably point to either creation or evolution? (Why would we trust a faulty worldview to accurately judge a correct worldview?) Alternatively, if the "neutral" interpretation is *correct*, then obviously the creation and evolution interpretations are both wrong — in which case neither is the correct worldview. Everyone must have an ultimate standard by which evidence is evaluated. That ultimate standard cannot itself be judged by a lesser "neutral" standard, otherwise it would not be the *ultimate* standard![3] Clearly, a "neutral" position is logically impossible.

Second, a neutral approach is incompatible with the Bible. Jesus indicates that there is no neutral when it comes to an ultimate commitment. In Matthew 12:30 He says, "He who is not with me is against me; and he who does not gather with me scatters" (NASB). Many other verses could be listed (Rom. 8:7; James 4:4; etc.). At first it may seem that this reason only applies for the Christian, since only the Christian regards the Bible as an infallible source of truth. But the nature of the claim forces the unbeliever to be non-neutral as well. Since the Bible indicates that there is no neutral ground, anyone who says that there is neutral ground is necessarily saying that the Bible is wrong. But anyone who says that the Bible is wrong is not being *neutral* since he has taken the position that the Bible is wrong. It is therefore impossible to be neutral with regard to biblical authority!

Resolving the Debate: Consistency

So far, we have shown that scientific evidence by itself will not settle the debate since we all interpret our observations of the universe to match with our worldview. And we have shown that everyone must have a worldview. We have also shown that we cannot settle the debate by attempting to be neutral; such a position cannot possibly exist. How then can the debate over origins (which is really a debate over worldviews) be rationally resolved? The solution is to realize that worldviews have consequences. Whatever a person chooses as his or her ultimate standard will lead to other beliefs, which will lead to others, and so on.

However, some beliefs do not comport with each other — they don't "go well together." This provides us with one criterion by which we can distinguish a true worldview from a false one: **a true worldview must be logically consistent**. If a worldview has internal contradictions, then it cannot be entirely true since contradictions cannot be true. Moreover, some worldviews lead to the strange consequence that it would be impossible to actually know anything. Such a worldview is rationally defective since it would be impossible to know that it is true. So although everyone has an ultimate standard, not all ultimate standards will provide a self-consistent worldview in which knowledge is possible. If a worldview is self-contradictory, or has absurd consequences, then it cannot be correct.

As an example, consider the philosophy of *relativism*. Relativists believe that truth is "relative" — that it varies from person to person. Relativism includes the idea that there are no absolutes. But the proposition that "there are no absolutes" is itself an absolute proposition. Relativists assert that it is absolutely true that truth is not absolute.

This is a self-defeating philosophy. If relativism were absolutely true, it would lead to the consequence that it cannot be absolutely true. So, if it were true, it would be false; therefore it is false.

As another example, consider the philosophy of *empiricism*. This is the idea that all knowledge is gained through observation. Now of course I do believe that *some* knowledge is gained through observation — this is perfectly consistent with Scripture.[4] God made our senses to reliably probe the universe, and so there is nothing wrong with empirical methods. But the philosophy of empiricism goes much further than this. Empiricists believe that *all* knowledge is acquired by observation.[5] Or to put it another way, observation is the ultimate standard by which all truth claims are tested. And that I do not believe. I have found, however, that many evolutionists are empiricists.

We must eventually ask the empiricist how he *knows* that "all knowledge is gained through observation." Clearly this is not something that the empiricist has observed (since knowledge cannot be "seen.") So then how could anyone possibly *know* that empiricism itself is true, if all things are indeed known by observation? If empiricism is proved in some way other than through observation, then it refutes itself. If the empiricist's ultimate standard did happen to be true, the empiricist could never actually *know* that it is true; he could never prove it. And if a person's ultimate standard is uncertain, then all his other beliefs (which are based on that standard) are called into question. Empiricism destroys the possibility of actually *knowing* anything.

Resolving the Debate: The Preconditions of Intelligibility

In order for a worldview to be rationally defensible, it must be internally consistent. But just because a worldview is self-consistent does not necessarily mean that it is correct. There is another criterion as well. **A rational worldview must provide the *preconditions of intelligibility*.** These are conditions that must be accepted as true *before* we can know anything about the universe. The preconditions of intelligibility are things that most people take for granted.

The reliability of memory is one example. Everyone assumes that his or her memory is basically reliable, but this turns out to be rather difficult to prove. How do you really know that your memory is reliable? Some might say, "Well, I took a memory test two weeks ago, and I did very well on it." But we could reply, "How do you *know* you took a test two weeks ago? Just because you remember this doesn't prove it happened unless we already knew your memory is reliable." That our memories are basically reliable is something that we all assume *before* we begin to investigate the universe.

Another example is the reliability of our senses. We suppose that our eyes, ears, and other senses reliably report the details about the universe in which we live. Without this assumption, science would be impossible. We could draw no reliable conclusions from any experiment if our observations of the experiment are unreliable. If our sensory experiences are merely illusions, then science would be impossible.

Consider one more crucial example: laws of logic. We all presume that there are laws of logic that govern correct reasoning. Earlier in this chapter I stated that contradictions cannot be true. It probably didn't occur to any reader to question that claim; it is a law of logic that we all take for granted. And yet how could we prove that the laws of logic are correct? We would have to first assume that they are true in order to begin a logical proof. Therefore, laws of logic constitute a precondition of intelligibility. They must be assumed before we can even begin to reason about anything — including reasoning about the laws of logic themselves.

We take for granted that our senses and memory are basically reliable, and that there are laws of logic. Yet most of us do not stop to think *why* these things are so. In a biblical creation worldview, these preconditions make sense; they are what we would expect if the Bible is true. It is reasonable that our memory and senses would be basically reliable since they have been designed by God. We will show in the next chapter that laws of logic make sense in the Christian worldview as well; they reflect God's thinking.

A logically correct worldview must provide these preconditions of intelligibility, because without them we could not know anything about the universe. Both creationists and evolutionists must assume the preconditions of intelligibility at the outset in order to know anything. But we will see in the next chapter that only in the biblical creation worldview do the preconditions of intelligibility make sense. Only a consistent Christian can have justification (a sound reason) for things like laws of logic and the reliability of our senses. Without justification for the things we take for granted, we can't really know that any of our thinking or observations of the world are correct. And if our thinking and observations are unreliable, then we really can't be certain about

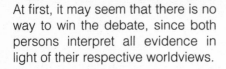

At first, it may seem that there is no way to win the debate, since both persons interpret all evidence in light of their respective worldviews.

The secular worldview is "sinking sand." It is inconsistent and will not support a rational understanding of the things we take for granted.

anything at all. So only in a biblical creationist universe is it possible to actually know anything about anything.

Proverbs 1:7 indicates that knowledge begins with a respectful submission to the biblical God and that rejection of the wisdom of biblical instruction leads inevitably to irrationality — to "foolishness." This is the key to the ultimate proof of biblical creation, or, for that matter, the Bible, the Christian worldview, the existence of God, and so on.

The ultimate proof of creation can be summarized as follows: *if biblical creation were not true, we could not know anything!* The logical prerequisites for knowledge (which most people take for granted) are provided *only* in biblical creation, and would be impossible in an evolutionary or atheistic universe. In the next chapter we will see why this is so.

Some people might raise an immediate objection: "But there are people who haven't even read the Bible — who don't believe in creation; and they do indeed know things." But this response is fallacious.[6] It is not relevant to the claim that has been made. No one is arguing that people must have read the Bible or profess to believe in creation to know things. The argument is that the Bible's account of origins (along with its other accounts) must be *true* — not that people must profess or believe it to be true. Only the God described in the Bible can provide the rational foundation for the things we take for granted. Without God's Word, we would have no good reason to believe in the preconditions of intelligibility: the basic reliability of memory and senses, laws of logic, uniformity of nature, morality, personal dignity and freedom, and so on. Thus, we would be unable to justify our beliefs about anything whatsoever.

The Necessity of Being Non-Arbitrary

In response to the above argument, some may be tempted to respond like this: "It is not important that we have a reason for things like logic and the reliability of senses and memory. It is enough that we are able to act upon them. We can know lots of things, even though we may not have a reason for those things we take for granted." But such reasoning is arbitrary and specious. Believing in something is not the same as knowing something. Children believe that Santa Claus brings presents to them at Christmas, and they act on that belief (by setting out milk and cookies) — but they clearly do not know this.

Obviously, a belief must be true in order for it to be considered genuine *knowledge*. But the fact that a belief may happen to be true does not mean that the person really has *knowledge* of it. If a person has enough arbitrary beliefs, probably a few of them will happen to be true just by accident. But if the person does not have a good reason for those beliefs (even the true ones), it would be inappropriate to say he or she has actual knowledge. In order for a belief to count as knowledge, a person needs to have a good *reason* for a true belief. Therefore, it is not possible to have *knowledge* of something without having a *reason* for it. This is an extremely important principle, so let us illustrate it with an example.

Suppose someone said, "I just *know* it is going to be warm and sunny for the church picnic next month." Does this person really *know* this? Clearly not. She may believe this, but there is no guarantee that her belief is true. Suppose that it turned out to be true; the day of the picnic really happened to be warm and sunny and the person responded, "See, I *knew* it would be sunny!" But did she really *know* it all along? Even though her belief turned out to be true, it would be wrong to say that she had *knowledge* of the future. She did not really know that it would be sunny because she did not have justification; that is, she did not have a good reason for her belief. Knowledge is true, *justified* belief.

Evolutionists rightly expect creationists to be non-arbitrary — to have a reason for our beliefs. But many evolutionists feel no need to have a reason for their own beliefs; this is a double standard. Just imagine if an evolutionist asked a creationist why he believes in creation, and the creationist responded, "Oh, I don't need a reason. Creation is true, and that's all there is to it." The evolutionist would rightly consider such a response to be without merit, because it is arbitrary. Yet when asked about the preconditions of intelligibility, some evolutionists will say, "Oh, we don't need a reason for such things. It is enough that we act on them." Such a response is equally arbitrary. The rational person has a reason for what he or she believes.

Much more could be said about knowledge, arbitrariness, and inconsistency. We will revisit these topics again in chapter 5. For now, it should suffice to say that if we don't have a reason to believe something, then we don't really know it. Those who deny biblical creation do not have a *reason* for the things they take for granted (within their own worldview), and thus they could not really *know* any of these things if their professed worldview were true. To the extent that unbelievers know anything, it is because they are ultimately relying on biblical creation, as we will explore in the next chapter. The fact that unbelievers act upon their beliefs is not in question. The point is that *if their worldview were true*, they would have no justification for their most basic convictions, and without justification, there is no genuine knowledge — merely beliefs. Non-Christians do have beliefs, of course, and some of those beliefs happen to be true. But the non-Christian could never really *know* that those things are true unless biblical creation is also true.

What remains now is to see specifically how the Bible accounts for these things, and to show why evolutionary worldviews cannot account for them. We will therefore provide some illustrations of the ultimate proof — examples showing how it works. We will concentrate on three of the many preconditions of intelligibility: laws of logic, uniformity of nature, and morality. Only a biblical creation worldview can make sense of these things that we all take for granted. The Bible must be true because if it were not, we could not actually know anything at all. For this reason, non-biblical worldviews such as evolution are necessarily ultimately *irrational*.

Endnotes

1. Everyone must have an ultimate standard, as shown in chapter 9. There can be secondary standards of course. Observation is an example of a secondary standard. We generally believe that what our senses perceive is the truth. But most of us do not trust our senses as an ultimate unquestionable standard; when we see an optical illusion, or a magic trick, we are inclined to disregard our observations in favor of a greater standard that tells us that such things cannot be what they appear to be.

2. In some cases, scientists prefer methodological naturalism rather than metaphysical naturalism. The latter is the belief that nature is all there is, and that is usually what is meant by the term "naturalism." The former is the belief that science should be conducted as if nature were all that there is, regardless of whether or not it is actually true.

3. More details are provided in chapter 9. The purpose here is only to give the "flavor" of the argument.

4. Empirical methods can serve as a secondary standard. But they are not the ultimate standard for the consistent Christian, because (1) they themselves require justification by non-empirical means, and (2) knowledge of non-empirical things (like laws of logic) is possible.

5. In many cases this is supplemented with the need for logical consistency.

6. This is the fallacy of irrelevant thesis (see chapter 7).

Chapter 3

Illustrations of the Ultimate Proof

A debate over biblical creation is a lot like a debate over the existence of air. Can you imagine two people debating whether or not air exists? What would the critic of air say? Whatever his arguments, he would have to use air in order to make them. Not only is air crucial to the survival of the critic, but air would have to exist in order for his arguments to be heard and understood. It would seem strange for someone to argue against the existence of air, while simultaneously breathing, and expecting his arguments to be heard as the sound travels through the air. In order for the critic of air to be able to make an argument, it would have to be wrong.

Likewise, the evolutionist must use biblical creation principles in order to argue against biblical creation. In order for his argument to make sense, it would have to be wrong. Ironically, the fact that evolutionists are able to argue against creation proves that creation is true! Evolutionists must assume the preconditions of intelligibility in order to make any argument whatsoever; they must assume things like laws of logic and uniformity of nature. But these preconditions of intelligibility

The unbeliever cannot consistently stand on his own worldview because it is irrational.

Therefore, the unbeliever must stand on the Christian worldview in order to be rational.

do not comport with an evolutionary worldview; they only make sense if creation is true. Hence, we have an ultimate proof of creation: we know that biblical creation must be true because if it were not, we could not know anything at all.

Sometimes an evolutionist will object to this in the following way. He will say, "Creation doesn't have to be true in order for us to know things. After all, I don't even believe in creation; and I know lots of things!" But this response is fallacious. It would be like the critic of air saying, "We don't need air to breathe. After all, I don't even believe in air; and I can breathe just fine!" The argument is not that breathing requires a profession of belief in air — but it does require air. Likewise, knowledge does not require a *profession of belief* in biblical creation — but it does require that biblical creation is true. Yes, evolutionists can know lots of things, but only because their worldview is wrong.

To illustrate the ultimate proof, we are going to look at three specific examples. These are preconditions that only make sense in a biblical worldview, yet they are required in order to learn anything about the universe. Although these are not the only three preconditions that are important, they are some of the most easily understood and commonly used. They are laws of logic, uniformity of nature, and absolute morality.

Clearly, in order for us to reason logically, there must be laws of logic. In order for us to study nature, the universe must have an underlying orderliness: it must have some regularity in time and space, which we will refer to as *uniformity*. At first it may seem odd that absolute morality is required for a rational worldview. But the idea that we *should* be rational at all is a moral obligation. So morality is required if we are to argue that people *ought* to have a rational basis for their worldview. And, without morality, we could have no knowledge of right and wrong. In any case, most evolutionists do believe in morality; yet as we will see, they have no basis for morality within their own worldview. These three preconditions should not

The unbeliever stands on Christian principles: logic, uniformity, and morality. But he denies that these are Christian principles.

The unbeliever must use Christian principles to argue against the Bible. The fact that he is able to argue at all proves that he is wrong.

be thought of as separate arguments, but rather as three illustrations of a single argument. Since morality may be the easiest to understand, we begin with this illustration.[1]

1. Morality

Morality is a very difficult problem for the evolutionary worldview. This isn't to say that evolutionists are somehow less moral than anyone else. Most of them adhere to a code of behavior. Like the biblical creationist, they do believe in the concepts of *right* and *wrong*. The problem is that evolutionists have no logical reason to believe in any sort of moral imperative within their own worldview.

Both creationists and evolutionists have a sense about what is morally right and what is morally wrong. For the biblical creationist, this makes sense. Right is what corresponds to God's approval, and wrong to His disapproval, and these are rooted in His unchanging character. Moreover, God made us in His image and gave us a sense of His character so that we can understand right and wrong.

But in the evolutionary, naturalistic universe, how can anything whatsoever be "right" or "wrong"? And who decides? In a chance universe, what happens simply happens. There's no right or wrong about it. And if people are merely accidents resulting from chemical reactions over billions of years, as the evolutionist asserts, how can they be morally obligated to behave in a particular way? To whom are they accountable? On what basis could we say that any action is objectively (not merely subject to personal opinion) right or wrong? After all, chemical reactions have no choice but to follow the laws of physics, and therefore can have no genuine moral obligation to anything.

If the concepts of right and wrong are to be meaningful, evolution cannot be true. Right and wrong are Christian concepts that go back to Genesis. By attempting to be moral, therefore, the evolutionist is being irrational, for he must borrow biblical concepts that are contrary to his worldview.

The Bible teaches that God is the Creator and owner of all things (Gen. 1:1; John 1:3). All things belong to God (Ps. 24:1), and thus God has the right to make the rules. And God will hold us accountable to

His standard, invoking punishments and blessings for our wicked and good deeds respectively. So the biblical creationist has (1) a good reason to believe that objective morality exists, (2) an objective standard for knowing what is right and what is wrong — namely the Bible, and (3) a very good, objective reason to behave according to that moral standard articulated in the Bible — the final judgment.

So an absolute moral code makes sense in a biblical creation world-view. But if the Bible were not true, if human beings were merely the outworking of millions of years of mindless chemical processes, then how could there be an objective basis for right and wrong? And who decides what it is? How is it discovered? Why would we be obligated to follow any moral code at all? Would the concepts of right and wrong have any objective meaning if evolution were true?

Certainly, evolutionists can express opinions of what they believe to be right or wrong. But two problems immediately arise. First, what happens when two people disagree on a moral claim? One person says abortion is morally right and acceptable; the other claims that it is mor-ally wrong and detestable. What objective standard can we bring in to settle the issue?

The Christian stands upon the Bible as the written Word of our Creator. It is by God's revealed standard alone that everyone will be judged, and thus God's standard is the only objective basis for morality. After all, we will not be judged by our neighbor's feelings of right and wrong, but rather by God's commandments (Rev. 20:12).

But the evolutionist is in a bind — he has rejected God's Word, at least in Genesis where we learn that God is our Creator — the one to whom we are morally obligated. Yet the evolutionist has no objective alternative. He might say "me — I am the standard. What I believe to be right is indeed right." But then the other person disagrees, saying "No, I am the standard, and you are wrong." So the question cannot be answered. We end up like the situation in Judges 17:6 and 21:25 where everyone "did what was right in his own eyes."

Second, what would the concepts of "right" and "wrong" even mean in an evolutionary worldview. In the biblical worldview, morality refers to the absolute, objective standard that God applies to all people as revealed in His Word and in our conscience. But in the secular world-view, can morality even be defined? And how can there be any standard that is objective (open to observation by all), absolute (as opposed to relative to the individual), and universal (in the sense that it applies to everyone)? A person might just make up his own personal "morality." But there is nothing to prevent his neighbor from making up a different personal "morality." Such artificial moral codes are subject to change at the whim of the person. Thus, morality can never be objective, absolute, or universal in an evolutionary universe. It can only be subjective, relative, and arbitrary.

Now, some people might say, "That's true. Morality is just relative. There's no such thing as absolute morality, and therefore you should not try to enforce your personal moral code on other people!" But when they say "you should not . . ." they are doing just what they are telling others not to do: enforcing their personal moral code on other people. In essence, they are saying that it is objectively wrong for us to tell others that some things are objectively wrong. Relative morality is self-refuting.

If morality were relative to the individual, then ethics would be reduced to mere personal preference. In that case, one person could never rationally declare any actions of another person to be objectively wrong. He could only say that such actions displease him. And so murder would be on the same level as putting ketchup on eggs — it might be unpleasant to some, but nothing more could be said.

For example, a person might choose for himself a moral code in which murder is perfectly acceptable. This might seem upsetting to us, but how could we argue that it is wrong for others to murder if morality is nothing but a personal standard? If morality is a subjective personal choice, then even Hitler cannot be denounced for his actions since he was acting in accord with his chosen standard. Clearly this is an unacceptable position.

Furthermore, "relative morality" is a position that no one would hold when pressed on the matter. After all, what would happen if a moral relativist were held at gun point and asked, "Can you give me any reason why I should not pull the trigger if I can get away with it?" He would very quickly become a moral absolutist, and would insist that murder is objectively wrong, not just for himself, but for the person holding the gun as well. People cannot live consistently by such an amoral standard.

Objective Evolutionary Morality?

Some might respond, "Well, I do believe in objective morality, and I also believe in evolution, so obviously biblical creation is not required for objective morality." The absurdity of this answer is quickly revealed by analogy. Consider two people debating the existence of air. The air-affirmer points out that air is necessary to breathe. Now, suppose the critic responded, "That's absurd! I don't even believe in air at all, and yet I can breathe just fine. So clearly, air is not required for breathing!" Would that response be rational?

The critic has not responded cogently, because the argument is not that a belief in air is required to breathe (for which he can present himself as a counterexample), but rather that air is required to breathe. So his lack of belief in air is not relevant to the claim. He is able to breathe despite his lack of belief in air only because his belief is wrong: air does indeed exist. Likewise, the evolutionist is able to have awareness of the objective nature of morality despite his belief in evolution only because his belief in evolution is wrong.

People can be irrational; they can profess to believe in things that are contrary to each other. They can profess to believe that air does not exist while still breathing air. They can profess to believe in evolution and still assert that an objective moral code exists. The question is not about what people believe to be the case (which may be self-contradictory), but rather what actually is the case (which can never be self-contradictory). And evolution cannot coexist with real objective morality any more than breathing can exist without air. Any moral standard proposed by the evolutionist ends up being a subjective and arbitrary preference — not genuine morality.

Some evolutionists argue that there *is* an absolute standard; they say, "Right is what brings the most happiness to the most people." But this is also arbitrary. Why should *that* be the selected standard as opposed to some other view? And why would other people be obligated to follow that particular opinion? Even here, the evolutionist has tacitly borrowed from the Christian position. In the Christian worldview, we should indeed be concerned about the happiness of others since they are made in God's image.[2] But if other people were simply chemical accidents, how could one chemical accident have any sort of moral obligation to care about another? Concern for others does not make sense in an evolutionary universe.

Perhaps the evolutionist will claim that morality is what the majority decides it to be. But this view has the same defects as the others. It merely shifts an unjustified opinion from one person to a group of people. It is arbitrary and leads to absurd conclusions. Why should I be obligated to follow the opinions of the majority? Again, we find that we would not be able to denounce certain actions that we know to be wrong. After all, Hitler was able to convince a majority of his people that his actions were right, but that doesn't really make them right.

Morality requires a mind in order to make a value judgment about what *should* be the case. But for morality to be objective, it must be true for all people, and exist in the universe beyond their personal minds. Hence, morality cannot be based on a human mind because our thoughts do not control or determine the external universe, and are not necessarily true. However, the mind of God does control and determine the entire universe (Isa. 46:9–10), and His thoughts are necessarily true because His mind determines truth (Col. 2:3; John 14:6).[3] Objective morality requires the biblical God.

Without the biblical God, *right* and *wrong* are reduced to mere personal preferences, with no objective moral obligation whatsoever. In an evolutionary universe, the statement "murder is wrong" is nothing more than a personal opinion on the same level as "blue is my favorite color." And if others have a different opinion, we would have no basis for arguing with them. Thus, when evolutionists talk about morality as if it is a real standard that other people should follow, they are being inconsistent with their own professed worldview. Moreover, they show that in their heart of hearts they really do believe in the biblical God (Rom. 1:18–20).

Evolutionary Inconsistency

As one example, consider those evolutionists who are very concerned about children being taught creation. "This is wrong," they say, "because you're lying to children!" Now, obviously this begs the question since the truth or falsity of creation is the concern at issue: we are convinced that creation is true, and evolution is the lie. But the truly absurd thing about such evolutionary arguments is that they are contrary to evolution! That is, in an evolutionary worldview, why shouldn't we lie — particularly if it benefits our survival value?

Certainly the Christian believes that it's wrong to lie, but then again, the Christian has a reason for this. God has indicated in His Word that lying is contrary to His nature (Num. 23:19), and that we are not to engage in it (Exod. 20:16). But apart from the biblical worldview, why should we tell the truth? For that matter, why should we do anything at all? Words like "should" and "ought" only make sense if there is an absolute standard given by one who has authority over everyone.

If human beings are merely chemical accidents, why should we be so concerned about what they do? We wouldn't become angry at baking soda for reacting with vinegar; that's just what chemicals do. So why would an evolutionist be angry at anything one human being does to another, if we are all nothing more than complex chemical reactions? If we are simply evolved animals, why should we hold to a code of conduct in this "dog-eat-dog" world? After all, what one animal does to another is morally irrelevant. When evolutionists attempt to be moral, they are "borrowing" from the Christian worldview.

One humorous example of this happened at the opening of the Creation Museum. A group opposing the museum (Defcon — "The Campaign to Defend the Constitution") hired a plane to circle above with a trailing banner that read, "Defcon says thou shalt not lie." Of course, we couldn't agree more! After all, this is one of the Ten Commandments. In fact, the purpose of the Creation Museum is to present the truth about origins. So the evolutionists had to borrow from the biblical worldview in order to argue against it. In an evolutionary universe, Defcon's moral objection makes no sense (although we certainly appreciated the free advertising).

Understanding the Evolutionary Position

The Christian worldview not only accounts for morality, it also accounts for why evolutionists behave the way they do. Even those who have no basis for morality within their own professed worldview nonetheless hold to a moral code; this is because in their heart of hearts they really do know the God of creation despite their profession to the contrary. Scripture tells us that everyone knows the biblical God, but that they suppress the truth about God (Rom. 1:18–21). Why would anyone do this?

We have inherited a sin nature (a tendency to rebel against God) from Adam (Rom. 5:12), who rebelled against God in the Garden of Eden (Gen. 3). John 3:19 indicates that people would rather remain in spiritual darkness than have their evil deeds exposed. Just as Adam tried to hide from God's presence (Gen. 3:8), so his descendents do the same. But the solution to sin is not suppression, it is confession and repentance (1 John 1:9; Luke 5:32). Christ is faithful to forgive anyone who calls on His name (Rom. 10:13).

Nearly everyone believes that people ought to behave in a certain way — a moral code. Yet in order for morality to be meaningful, biblical creation must be true. Since God created human beings, He determines what is to be considered *right* and *wrong*, and we are responsible to Him for our actions. We must therefore conclude that evolutionists are being irrational when they talk about right and wrong, for such concepts make no sense in an evolutionary universe.

2. Laws of Logic

Rational reasoning involves using the laws of logic.[4] Therefore, a rational worldview must be able to account for the existence and properties of such laws. Remember: rationality requires that we must have a good reason for our beliefs. Therefore, we must have a good reason to believe that laws of logic correctly guide our reasoning if we are going to believe in them and rely upon them.

As an example, let's just consider one of the laws of logic: the law of non-contradiction. This law states that any self-contradictory statement is false: you can't have A and not-A at the same time and in the same relationship (where the letter A represents any claim). For example, the statement "My car is in the garage *and* it is not the case that my car is in the garage" is necessarily false by the law of non-contradiction. Any rational person would accept this law. But few people stop to ask, "*Why* is this law true? Why should there be a law of non-contradiction, or for that matter, any laws of reasoning?"

The Christian can answer these questions. For the Christian there is an absolute standard for reasoning; we are to pattern our thoughts after God's. And we know (in a finite, limited way) how God thinks because He has revealed some of His thoughts through His Word.[5] According to Genesis, God has made us in His image (Gen. 1:26) and therefore we are to follow His example (Eph. 5:1). The laws of logic are a reflection of the way God thinks, and thus the way He expects us to think. The law of non-contradiction is not simply one person's opinion of how we ought to think, rather it stems from God's self-consistent nature. God cannot deny Himself (2 Tim. 2:13), and all truth is in God (John 14:6; Col. 2:3), therefore truth will not contradict itself. Since God is constantly upholding the universe by His power (Heb. 1:3), the consistent

Christian expects that no self-contradictory statement will ever be true anywhere in the universe.

Not only do we all take for granted that laws of logic exist, we also presume that they have certain properties. For example, laws of logic are abstract and immaterial. That is, they are non-tangible. You cannot stub your toe on a law of logic, or accidentally swallow one. They are not made of matter and do not have a location in space. They deal with ideas not physical things. No one uses a law of logic like a hammer to drive in a nail, or like a shovel to dig a ditch. Rather, we use them to analyze ideas and to reason properly.

Laws of logic are universal — meaning they apply everywhere. We take this for granted. They apply just as legitimately in Europe as in Australia. Imagine someone visiting a foreign country and worrying, "I sure hope the laws of logic apply here." That would be absurd. Local customs vary from country to country, but laws of logic are the same everywhere in the universe.

Laws of logic are invariant — meaning they do not change with time. People take this for granted. No one says, "Sure, laws of logic worked yesterday. But who knows if they will work today? And I'm really concerned that they will not work tomorrow!" Rather, we all pre-suppose that laws of logic do not change with time.

Also, laws of logic are exception-less. They are not merely general trends that hold most of the time. Rather, they are always true and mark the correct standard of reasoning without exception.

All these properties of logic make sense in the Christian worldview, where laws of logic are God's standard for thinking. Since God is an unchanging, sovereign, immaterial Being, His thoughts would neces-sarily be abstract, universal, invariant entities. Consider, God is imma-terial — meaning He does not have a specific location in space, and is not made of atoms like we are (John 4:24; Luke 24:39). His thoughts are abstract and immaterial because all thoughts are. Hence, laws of logic are abstract and immaterial.

God is omni-present (Jer. 23:24; Psalm 139:7–8), meaning His power is instantly available everywhere, and God is sovereign over the entire universe. Hence, His thoughts are the absolute standard for right reasoning everywhere in the universe. Laws of logic are thus universal.

God is beyond time (2 Pet. 3:8) and does not change with time (Mal. 3:6). Thus, His thinking does not change with time. Laws of logic are therefore invariant. Moreover, laws of logic are exception-less because all truth exists in the mind of God (Col. 2:3), not just some. There are no exceptions.

So the consistent Christian who takes the Bible as written, has a good reason to believe that laws of logic exist and are abstract, universal, invariant, exception-less, correct standards for all reasoning. Laws of logic make sense in a Christian worldview.

But other worldviews cannot account for them. For example, apart from the Bible, how could we know that contradictions are *always* false? That is, how could we know that the law of non-contradiction is universal, invariant, and exception-less? We could only say that *in our experience*, there have been no exceptions, and the law of non-contradiction seems to apply everywhere that we have experienced. But our experiences are very limited, and no one has experienced the future. So if someone asserted that he or she has finally discovered two contradictory claims that are both true, the non-Christian has no basis for dismissing such an assertion. Only in a biblical worldview can we know that contradictions cannot occur in reality; only the Christian has a basis for the *law* of non-contradiction, or laws of logic in general.

Possible Responses

An evolutionist might respond by saying, "Well, I can reason just fine, and I don't believe in the Bible." But this is the same mistake as the critic of air saying, "Of course air isn't necessary to breathe, because I don't believe in air and I can breathe just fine." No one is suggesting that *belief* in air is necessary to breath, but rather the *fact* of air. Likewise, no one is suggesting that professing belief in the Bible is necessary to use logic, but rather that the Bible must be factual in order for use of logic to be reasonable.

So the critic's response just isn't rational. The ultimate proof is that logical reasoning (and the other things required for knowledge) requires the biblical God, not a profession of belief in Him. Yes, of course the evolutionist can reason; it's because God has created the human mind and given mankind access to the laws of logic — and that's the point. Logical reasoning is possible because biblical creation is true. The evolutionist can reason, but within his own worldview he cannot account for his ability to reason.

Another possible response would be this: "Laws of logic do not require biblical creation. They are simply conventions made up by human beings." However, this response will not suffice. Conventions are (by definition) conventional. That is, we all agree to them and so they work — like driving on the right side of the road. But if laws of logic were conventional, then different cultures could adopt *different* laws of logic (like driving on the *left* side of the road). So in some cultures it might be perfectly fine to contradict yourself. In some societies truth could be self-contradictory. Clearly, that wouldn't do. If laws of logic are just conventions, then they are not universal laws. Rational debate would be impossible if laws of logic were conventional, because the two opponents could simply pick different standards for reasoning. Each would be "right" according to his own arbitrary standard.

Also, there would there be no reason to think that laws of logic are unchanging if they were merely human conventions, and every reason to think otherwise. After all, human conventions often change with time. And there would be no reason to think that the universe would obey — without exception — humanly stipulated conventions. After all, the universe does not respect humanly imposed laws like speed limits. Yet, the universe never violates in reality a law of logic. Clearly, laws of logic cannot be merely conventional.

Some evolutionists might respond, "Laws of logic are chemical reactions in the brain that have been preserved because they have survival value." There are several problems with this response. First, survival value does not equate to truth. My left arm has survival value, but we wouldn't say that it is "true" or "false"; it simply is. So we would have no reason to think that the law of non-contradiction (or any law of logic) is *true*, if it is simply a chemical reaction.

Some might ask, "But wouldn't chemical reactions that give us a sense of truth have survival value?" But this is not necessarily so. Photosynthesis has tremendous survival value in plants. If it produces a sensation in plants that "2+2=17", such a sensation wouldn't be true even though the chemistry would continue to have survival value. How can an evolutionist possibly know (on his own worldview) that he's not a plant and that his thoughts and reasoning about the world are nothing more than a side-effect of photosynthesis? It won't do to say that he observes with his senses that he's not a plant, because the reliability of his senses is the very thing in question.

Second, if laws of logic were just chemical reactions, then they would not be laws at all. And they couldn't possibly be universal, because these reactions occur only within the brain — not everywhere in the universe. In other words, we couldn't argue that self-contradictory claims cannot be true on Mars, since no one's brain is on Mars. In fact, if the laws of logic were just electro-chemical reactions in the brain, then they would differ somewhat from person to person, because everyone has different reactions in his or her brain.

Perhaps someone would argue, "Laws of logic are a description of how the physical universe behaves." This response also fails for a number of reasons. First, laws of logic are conceptual in nature. They do not really describe aspects of the physical universe. Rather, they describe the correct chain of reasoning from premises to conclusions. Laws of *nature* describe how the physical universe behaves. Laws of logic describe the correct chain of reasoning from premises to conclusions.

Second, if laws of logic were descriptions of the physical universe, then we might expect different regions of the universe to have different laws of logic, since different regions of the universe are described differently; but laws of logic apply everywhere. A description of the surface of Mars is very different from a description of the core of the sun. Yet, we all presume that laws of logic apply equally well in both places.

Third, we would have no way of knowing (and therefore no reason to expect) that laws of logic apply in the future as they have in the past, since no one has experienced the universe's future. After all, conditions in the universe are constantly changing. If laws of logic were descriptions of such conditions, then they would have to change as well.

Some have said that "laws of logic are descriptions of how the brain thinks." But if this were true, then why would we need laws of logic to *correct* the way the brain thinks? If laws of logic simply describe how people think, then no one could ever violate a law of logic, since people necessarily think the way they think. As with the other responses, laws of logic would lose their law-like power to govern correct reasoning if they were mere descriptions of thought processes.

Sometimes the evolutionist may simply take a pragmatic position: "I use laws of logic because they work." Unfortunately for the evolutionist, that isn't the question. We all agree that laws of logic work; they work because they're true. The question is whether the evolutionist can justify his belief in the existence and properties of laws of logic. The fact that laws of logic have been useful to us in our limited, finite experiences in the past does not in any way justify our belief that they will continue to be useful in the future, or that they are universal or exception-less. Nor does it account for why these laws should even exist in the first place. How can the evolutionist account for absolute standards of reasoning like the laws of logic? In an accidental evolutionary universe, why would there be universal, unchanging standards?

Additional Responses

Almost all evolutionists will use some variation of one of these responses. So if you have studied these responses and understand why they are defective, you will have no trouble at all answering any attempted rebuttal of the ultimate proof. But it may also be helpful to prepare for some less-common responses. Often as a last resort, the critic will admit that he cannot account for laws of logic, and he will add, "But neither can you!" This response is actually fallacious since it merely sidesteps the argument; it's called a *Tu Quoque* fallacy. And in any case, the Christian can indeed account for laws of logic; we have a universal standard for reasoning because Almighty God has revealed some of His thoughts to us.

Very rarely the critic will actually claim to give up logic in order to protect his worldview. But he can't really do this. He will say, "I don't believe in laws of logic, therefore I don't need to have a reason for logic within my worldview." But this response is self-refuting. The critic is attempting to use logic (when he says "therefore") in order to argue that he doesn't need logic. In any case, by giving up logic, the critic has lost the debate. The argument I am making is that only biblical creationists have a *logical*, rational basis for laws of logic, and thus evolutionary worldviews are inherently irrational. So for the evolutionist to give up logic is to concede defeat.

Laws of logic pose a very serious problem for the evolutionist. Almost all evolutionists know they should be logical, and yet they have no basis for laws of logic within their own professed worldview. The problem is particularly embarrassing for the materialistic atheist.[6] A materialistic atheist does not believe in anything beyond the physical universe. In his view, all that exists is matter in motion. But of course laws of logic are not matter; they are not part of the physical universe. Therefore, laws of logic cannot exist if materialism is true! Not only is the materialistic atheist unable to account for the existence of laws of logic, but they are actually contrary to his worldview. His worldview is necessarily irrational.

Laws of logic reflect the thinking of God and do not make sense in an evolutionary universe. Some people have supposed that theistic evolution might alleviate the problem. Many evolutionists do believe in some sort of god, and they might attempt to appeal to their god as the basis for laws of logic just as the biblical creationist does. In fact, a number of evolutionists and old-earth creationists profess to believe in the Christian God. Do they therefore have a basis for laws of logic?

No, they do not. Recall that laws of logic are a reflection of the way God thinks. But how can we know how God thinks? God has revealed some of His thoughts in His Word — the Bible. And we are able to be logical since God has made us in His image according to Genesis. But evolutionists and old-earth creationists reject Genesis, or at least a straightforward reading of it, so they have no reason within their own worldview to suppose that we are able to pattern our thoughts after God's. Nor do they believe that God has accurately recorded His thoughts in the Scriptures, since they reject (at least many portions of) the Scriptures.[7]

Other "Religious" Positions

Although our primary purpose is to refute evolution, I again feel compelled to point out that only the biblical worldview can account for the preconditions of intelligibility — such as laws of logic. It's not just evolutionists who have this serious defect. Some persons from other religious persuasions may claim that they, too, can account for the laws of logic. They might say, "We can account for laws of logic by appealing to our god, just as you appeal to yours." But upon analysis, we will find that these other gods turn out to be mere idols that cannot do what the biblical God does.

Consider the Mormon gods. Mormons are actually polytheistic because they believe that God the Father is a different god than Jesus. If laws of logic are a reflection of the way God thinks, then which of the Mormon gods' thoughts should we follow? There cannot be a single universal set of laws of logic if there is more than one god. Therefore, no polytheistic religion can account for laws of logic. (Nor can they account for laws of morality either: which god's commands should we follow?) Moreover, the Mormon gods change with time. Mormons teach that God the Father is flesh, and that He ascended to deity over time — as they believe they will too. If God's nature changes, then there is no reason to believe that laws of logic do not change. Laws of logic could not be universal, invariant laws if Mormonism were true.

Consider Allah, the god of Islam. Could laws of logic be a reflection of the way Allah thinks? According to the Islamic doctrine of *tanzih,* Allah is so superior that nothing in human experience is comparable to him (Sura 42:11). But laws of logic are part of human experience — we use them all the time. Therefore, laws of logic cannot relate to Allah and cannot be a reflection of the way he thinks. So Islam also fails to provide a basis for the preconditions of intelligibility.

Biblical Creation Can Account for Logic

Since the God of Scripture is immaterial, sovereign, and beyond time, it makes sense to have laws of logic that are immaterial, universal, and unchanging. Since God has revealed Himself to man, we are able to know and use logic. Since God made the universe, and since God made our minds, it makes sense that our minds would have an ability to study and understand the universe. But if the universe and our minds are simply the results of time and chance as the evolutionist contends, why would we expect that the mind could make sense of the universe? How could science and technology be possible?

Rational thinking, science, and technology make sense in a biblical creation worldview. The consistent Christian has a basis for these things; the evolutionist does not. This is not to say that evolutionists cannot be rational about some things. They can because they too are made in God's image and have access to God's laws of logic. But they have no rational basis for rationality within their own worldview. Likewise, as we showed earlier, evolutionists can be moral, but they have no basis for that morality according to what they claim to believe. An evolutionist is a walking bundle of contradictions. He reasons and does science, yet he denies the very God who makes reasoning and science possible. On the other hand, the Christian worldview is consistent and makes sense of human reasoning and experience.

3. Uniformity of Nature

This brings us to the third illustration of the ultimate proof — and my personal favorite: uniformity of nature — also called the *inductive principle.* Some evolutionists have argued that science isn't possible without evolution. They teach that science and technology actually require the principles of molecules-to-man evolution in order to work.

They claim that those who hold to a biblical creation worldview are in danger of not being able to understand science![8]

I must admit that as a scientist myself, I find these claims particularly silly because they are so easy to refute. Ironically, evolution is actually contrary to the principles of science. That is, if evolution were true, the concept of science would not make sense. Science actually requires a biblical creation framework in order to be possible. Therefore, evolution turns out to be more of an "anti-science" than a science.[9] Here's why.

The Preconditions of Science

In order to do science we take for granted that the universe is understandable — that it can be quantified in a way the mind can comprehend. We assume that the universe is logical and orderly and that it obeys mathematical laws that are consistent over time and space. Even though conditions in different regions of space and eras of time are quite diverse, there is nonetheless an underlying uniformity.[10] Because there is such regularity in the universe, there are many instances where scientists are able to make successful predictions about the future.[11] For example, astronomers can successfully compute the positions of the planets, moons, and asteroids far into the future. Without uniformity in nature, such predictions would be impossible, and science could not exist. The problem for evolutionism is that such regularity only makes sense in a biblical creation worldview.

The biblical creationist expects there to be order in the universe because God made all things (Gen. 1:1; John 1:3) and has imposed order on the universe. Since the Bible teaches that God upholds all things by His power (Heb. 1:3), the creationist expects that the universe

The future resembles the past because God upholds the future as He has upheld the past (the laws of nature are constant). Since none of us have experienced the future, the only way we could know that the future is like the past is by revelation from God. Everyone relies on this vital principle.

would function in a logical, orderly, law-like fashion.[12] Furthermore, God is consistent (1 Sam. 15:29; Num. 23:19) and omnipresent (Psalm 139:7–8). Thus, the creationist expects that all regions of the universe will obey the same laws, even in regions where the physical conditions are quite different. The entire field of astronomy depends upon this important biblical principle.

Moreover, God is beyond time (2 Pet. 3:8) and has chosen to uphold the universe in a consistent fashion throughout time for our benefit. So even though conditions in the past may be quite different than those in the present and future, the way God upholds the universe (what we would call the "laws of nature") will not arbitrarily change.[13] God has told us that there are certain things we can count on to be true in the future — the seasons, the diurnal cycle, and so on (Gen. 8:22; Jer. 33:20–21). Therefore, under a given set of conditions, the consistent Christian has the right to expect a given outcome because he or she relies upon the Lord to uphold the universe in a consistent way.

These Christian principles are absolutely essential to science. When we perform a controlled experiment using the same preset starting conditions, we expect to get the same result every time. The "future reflects the past" in this sense. Scientists are able to make predictions only because there is uniformity as a result of God's sovereign and consistent power. Scientific experimentation would be pointless without uniformity; we would get a different result every time we performed an identical experiment, destroying the very possibility of scientific knowledge.

Since science requires the biblical principle of uniformity (as well as a number of other biblical creation principles), it may seem rather amazing that one could be a scientist and also be an evolutionist. And yet there are scientists who profess to believe in evolution. How is this possible?

The answer is that evolutionists are able to do science only because they are *inconsistent*. They accept biblical principles such as uniformity, while simultaneously denying the Bible from which those principles are derived. Such inconsistency is common in secular thinking; secular scientists claim that the universe is not designed, but they do science as if the universe *is* designed and upheld by God in a uniform way. Evolutionists can do science only if they rely on biblical creation assumptions (such as uniformity) that are contrary to their professed belief in evolution.[14]

How Would an Evolutionist Respond?

The consistent Christian can use past experience as a guide for what is likely to happen in the future, because God has promised us that (in certain ways) the future will reflect the past (Gen. 8:22). But how can those who reject Genesis explain why there should be uniformity of nature? How would an evolutionist respond if asked, "Why will the future reflect the past?"

One of the most common responses is: "Well, it always has. So I expect it always will." But this is the fallacy of begging the question — arbitrarily assuming the very thing that is to be proved for the sake of proving it. This is sometimes called *circular reasoning*, and it doesn't really prove the point beyond merely assuming it. I'll grant that in the past there has been uniformity.[15] But how do I know that in the future there will be uniformity, unless I already assumed that the future reflects the past (i.e., uniformity)? Whenever we use past experience as a basis for what is likely to happen in the future, we are assuming uniformity. So when an evolutionist says that he believes there will be uniformity in the future since there has been uniformity in the past, he's trying to justify uniformity by simply assuming uniformity — a vicious circular argument.

The circular nature of this response is often hard for people to grasp at first. The difficulty is perhaps because uniformity is so foundational

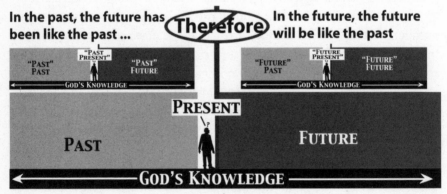

The above argument is circular. The "therefore" of this argument *assumes* that the future will be like the past (otherwise past experience would be totally irrelevant to the future). But this is the very thing that the argument is trying to prove.

to our thinking, so constantly assumed, that we seldom take notice of it. It's like breathing. We need air to survive and we breathe all the time without thinking about it. Hence, when evolutionists are first challenged to justify uniformity, they often arbitrarily (and unconsciously) assume it for the purpose of proving it. That is, they rely upon past experiences to justify their expectation that, in the future we may use past experiences to justify our expectation of the future. The error is subtle and yet very common. So it is worthy of careful reflection.

In their textbook *Introduction to Logic*, Copi and Cohen cite this fallacious way of arguing for uniformity/induction as the quintessential example of the fallacy of begging the question. They write:

> Powerful minds sometimes are snared by this fallacy, as is illustrated by a highly controversial issue in the history of philosophy. Logicians have long sought to establish the reliability of inductive procedures by establishing the truth of what is called the "principle of induction." This is the principle that the laws of nature will operate tomorrow as they operate today, that in basic ways nature is essentially uniform, and that therefore we may rely on past experience to guide our conduct in the future. "That the future will be essentially like the past" is the claim at issue, but this claim, never doubted in ordinary life, turns out to be very difficult to prove. Some thinkers have claimed that they could prove it by showing that, when we have in the past relied on the inductive principle, we have always found that this method has helped us to achieve our objectives. They ask, "Why conclude that the future will be like the past?" and answer "Because it always has been like the past."
>
> But as David Hume pointed out, the common argument is a *petitio*, it begs the question. For the point at issue is whether nature *will continue* to behave regularly; that it *has* done so in the past cannot serve as proof that it *will* do so in the future — unless one assumes the very principle that is here in question: that the future will be like the past. And so Hume, granting that in the past the future has been like the past, asked the telling question with which philosophers still tussle: How can we know that future futures will be like past futures? They *may* be so, of course, but we may not assume that they will be for the sake of *proving* that they will.[16]

Some people will admit, "Well, of course I don't know for certain that the laws of nature will be in the future like they have been in the past. But it is very *probable* that they will." But this too begs the question because any argument from probability also tacitly assumes the truth of uniformity in nature. Consider the following.

When the weatherman says that there is a 90% chance of rain today, he is relying upon past experiences to make a prediction about the future. The number (90%) means that in the past, when conditions were similar to those of today, it rained on 90% of those days. Hence, the weatherman assumes that in the future, when conditions are similar to those of the past, it will rain on 90% of those days. That the future will reflect the past is assumed.

Thus, probability cannot serve as the foundational reason for the inductive principle, because probability assumes the truth of the inductive principle. So it is not simply that evolutionists could not know *for certain* that uniformity is true on their own worldview, but rather they could not even know that it is *probably* true. That is, they could not have any good reason to believe that uniformity is even likely to be true if evolution were true. Evolutionists believe in uniformity, as do creationists. But only the latter have genuine *knowledge* of uniformity on their own worldview because only the biblical worldview gives us an objective reason to believe in uniformity without begging the question.

An evolutionist might argue that the nature of matter is such that it behaves in a regular fashion;[17] in other words, uniformity is just a property of the universe. This answer fails for several reasons. First, it doesn't really answer the question. Perhaps uniformity is one aspect of the universe, but the question is *why*? What would be the basis for such a property in an evolutionary worldview? Second, we might ask how an evolutionist could possibly *know* that uniformity is a property of the universe. At best, he can only say that the universe — in the past — seems to have had some uniformity.[18] But how do we know that will continue into the future unless we already knew about uniformity some other way? Many things in this universe change; how do we know that the laws of nature will not?

Some evolutionists might try a more pragmatic response: "Well, I can't really explain why. But uniformity seems to work, so we use it." This answer also fails for two reasons. First, we can only argue that uniformity seems to have worked in the *past*; there's no guarantee it will continue to work in the future unless we already have a reason to assume uniformity (which only the Christian does). Yet evolutionists do assume that uniformity will be true in the future. They couldn't even get out of bed without making this assumption.

Second, anyone using this answer has admitted that uniformity is without justification in the evolutionary worldview — which is exactly the point. No one is denying that there is uniformity in nature; the point is that only a biblical creation worldview can make sense of it. Evolutionists can only do science if they are inconsistent — that is, if they assume biblical creationist concepts while denying biblical creation.

Theistic Evolution Won't Save the Day

Some evolutionists[19] might argue that they can account for uniformity just as the biblical creationist does — by appealing to a God who upholds the universe in a law-like fashion. After all, evolutionists are not necessarily atheists. Many of them believe that some sort of god used evolution to form the various living creatures: this is "theistic evolution." However, simply adding a god to evolution will not resolve the problem. This is because there is no guarantee that their god will uphold the future in a consistent fashion as the Christian God does.

Even if they say that they believe in the Christian God, this will not solve the problem. We could ask, "How do you *know* that God will uphold the future as He has upheld the past?" The biblical creationist can answer this question: "The Bible teaches this." But the theistic evolutionist cannot give a good answer to this because he does not accept the Bible (at least not all of it, e.g., Genesis).

To be clear, a theistic evolutionist may very well *believe* that God (or *a* god) will uphold the future as He has upheld the past (and thus that the laws of nature will not change with time). But remember, a belief must have a good reason if it is to be considered rational, and not simply an arbitrary opinion. A biblical creationist does have a good reason for this belief: God has revealed in His Word that He will uphold the universe in a consistent fashion. But a theistic evolutionist must deny the Bible as his authoritative standard (because he rejects Genesis), and therefore cannot appeal to the Bible as the basis for his knowledge of God.

As a last resort, the theistic evolutionist may say, "But I accept much of the Bible. I just don't believe in a literal Genesis. So I do believe in uniformity based on the teaching of Scripture." But this fails for two reasons. First, the same Bible that teaches uniformity also teaches that God created the universe in six days. It is arbitrary and inconsistent to accept one while denying the other.[20] Second, the basis of uniformity is found in Genesis (e.g., Gen. 8:22), which a theistic evolutionist does not accept.[21] Without biblical creation, the rational basis for uniformity is lost. A theistic evolutionist does not have a good reason to believe in uniformity, and thus has no foundation for science.

It's not just any god that is required in order to make sense of uniformity; it is the Christian God as revealed in the Bible. Only a God who is beyond time, consistent, faithful, all-powerful, omnipresent, and who has revealed Himself to mankind can guarantee that there will be uniformity throughout space and time. Therefore, only *biblical* creationists can account for the uniformity in nature. Additional information showing the irrationality of theistic evolution and day-age creationism is found in appendix A.

Evolution Is Irrational

In fact, if evolution were true, there wouldn't be any rational reason to believe it! If life is the result of evolution, then it means that an evolutionist's brain is simply the outworking of millions of years of random-chance processes. The brain would simply be a collection of chemical reactions that have been preserved because they had some sort of survival value in the past. If evolution were true, then all the evolutionist's thoughts are merely the necessary result of chemistry acting over time. Therefore, an evolutionist *must* think and say that "evolution is true," not for rational reasons, but as a necessary consequence of blind chemistry.

Scholarly analysis presupposes that the human mind is not just chemistry. Rationality presupposes that we have the freedom to consciously consider the various options and choose the best. Evolutionism undermines the preconditions necessary for rational thought, thereby destroying the very possibility of knowledge and science.

Evolution is anti-science and anti-knowledge. If evolution were true, science would not make sense because there would be no reason to accept the uniformity of nature upon which all science and technology depend. Nor would there be any reason to think that rational analysis would be possible since the thoughts of our mind would be nothing more than the inevitable result of mindless chemical reactions. Evolutionists are able to do science and gain knowledge only because they are inconsistent — professing to believe in evolution while accepting the principles of biblical creation.

Why So Inconsistent?

When we consider the concepts of morality, logic, and science, we find that evolution simply cannot account for these things, yet evolutionists do believe in them. How are we to account for such inconsistency? Not only does the Bible give us a basis for such concepts, but it also tells us why unbelievers know such things and yet are unwilling to acknowledge God as the source. The Bible tells us that God has revealed Himself to mankind, and thus all people have innate knowledge of God. But people have rebelled against God. They have an ax to grind and are unwilling to be thankful or give glory to the Lord. Instead they suppress what they know to be true. Romans 1:18–25 states:

> For the wrath of God is revealed from heaven against all ungodliness and unrighteousness of men who suppress the truth in unrighteousness, because that which is known about God is evident within them; for God made it evident to them. For since the creation of the world His invisible attributes, His eternal power and divine nature, have been clearly seen, being understood through what has been made, so that they are without excuse. For even though they knew God, they did not honor Him as God or give thanks, but they became futile in their speculations, and their foolish heart was darkened. Professing to be wise, they became fools, and exchanged the glory of the incorruptible God for an image in the form of corruptible man and of birds and four-footed animals and crawling creatures. . . . For they exchanged the truth of God for a lie, and worshiped and served the creature rather than the Creator, who is blessed forever. Amen (NASB).

Conclusions

In logic, no one is allowed to be arbitrary — to simply assert assumptions that have no foundation whatsoever.[22] A rational person has a reason for what he or she believes. We have demonstrated that the consistent Christian has a good reason to believe in the preconditions

of intelligibility: they are consistent with biblical creation. The biblical worldview provides a basis for those things we take for granted. And although this may not be the only reason to accept the Bible as our ultimate standard, it is certainly a good one: the Bible provides a consistent worldview that contains the necessary principles for logical reasoning, science, and morality.

Evolutionists, however, have no justification for these principles. Yes, evolutionists believe in logic, morality, and science, but such things do not make sense in an evolutionary universe. Evolutionists must borrow biblical creation principles in order to make sense of anything. They are intellectually schizophrenic — relying on one worldview while professing another. Like the critic of air, evolutionists must use that which is *contrary* to their position in order to make an argument *for* their position.

In particular, evolutionists sometimes argue that it is *wrong* to teach creation "because this is lying." But since such a moral claim relies on biblical principles (that lying is wrong), the argument only makes sense if creation is true. Or evolutionists will argue that creationists are irrational. But rationality presupposes the existence of laws of logic — which only make sense in a biblical worldview. Finally, evolutionists will argue that science supports their position. But science requires the uniformity of nature, which only makes sense if biblical creation is true.

Evolutionists are in the unenviable position of having to rely on the fact that their worldview is false in order to argue that it is true.

The ultimate proof of biblical creation is that without it we could not know anything. We've seen three illustrations of the ultimate proof in this chapter. Although many other examples could have been used, these three examples certainly suffice to refute the evolutionary worldview. In the following chapters, we will explore how to use these illustrations in a rational dialogue with evolutionists, or supporters of other non-biblical positions.

Endnotes

1. This section is an adaptation of an article I originally wrote for the Answers in Genesis website. The original article is entitled "Evolution and the Challenge of Morality."

2. The happiness of others, though important, is not the primary concern within the Christian worldview. To love and obey the God who has created and saved us should be our primary focus (Mark 12:30; Eccles. 12:13). One aspect of this is that we should treat others with love and respect (Matt. 7:12; Mark 12:31).

3. God's mind is not like ours. God's mind is the source of all truth, whereas our minds are the recipients of some truth.

4. Christian philosopher Dr. Greg Bahnsen masterfully used the concept of laws of logic to demonstrate the existence of God in the famous Bahnsen-Stein debate. Dr. Bahnsen pointed out that since debates presuppose laws of logic, and since atheism cannot account for such laws, the very debate itself proved the existence of God. His opponent, Dr. Gordon Stein, was not able to counter the argument. This debate has become something of a legend. Audio CDs of the debate are available at the Covenant Media Foundation website: http://www.cmfnow.com/.

5. Clearly, our thoughts are not as "high" as God's, for we are finite and He is infinite. Nonetheless, we are made in God's image, and therefore have a limited capacity to reason logically — to "think God's thoughts after Him."

6. This section is adapted from an article that was originally designed to refute the atheist's worldview. The article appears on the Answers in Genesis website and is entitled "Atheism: An Irrational Worldview." Note that both evolutionists and atheists can be refuted by essentially the same argument since both worldviews have the same defects.

7. We will deal with the claim that it's just a different "interpretation" of Scripture in the appendix.

8. Theodosius Dobzhansky wrote that "Nothing in biology makes sense except in the light of evolution." This was also the title of his 1973 essay first published in the *American Biology Teacher*, vol. 35, p. 125–129.

    The National Academy of Sciences issued a document titled "Science, Evolution, and Creationism," which stated that evolution is a "critical foundation of the biomedical and life sciences" and that evolutionary concepts "are fundamental to a high-quality science education."

The National Academy of Sciences also published a document titled "Teaching about Evolution and the Nature of Science" (1998) with a similar theme. In the preface (p. viii), the authors indicate that biological evolution is "the most important concept in modern biology, a concept essential to understanding key aspects of living things." They chose to publish the document in part "because of the importance of evolution as a central concept in understanding our planet."

9. The term "anti-science" was the inspiration for the original article on which this section is based. This section has been expanded and modified from the original article, which was posted on the Answers in Genesis website under the title "Evolution: The Anti-Science."

10. Uniformity should not be confused with "uniformitarianism." Uniformity simply insists that the laws of nature are consistent and do not arbitrarily change with time or space, though specific conditions and processes may change. Uniformitarianism is the (unbiblical) belief that present processes are the same as past processes; it asserts a consistency of *conditions* and *rates* over time and is summed up in the phrase: "The present is the key to the past."

11. There are some situations (such as chaotic systems) where the outcome is not computable because the initial conditions can never be known precisely enough. Weather is one example. But even chaotic systems are predictable in principle — if the initial parameters could be known with sufficient precision. Even quantum mechanical systems are predictable *statistically*. The probabilistic nature of quantum mechanics does not conflict with uniformity. As the principles of quantum mechanics have worked in the past, so we expect them to work in the future; this is the essence of uniformity.

12. The "ordinances of heaven and earth" are specifically mentioned in Jeremiah 33:25.

13. Granted, God can use unusual and extraordinary means on occasion to accomplish an extraordinary purpose — what we might call a "miracle." But these are (by definition) exceptional; natural law could be defined as the ordinary way that God upholds the universe and accomplishes His will. We will discuss miracles in chapter 9.

14. Why would someone who professes to believe in evolution also accept creation-based concepts? Although they may deny it, evolutionists are also made in the image of God (Gen. 1:26–27). In their heart of hearts, they know the biblical God (Rom. 1:19–20), but they have deceived themselves (James 1:22–24). They have forgotten that the principles of science come from the Christian worldview.

15. In granting this assumption, I'm actually being very generous to the evolutionist. I could have been very thorough and asked, "How do we really know that even in the past nature has been uniform?" One might argue that we *remember* that the past was uniform. But since the memory portions of our brains require that the laws of chemistry and physics are constant over time, you would have to assume that the past is uniform in order to argue that we correctly remember that the past is uniform! Any non-Christian response would necessarily be a vicious circle.

16. I.M. Copi and C. Cohen, *Introduction to Logic*, 10th edition (Upper Saddle River, NJ : Prentice-Hall, Inc., 1994,1998), p.187.

17. The atheist Dr. Gordon Stein used essentially this response in the famous 1985 debate with Christian philosopher Dr. Greg Bahnsen on the existence of God.

18. Again, I'm being generous here. Even this response is begging the question, since the evolutionist would have to assume uniformity in the past in order to argue that his memories of the past are accurate.

19. A "day-age" creationist might also try to use this argument, but it also fails for the same reason. Day-age creationists do not believe that Genesis really means what it says (that God literally created in six ordinary days). So, how could we trust that Genesis 8:22 really means what it says? And if Genesis 8:22 does not mean what it says then there is no reason to believe in uniformity. Therefore, the day-age creationist has the same problem as the evolutionist. Neither can account for science and technology within his own worldview.

20. This is because a person would need a greater standard than the Bible to judge which sections of the Bible to accept, and which to reject. But any standard other than God's cannot be an ultimate standard, as we show throughout this book. See chapter 9 for an extended discussion on the rational necessity of an ultimate standard. See appendix A for a discussion of compromised positions, such as day-age creationism and theistic evolution.

21. Genesis 8:22 is one example. Even passages outside of Genesis that could be used to support uniformity are still based in Genesis. For example, in Jeremiah 33:20–21, God's covenant with day and night was clearly established during the creation week.

22. Otherwise, why not assert the exact opposite? If people are allowed to be arbitrary, then logical debate would be impossible since each of the opponents could "prove" his position by simply arbitrarily assuming it.

CHAPTER 4

REASONING WITH THE CRITIC

Now that we've seen that there is an irrefutable proof of creation, how can we use this proof in dialogues with evolutionists? We have studied three illustrations of the ultimate proof applied to three different areas of knowledge. People cannot even begin to know anything about science, rationality, or morality without borrowing biblical concepts. For any argument against creation to make sense, the evolutionist must secretly assume that biblical creation is *true*. For this reason, if it is used properly, the ultimate proof can turn any argument that is allegedly against creation into an argument *for* creation. To do this well, it is helpful to understand the thinking of the unbeliever, and how this differs from the thought process of the consistent Christian.

Presuppositions

All people have things that they believe to be true. Some of our beliefs are held somewhat loosely; others are held very strongly. As an example of a loosely held belief, I happen to believe that Mars has two and only two moons. However, if someone claimed to discover a third moon, and if the evidence seemed compelling, I would quickly change my belief to match. On the other hand, I also have strongly held beliefs — such as the law of non-contradiction. If someone claimed that they had discovered two contradictory claims that are both true,[1] I would be very skeptical of this. In fact, I would probably dismiss such a claim out-of-hand, because I am convinced that two contradictory claims cannot both be true. The beliefs that we hold to most strongly are called "presuppositions." People are very reluctant to give up their presuppositions.

Presuppositions are assumed at the outset, before any investigation of evidence; they are pre-supposed and control our interpretation of evidence. We are often not aware of our presuppositions, but they are always present. Just as we are always breathing, even though we are not often conscious of it until we stop and think about it, likewise, our presuppositions are constantly guiding our understanding of our experiences.

Presuppositions must be assumed before we can investigate other things. For example, laws of logic are a presupposition. I must assume that such laws exist before I can begin to reason. We learned previously that laws of logic are a precondition of intelligibility too. It is common that many presuppositions are also preconditions of intelligibility, but some are not. A number of evolutionists accept naturalism as a presupposition, but this is certainly not a precondition for being able to understand the universe.

All your presuppositions taken together form your worldview. So this leads us to a more precise definition of a worldview than the one we used in the first chapters. A worldview is a network of *presuppositions* in light of which all reasoning and experiences are interpreted. So although we have not mentioned the term until now, we have already dealt with presuppositions in the previous chapters because we have been talking about worldviews all along. To understand the difference between the way creationists and evolutionists think about the universe, we must examine their respective presuppositions.

A consistent Christian believes that the Bible is true, God exists, there are laws of logic, there is uniformity in nature, there is an absolute and binding moral code, and our senses and memory are basically reliable. These presuppositions comport; they go well together. We'd expect that there would be laws of logic if the Bible is true — since the Bible uses laws of logic. But both are presuppositions since they are supposed before investigation. Even though logic would be unjustified apart from the biblical God, we must use logic to read the Bible anyway — it must be presupposed. Laws of logic (and the Bible) are provable, but they must be supposed *before* they can be proved.[2] Hence, they are presuppositions. The Christian's presuppositions form a rationally consistent worldview in which knowledge is possible.

Evolutionists have their presuppositions too. Many evolutionists believe a number of the following: the Bible is irrelevant to science, empiricism (all things are known by observation), naturalism (nature is all that there is), evidence can be interpreted "neutrally," and unaided human reasoning is capable of determining truth. Some evolutionists accept evolution itself as a presupposition — an unquestionable fact through which other evidences are interpreted.

However, evolutionary presuppositions do not form a consistent worldview in which knowledge is possible. In many cases, secular presuppositions turn out to be self-refuting (as we demonstrated with empiricism in chapter 2). In all cases, they fail to provide the preconditions of intelligibility. If evolution were true, science and reasoning would not be possible: there would be no basis for logic, nor would there be any basis for uniformity in nature. So if evolutionists were consistent with their worldview, they would not be able to reason or do science. Yet evolutionists are able to reason and to do science. Thus it follows that evolutionists do not consistently rely upon their own worldview. They rely upon creationist presuppositions! How can we account for this inconsistency?

The Nature of the Unbeliever

The Bible gives us the reason why all unbelievers do rely (to some extent) on biblical principles. All people do know in their heart of hearts the biblical God, because God has revealed Himself to everyone. Romans 1:19–20 states, "Since what may be known about God is plain to them, because God has made it plain to them. For since the creation of the world God's invisible qualities — his eternal power and divine nature — have been clearly seen, being understood from what has been made, so that men are without excuse." The problem is not that people are unaware of God. The problem is that they "suppress the truth by their wickedness" (Rom. 1:18).

God has "hardwired" certain information into us — including an innate knowledge of Him and His principles. This is why everyone believes in laws of logic, uniformity of nature, and absolute morality (even those who say they don't). God has made Himself known to everyone. But not everyone honors God or is thankful for His revelation. Romans 1:21–23 states: "For although they knew God, they neither glorified him as God nor gave thanks to him, but their thinking became futile and their foolish hearts were darkened. Although they claimed to be wise, they became fools, and exchanged the glory of the immortal God for images made to look like mortal man and birds and animals and reptiles." This verse confirms what we have already seen: a rejection of biblical principles leads to futile thinking — it destroys the possibility of knowledge.

Ephesians 4:17–18 further illustrates this. We are not to walk as the Gentiles, ". . . in the futility of their thinking. They are darkened in their understanding and separated from the life of God, because of the ignorance that is in them due to the hardening of their hearts." The futility of unbelievers' thinking stems ultimately from a hardness of their hearts — a stubborn rebellion against God. This results in ignorance, which results in darkened understanding, leading to a type of useless, futile thinking.

Fortunately, unbelievers are not totally consistent with their faulty, futile presuppositions. If they were, they couldn't function at all. They must rely on biblical principles in order to know anything. Unbelievers are "presuppositional kleptomaniacs." They cannot stop themselves from stealing biblical presuppositions in order to function and make sense of the universe. But they have "forgotten" where those principles come from. Unbelievers do believe in God, but they have convinced themselves that they don't. They are self-deceived (James 1:22–24). How can we expose the inconsistency of the secular position?

The Bible gives us one more important piece of information about the unbeliever: he is a *fool* (Prov. 1:7; Rom. 1:22). Now please don't be upset by the biblical use of the term "fool." The Bible is not simply engaging in name-calling. Nor am I; rather, I am using biblical terminology to describe a biblical strategy. A fool (in the biblical sense of the word) is someone whose thinking is futile because he has rejected God's revelation (Rom. 1:21; 1 Cor. 3:19; Prov. 1:7). The fool may have very high intelligence, but he refuses to use his intellect in the way that God has designed — in a way that is faithful to God's revelation. As a result, his thinking is reduced to absurdity.

The "fool" arbitrarily (and inconsistently) rejects the biblical presuppositions that lead to knowledge, and replaces them with secular presuppositions that lead to futile, self-defeating reasoning. The only reason the fool is able to know anything at all is because he does not do this consistently. In his heart of hearts, he does believe in biblical presuppositions. We should never disparage or mock a fool. After all, the fool is also made in God's image and is entitled to dignity on that basis. And besides, every one of us has been the fool at some point in our lives. Therefore, as we now learn to expose the foolishness of secular thinking, we must always remember to answer with gentleness and respect (1 Pet. 3:15).

How to Argue with a "Fool": Don't Answer, Answer

The Bible not only tells us how to identify a fool, but also how to converse with one. We've already seen that we cannot simply use scientific evidence — by itself — on those people who have different presuppositions; they will simply re-interpret the evidence to fit into their worldview. God knew that this would be the case, and so He provided us with a crucial tool: a strategy for answering those people who have foolishly embraced erroneous, unbiblical presuppositions. It is a two-part strategy found in Proverbs 26:4–5.

Proverbs 26:4 is part 1. This verse states: "Do not answer a fool according to his folly, lest you also be like him" (NKJV). Here we learn that we are not to answer the unbeliever according to his folly — according to his fallacious presuppositions. We are not to accept his standards for the debate, because they are nonsense. His ultimate standard

DO NOT ANSWER A FOOL ACCORDING TO HIS FOLLY,   **LEST YOU ALSO BE LIKE HIM.**

We should never embrace the foolish presuppositions of an unbeliever.

Otherwise, we too will be reduced to foolishness (Prov. 26:4).

leads to the conclusion that knowledge is impossible, in which case there is nothing to debate anyway. If we were to accept his ludicrous terms, we, too, would be reduced to futile, contradictory thinking, and this will get us nowhere.

As an example, consider an argument with an empiricist. The empiricist will only want to accept arguments that are based on empirical observation. Recall, his standard is that "all knowledge is based on observation." But this standard is self-defeating; if all knowledge is based on observation, then we could never *know* that "all knowledge is based on observation," since this has not been observed. The empiricist couldn't really *know* anything at all by such thinking since his standard (by which he tests other things) is uncertain. Therefore, if we accept his self-defeating standard, we, too, will be in the position of not being able to know anything. We will have become like him.

As another example, evolutionists often try to frame the origins debate as "science versus faith" where they take "science" to mean "evolution." Sadly, many Christians fail to challenge this claim; instead they accept it and attempt to argue by this erroneous standard. Such Christians respond by disparaging science: "Science is not reliable, and evolution is just a theory anyway." They essentially argue: "The Bible is good. Science is bad." And that's very unfortunate. The origins debate is not "science versus faith" at all. Science (though fallible) is a wonderful and very powerful tool that the Lord has given us; it confirms creation when used properly. Moreover, evolution is contrary to the principles of science, as we saw in the last chapter. So don't let an evolutionist get away with this type of claim; don't "answer the fool according to his folly."

Here is another example of a very common mistake made by creationists when conversing with an evolutionist. The evolutionist will say

something like this: "We can talk about origins, but let's leave the Bible out of the discussion. I'm only interested in the scientific evidence." Many creationists are tempted to say, "okay" and then proceed to try and convince the evolutionist by mere scientific evidences. This procedure is *wrong* according to Proverbs 26:4.

First, we've already seen that mere evidence will not motivate a person to change his presuppositions (because our presuppositions tell us how to interpret the evidence). There's no getting around it: we all interpret evidence to match our worldview. Scientific evidence has its place, certainly. And it may be used as a secondary standard by which to confirm biblical creation. But it must not be divorced from its biblical foundation.

Second, this is really an example of the "pretended neutrality fallacy." The biblical creationist is trying to show that the Bible is the ultimate authority by which all evidence (and that pertaining to origins in particular) should be interpreted. If it were possible to correctly interpret evidence about origins without biblical presuppositions, then the Bible really isn't the ultimate standard. So if we agree that the biblical worldview isn't necessary to settle the matter, we've immediately lost the debate — for this is the real issue behind the origins debate.

Third, the idea of leaving the Bible out of the discussion when talking about origins really does not make any sense. The Bible is the only infallible record we have regarding origins. Why on earth would we want to leave that out of the discussion? Furthermore, the Bible is the only ultimate standard that can provide the preconditions of intelligibility that

ANSWER A FOOL ACCORDING TO HIS FOLLY,   **LEST HE BE WISE IN HIS OWN EYES.**

Without embracing the unbeliever's philosophy, we take it to its logical conclusion . . .

. . . so that he can see how absurd his position is (Prov. 26:5).

make knowledge possible. The evolutionist's ultimate standard leads to nonsense (as we saw in the last chapter). If we trade in our correct worldview for a faulty one that can't lead to knowledge, then we, too, will be reduced to foolishness. Do not "answer a fool according to his folly" — according to his erroneous presuppositions — otherwise you will be just like him.

Now, Answer

Proverbs 26:5 is part 2. This verse states: "Answer a fool according to his folly, Lest he be wise in his own eyes" (NKJV). At first this may seem like a contradiction — didn't we just read that we should *not* answer a fool according to his folly? But it's not a contradiction at all because the sense is different. In verse 4 we learn that we should not embrace the folly of the unbeliever lest we be like him. But in verse 5 we are instructed to show where his folly would lead if it were true. We are going to accept his standard only *hypothetically* to show *for the sake of argument* that it would lead to nonsense. We make it clear that we do not actually accept his standard (Prov. 26:4), but if we hypothetically did, it would lead to an absurd conclusion; thus the fool cannot be wise in his own eyes (Prov. 26:5). When we do this, we are reflecting back the absurd philosophy of the "fool" for argument's sake, so that he can see how ridiculous it is.

As an example of this, consider debating with a relativist. He says, "I don't believe in absolutes. We can talk about the Bible if you like, but you can't use any absolute statements, because I don't believe in such things." What is the biblical way to respond to this foolish standard? First, we don't answer him according to his folly or we would be like him (Prov. 26:4). We might say, "I don't accept your claim that there are no absolutes." But then we do show for the sake of argument where such a standard would lead if it were true so that the relativist cannot be wise in his own eyes (Prov. 26:5), saying something like this: "But for the sake of argument, if there were no absolutes, you couldn't even say that 'there are no absolutes' since that is an absolute statement. Your standard is self-refuting: it leads to the conclusion that it cannot be true."

The "don't answer, answer" strategy is a very powerful tool that can be used to expose faulty presuppositions. In fact, we've really been using this tool all along. In the previous chapters we never abandoned the Bible as the ultimate standard. But we did show the consequences of hypothetically accepting alternative, evolutionary worldviews. The non-biblical worldviews lead to the absurd consequence that there is no basis for logic, science, or morality. Let's consider one more hypothetical scenario.

Suppose someone said, "I don't believe in words. Prove to me that creation is true without using words." For some reason, Christians are very tempted to answer the fool according to his folly and become like him; we are tempted to accept the ludicrous standard of the critic. But if we do, we, too, will be reduced to foolishness. Why would a creationist accept such an absurd standard? Just imagine a creationist trying to show that creation is true using charades! This is exactly what I picture in my mind whenever I see a creationist try to prove creation without using the Bible. Don't accept the critic's standard! If he wants to leave the Bible out of the discussion, or if he doesn't believe in words, that's *his* foolishness. Don't make it yours!

Instead, use the "don't answer, answer" strategy. First, we use the "don't answer" part: say, "I don't accept your claim that words don't exist." Then, answer, "But for the sake of argument, if words didn't exist, you couldn't argue anyway. The fact that you are able to articulate your position proves that your position is wrong." This is a devastating critique. After all, how can the critic really respond to it? If he says nothing, the point stands unrefuted. If he says anything at all, he reinforces the point that words do exist.

Of course, our answer to the critic would not have to be stated exactly this way. For that matter, we don't have to explicitly state both responses; the "don't answer" part may be implied by the way we state the "answer" part. Moreover, there is no particular order in which we must use this strategy. It may be more effective in some cases to "answer" first, and then state the "don't answer" part second. However we choose to articulate our response, we should keep in mind the overall strategy: (1) never embrace the foolish presuppositions of the critic, but (2) do show where they would lead if they (hypothetically) were true.

When we add this strategy to the information we've learned in the previous chapters, we have a very powerful set of tools for defending the Christian faith. Learn to recognize how evolutionists implicitly rely on creationist presuppositions. When they try to get you to debate on their inconsistent (foolish) standard, reject this ("don't answer"), but show where their inconsistent thinking would lead if it were true ("answer"). In particular, look for the preconditions of intelligibility. Show that on their own presuppositions, they would have no basis for laws of logic, uniformity of nature, or morality. Let's look at some examples.

Answering the Critics

Suppose an evolutionist said, "I believe in naturalism. Show me logically how the earth could possibly be 6,000 years old. But you can't invoke the supernatural — because I don't believe in things that you can't observe with your senses." Of course, normally the critic would not be so explicit about his worldview; the Christian must listen carefully and try to figure out what the presuppositions of the critic are. But since we're just practicing at this point, our hypothetical critic has been unusually upfront about his worldview. How then should we answer?

We must always avoid the temptation to embrace the critic's standards lest we become like him. Do not just throw evidential arguments at the critic according to his terms and expect him to reconsider his presuppositions. Instead, look for inconsistencies in his worldview. When you examined his statements, I hope you mentally "zoomed in" on certain words and phrases: "naturalism" and "logic," for example. These two ideas do not comport with each other. If nature is all that there is, then laws of logic cannot exist, since they are not a part of nature. After all, you can't stub your toe on a law of logic, or pull a law of logic out of the refrigerator.[3] Whenever a non-Christian asks you to be rational, you should ask him, "why?" Only in the Christian worldview do we have a *moral* obligation to follow the *laws of logic* — which themselves only make sense in a biblical worldview. Use the "don't answer, answer" strategy to respond to this critic:

Here's the "don't answer" part: "I don't accept your belief in naturalism, or your belief that all things must be observed by the senses." Then answer: "In fact, if (for the sake of argument) naturalism were true, you couldn't have laws of logic anyway since they are not a part of nature. You say you only believe things observed by your senses; if that's true, then you can't believe in laws of logic since they cannot be observed by the senses. Logical reasoning would be impossible if your beliefs were true. So why do you ask me to be logical? Laws of logic only make sense if biblical creation is true." This response makes use of the ultimate proof. As such, there can be no rational rebuttal.

Even though he has already lost the debate at this point, the naturalist may not concede defeat. He will most likely attempt to argue that laws of logic are compatible with his worldview. He might say that laws of logic are just conventions, that they are chemical reactions in the brain, or that they are descriptions of the way the brain thinks. But we have already shown that these responses are rationally deficient; laws of logic could not be universal laws (and thus would not have any prescriptive power) if any of these were true. (If this is not obvious by this point, please review section 2 on laws of logic under the sub-heading "Possible Responses" in the previous chapter.) Or the critic may argue that we use laws of logic because they work. But this answer sidesteps the question rather than answering it: laws of logic only make sense in a biblical creation worldview.

As another example, suppose an evolutionist says, "It's wrong to teach creation in schools. You're lying to children!" Again, we answer using Proverbs 26:4–5 as our guide. We do not embrace the presupposition of this evolutionist, but we do show where such thinking would lead if it were true. Look for inconsistencies in the person's statement. On the one hand, this person believes that lying is wrong. On the other hand, he or she believes that creation is not true, in which case there is no basis for morality. So we respond as follows.

First, we apply the "don't answer" part. We state, "I don't accept your claim that teaching creation is lying. I am convinced that evolution is the lie, and I have powerful scientific evidences that confirm this." It would be perfectly appropriate at this point to mention a few examples of scientific evidence — perhaps those used in chapter 1. But since these do not ultimately refute evolution, we must eventually "answer the fool" showing the absurdity of evolutionary reasoning. Answer: "But, for the sake of argument, why in your worldview would it be *wrong* to lie to children?"

Sometimes the evolutionist will respond by saying, "Well, everyone knows that it's wrong to lie. You don't seriously deny this, do you?" Of course, we're not arguing that lying is okay. We are arguing that *if evolution were true*, then there is no moral standard by which we could say that lying is objectively wrong.

So we could respond, "In my worldview, lying is wrong because it is contrary to God's commands, and we are responsible to Him since we were *created* by Him. But if evolution were true, why would it be wrong to lie to children? After all, human beings are just chemical accidents of nature in your view. So, why should we be concerned about what one chemical accident does to another chemical accident? *If evolution were true*, why would it be wrong for me to lie to someone, particularly if it has survival value?"

Additional Examples

Evolutionists often attempt to use "scientific arguments" to refute biblical creation. They'll say, "All the scientific evidence shows that life evolved over billions of years. And besides, science would be impossible if God were constantly interfering with the laws of nature." We respond using the biblical strategy.

Beginning with the "don't answer" part, we state, "I don't accept your claim that scientific evidence supports evolution. In fact, there are many evidences that challenge evolutionary notions." We could give some examples at this point, showing that information theory, irreducible complexity, and carbon-14 all confirm biblical creation. Continue by gently correcting their distorted view of what creationists believe: "Nor do I believe that God constantly interferes with laws of nature. In my view, laws of nature are a description of the consistent way God upholds the universe." Then answer, "But for the sake of argument, apart from biblical creation, why would the universe be understandable? If the universe is an accident, and our brains are the result of accidental mutations, then why would we expect that one sequence of accidents could correctly understand another accident? Why would there be an underlying uniformity in a constantly evolving universe? Why would there be laws of nature? In particular, why do we all presume that the laws of nature will work *in the future as they have in the past*?"

This last question is the "killer" — there just isn't any good response to it apart from the Christian worldview. Nine times out of ten, the evolutionist will respond, "Well, the laws of nature have been constant in the past, so I expect they will be in the future too." But this answer already assumes that the future reflects the past; it is vicious circular reasoning, as we discussed in the previous chapter. Any time you use past experience as a basis for what will probably happen in the future, you are assuming that the future reflects the past. You can't therefore merely use this assumption to prove that the future will be like the past. Yet most evolutionists will not realize that they are arguing in a circle. I can almost guarantee that you will have to explain this to them, so have an example in mind. Here's one that I like to use: "We can't just assume that things in the future will always be like the past; things change. It would be silly for me to argue that I'm never going to die. After all, I've never died in the past, so I assume I will never die in the future."

How do we know laws of nature will be tomorrow as they have been in the past? This may be the case, of course, but how would you *justify* it? Only the Bible gives us an answer: God (who is beyond time and knows the future) has promised us that He will uphold it in a consistent fashion (Gen. 8:22). We know this truth only by *revelation* from God.

Let's consider one last example of the "don't answer, answer" strategy. Suppose an unbeliever says, "You can't trust the Bible. It's full of contradictions!" There would be some value in addressing the specifics, to show the unbeliever how he or she has not properly read the text. But this might go on indefinitely, if we do not — at some point — challenge the unbeliever's faulty worldview. Rather than simply trying to explain all the alleged contradictions on the terms of the unbeliever, how much more powerful it would be to use the Proverbs 26:4–5 "don't answer, answer" strategy!

First, the don't answer part: we state, "I don't accept your claim that the Bible is full of contradictions." Then answer, "But, for the sake of argument, if it did, why in your worldview would that be wrong? As a Christian, I believe that contradictions cannot be true because all truth is in God and God is self-consistent. But what is your basis for the law of non-contradiction, or for that matter any of the laws of logic?" As we saw in the previous chapter, only the Bible provides a rational foundation for laws of logic. So, this puts the unbeliever on the "horns of a dilemma." If he accepts the Bible as his foundation for logic, then he can't argue against it. Yet, if he rejects the Bible, then he has no basis for saying that contradictions are always false. So how then can he say that the Bible cannot be trusted for allegedly containing contradictions?

It doesn't occur to most Christians to answer this way, and that's a shame. This biblical way of answering is very powerful. Keep in mind that we need not answer as explicitly as I have in the above hypothetical examples. Often the "don't answer" portion of the strategy will not need to be stated since it will be implied by the "answer" portion. On the other hand, sometimes it is necessary to clearly explain the Christian position to an unbeliever, requiring the "don't answer" part to be more explicit. Every conversation is different, and so the specific points will differ. But in all cases, we stand on the truth of God's Word and refute the fallacious standard of the "fool."

Truth, not Tricks

The "don't answer, answer" technique is not a debate gimmick. It is not a trick to win an academic debate or to persuade people to believe something that is not true. Rather, it is a way of exposing error, and revealing truth. Therefore, it can only be used effectively to show the truth of things that are actually true. Consequently, the "don't answer, answer" method cannot be used to prove Islaam, Mormonism, Buddhism, Hinduism, or atheism. It will only reveal the truth of the Christian worldview, and expose the defects in the others. Likewise, the method cannot be used to argue for evolution, or old-earth creationism. It will only expose the errors of these positions, and reveal the truth of biblical creation.

For this reason, I am always happy to share this technique with unbelievers. It won't help them defend their position; it will only help them realize the truth. And that is the goal. I want to believe what is actually true, and I want others to believe this too. Anything less would not honor the Lord.

Always Be Ready

First Peter 3:15 states, "But sanctify Christ as Lord in your hearts, always being ready to make a defense to everyone who asks you to give an account for the hope that is in you, yet with gentleness and reverence" (NASB). The Greek word used for "defense" (or "answer" in many translations) is "apologia" ($\alpha\pi\text{o}\lambda\text{o}\gamma\text{i}\alpha$), which is where we get the word apologetics. The word "apologia" means to give a reasoned argument in defense of one's position. So apologetics is the defense of the Christian faith. We are to provide a *reason* for the "hope" (the confidence)[4] that is in us whenever anyone asks. The ultimate proof gives us a wonderful reason: our faith in Christ provides a foundation for rational reasoning, science, and morality.

But too often we fail to appreciate the first part of 1 Peter 3:15: "sanctify Christ as Lord in your hearts." This is the key to accomplishing the rest of the verse. We must set apart Christ as Lord in our heart (in the core of our being) so that all our thinking is based on Him. When we do this, we can see how unbelievers already know God and secretly rely on biblical principles. And this forms the basis of our defense of the faith. As we get better at this, it's all the more crucial that we remember that last part of the verse as well: we must always answer "with gentleness and reverence."

If you really understand the ultimate proof, its various illustrations, and the "don't answer, answer" strategy, then you can take any argument that is alleged against the biblical worldview and show that it is actually an argument *for* the biblical worldview. In the next chapter we will learn some additional strategies and will codify a general approach for defending biblical creation against all opposition.

Endnotes
1. True at the same time and in the same sense or relationship.
2. Examples of such a proof are provided in chapter 9.
3. Dr. Bahnsen frequently used these examples. The point of course is that logic is immaterial, yet it does exist. Therefore, not all things that exist are material.
4. The Greek word for "hope" used in 1 Peter 3:15 is "elpis" (ελπις). This kind of hope is not a mere wistful dream, but indicates a confident expectation.

CHAPTER 5

THE PROCEDURE FOR DEFENDING THE FAITH

The previous chapters have given us an irrefutable argument for biblical creation and the Christian worldview in general. We have also seen that the Bible gives us a strategy by which we can expose the absurdity of antibiblical presuppositions. In this chapter, we will codify a generalized procedure for responding to any possible criticism of the biblical worldview. Our apologetic procedure will draw upon the facts that we have previously established. It is therefore instructive to briefly review what we have learned in chapters 1 through 4. These are things we should constantly keep in mind when debating with an evolutionist, an old-earth supporter, or any person holding a non-biblical position.

Summary of Chapters 1–4

First, everyone has presuppositions — basic beliefs that we take for granted before we begin to draw conclusions about the universe. These include things like laws of logic and the reliability of our senses. All of our presuppositions taken together form our *worldview*. Our worldview determines how we interpret the facts, and even what constitutes a "fact." Most people are not aware that they have a worldview, and consequently have not given much thought to it.

Second, the presuppositions of the unbeliever do not comport; they don't "go well together." They are inconsistent, often self-refuting, and would make knowledge impossible. The unbeliever's worldview cannot account for the preconditions of intelligibility — those things that are required in order for us to know anything. Preconditions of intelligibility include things like laws of logic, uniformity of nature, and absolute morality. Without a rational basis for the preconditions of intelligibility, the unbeliever cannot really *know* anything by his own worldview. He can certainly believe things, but he has no way to prove them, and thus he doesn't actually *know* them, based on his own worldview.

Third, unbelievers cannot *consistently* act upon their own professed worldview. If they did, they couldn't know anything; they wouldn't be able to function at all. Their own presuppositions cannot make sense of the universe. Therefore, unbelievers will compulsively "steal" Christian presuppositions in order to function. They are "presuppositional klepto-maniacs," constantly assuming things (like laws of logic) that make no sense upon their professed unbiblical worldview. The fact that unbeliev-ers consistently fail to embrace their own presuppositions shows that in their heart of hearts, they really do know the biblical God.

Fourth, to expose the inconsistency in unbelieving thought, we should use the "don't answer, answer" strategy. That is, we never embrace the presuppositions of the unbeliever; otherwise, we, too, will draw the wrong conclusions about the evidence and will be reduced to foolish-ness. However, we do show *for the sake of argument* where the non-biblical assumptions of the unbeliever would lead if they were true. We show that the unbeliever cannot make sense of anything as judged by his own standards. We are exposing the fact that the unbeliever does know the biblical God but has suppressed that truth in unrighteousness (Rom. 1:18). We expose the foolishness of the unbeliever with an attitude of reverence and humility, remembering that the unbeliever is also made in the image of God (Gen. 1:26–27), and is to be treated with respect.

Apologetic Guidelines

It is useful to have a mental "flow chart" to schematize our defense of the faith. Given the above information, we are now able to do this. Although I am convinced that there is one and *only one* correct approach to defending the faith (the way the Bible instructs us to defend it — to be discussed in chapter 10), there are several different ways we could schematize it. That is, there are several creative ways to remember the biblical principles outlined above. Analogously, there is one "cake," but it can be cut many different ways. Perhaps the simplest way is to divide it into two pieces. So we now introduce a twofold apologetic procedure.

(1) We present the biblical creation worldview and invite the evolutionist to stand on it for argument's sake. Although everyone thinks in terms of a worldview, most people do not *think that they think* in terms of a worldview. This is almost always the case with evolutionists, who tend to hold to the philosophies of empiricism and naturalism (which, ironically, *are* worldviews). They will not understand that the biblical creationist has a different standard for determining truth. We must therefore explain to the evolutionist that we reject their criteria for what is to be considered true or reasonable. This goes along with the "don't answer" part of the "don't answer, answer" strategy — we reject the presuppositions of the evolutionist. Instead, we embrace the Bible as our ultimate standard, since we consider it to be the infallible Word of the One who knows absolutely everything.

Most evolutionists are not aware of what biblical creationists believe; they have many misconceptions (thinking that creationists believe in fixity of species, or that we deny natural selection, etc.). In presenting the biblical worldview, we attempt to *educate* the evolutionist. We must make him aware of the fact that (A) everyone has a worldview through which all evidence is interpreted, and (B) our worldview can make sense of the evidence. We show that the biblical creation worldview is internally consistent, non-arbitrary, and can make sense of those things necessary for knowledge — the preconditions of intelligibility. We invite the evolutionist to consider our worldview, at least for argument's sake, so that he can see how we interpret evidence.

(2) We do an internal critique of the unbelieving/evolutionary worldview, showing that it is internally inconsistent and leads to absurdity. We show the evolutionist that he has not carefully considered the ramifications of his professed beliefs. If his beliefs were true, they would lead to the inescapable conclusion that we cannot know anything, since there would be no basis for laws of logic, or rationality by which we deduce other things. We "answer the fool according to his folly" for argument's sake, showing the self-defeating nature of the evolutionary

worldview. If his beliefs were true, then they would be false. Therefore, they are false.

Worldviews are a bit like kidneys. Everyone has them — you can't live or function without them. Yet, most people are unaware of their own ... until something goes wrong with them. To force the unbeliever to think through his worldview, we want to give him the intellectual equivalent of a kidney stone (for his own benefit!). We remind him of information that he already knows to be true but which he has not carefully considered — information that his worldview cannot process. Like a kidney stone, this procedure may be very painful for the evolutionist; he's not going to be happy about it. But his erroneous worldview must be exposed for the folly it is if he is ever going to come to the knowledge of the truth. An internal critique is therefore necessary so that the unbeliever cannot "be wise in his own eyes" (Prov. 26:5; NKJV).

The twofold apologetic method outlined above parallels the "don't answer, answer" strategy we discussed in the previous chapter. Just like the strategy, the two parts of this method do not have to be used in the order in which they are mentioned above. You may find it helpful to start with part 2, then move to part 1. You might then do a little more of part 2, a little of part 1, a lot of part 2, and so on. Most conversations or informal debates will consist of a volley of both parts in no particular order.

Introduction to the Apologetic Checklist: The "AIP" Test

While we are doing the internal critique of the unbiblical/evolutionary worldview, there are three things we must constantly keep in mind. This mental checklist is abbreviated by the letters "AIP." The first two are the key intellectual "sins" committed by unbelievers: arbitrariness and inconsistency. The third letter of "AIP" stands for the "preconditions of intelligibility." These three things show the evolutionary worldview to be utterly defective.

(A) **Arbitrariness:** In logical reasoning, no one is permitted to be arbitrary. That is, we cannot simply assert a claim that has no reason behind it and expect others to accept that claim. Our beliefs must have *justification*. Rational debate would be impossible if the two opponents decided they didn't need to give a reason for their position. If each person simply assumed what he was trying to prove, then there would be no point in arguing. Yet many evolutionists believe a number of things with no logical reason at all. It is unfair (and irrational) for an evolutionist to ask a creationist to provide a reason for his position, if the evolutionist himself is unwilling or unable to do the same thing. Such arbitrariness must be exposed as a fatal flaw in non-biblical worldviews.

Whenever an evolutionist asserts an arbitrary claim, simply ask him, "Why should I accept that claim?" If he insists that he doesn't need to give a reason, then we could simply assert the opposite and insist that we don't need a reason either. For that matter, we could just go ahead and assert that biblical creation is true: "creation is just a fact and we don't need to justify it." If the evolutionist is going to be arbitrary, then he has no right to criticize a creationist for being arbitrary either. After all, fair is fair. If we answer this way, we make it clear that we are being hypothetical; we creationists do indeed have a trustworthy reason for our position. Evolutionists do not.

Little children are often quite arbitrary. They believe lots of things with no good reasons at all. A child might believe that there is a monster under his bed or that Santa Claus comes down his chimney every Christmas. There is no good reason, yet children do believe these things sincerely and act upon their beliefs. They pull the bed sheets over their head to protect them from the monster; they leave out milk and cookies for Santa. We expect such arbitrariness from little children. But imagine if an adult were to behave in such a way. It would be disturbing to find an adult who seriously believed in monsters under the bed; we would be right to question his mental health. As we grow up, we are supposed to become *rational*, and part of being rational is learning to have a sufficient reason for what we believe. So when evolutionists fail to have a good reason for their beliefs, they are really behaving like uneducated children.

What are some beliefs that evolutionists hold arbitrarily? For some evolutionists, evolution itself is accepted as an unquestionable "fact." Believe it or not, you will encounter evolutionists who are actually offended if you ask them to defend their belief in evolution. For most evolutionists, naturalism, or at least methodological naturalism, is accepted without justification. Many hold to empiricism as an unquestionable fact. A few evolutionists will argue that they do not need to justify their own presuppositions. But presuppositions must also be justified if they are to be considered *rational* (however, by their nature, presuppositions must be assumed *before* they can be justified).[1] Many evolutionists claim that creationists have a "blind faith." And yet, ironically, we find that it is the evolutionists who are often quite arbitrary about what they believe.

Note that some evolutionists may give a *bad* reason for their position; this is not the same as being arbitrary. To be arbitrary is to give no reason at all: to just assume something and expect your opponent to assume it as well with no justification. If an evolutionist gives a *bad* reason, then the reason itself must be exposed as inadequate by further analysis using the AIP checklist. That is, the reason provided may itself be arbitrary, inconsistent, or may destroy the preconditions of intelligibility.

(I) **Inconsistency**: In logical reasoning, no one is allowed to be inconsistent — to have contrary beliefs. The reason is simple: if two beliefs are contrary to each other, then at least one of them must be false. Thus, a worldview that contains inconsistencies is necessarily false. It is often the case that the inconsistencies are indirect; one belief may lead to a conclusion that contradicts it. For example, a naturalist may try to defend his position using laws of logic, yet naturalism leads to the inescapable conclusion that there can be no laws of logic, since they are not part of the physical universe (as we saw in chapters 3 and 4).

(P) **Preconditions of Intelligibility**: A rational worldview must be able to provide justification for those things necessary for logical reasoning. We saw in chapter 3 that evolution fails to provide a foundation for laws of logic, uniformity of nature, and morality, yet these things are required for knowledge, rationality, science, and ethics. So how can evolution possibly be considered a rational worldview if it destroys the possibility of science and rationality?

Evolutionists regularly make use of science and reasoning (often successfully), but this is *inconsistent*

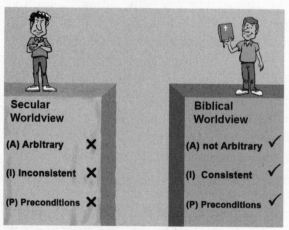

All secular worldviews fail the AIP test. The biblical worldview passes.

since such things would not make sense if evolution were true. An evolutionist might simply *assume* laws of logic, and uniformity of nature. But he has no justification for them within his own professed worldview. He is therefore being *arbitrary*. So the **P** part of the checklist is used in concert with the **A** and **I** parts. The Christian worldview can account for the preconditions of intelligibility in a consistent and non-arbitrary way. Evolution cannot. Nor can any non-biblical worldview.

The "AIP" test is performed primarily during part 2 of our apologetic procedure — the internal critique of the evolutionary worldview. We show that evolution is deficient because it is (A) arbitrary, (I) inconsistent, and it fails to provide (P) the preconditions of intelligibility. However, we can also point out that the biblical worldview passes the "AIP" test in part 1 of our apologetic method. The biblical worldview is non-arbitrary, it is self-consistent, and it provides a rational basis for the preconditions of intelligibility.

Expanding the Checklist

We must always be ready to expose arbitrariness and inconsistency in the unbeliever's worldview, and to show that his worldview cannot account for the preconditions of intelligibility. It is helpful to learn to recognize some common specific types, or sub-categories of arbitrariness and inconsistency committed by unbelievers, as well as additional preconditions of intelligibility. This expanded checklist is based on one of Dr. Greg Bahnsen's lectures; however, I have modified some of the examples so that they are particularly relevant for our purposes.

(A) Arbitrariness — Expanded

There are four common types of arbitrariness committed by unbelievers. These are (1) mere opinion, (2) relativism, (3) prejudicial conjecture, and (4) unargued philosophical bias. It may be helpful to remember these specific types of arbitrariness when conversing with an evolutionist, or any critic of Christianity. However, it is not necessary to identify these by name; it is perfectly sufficient to simply point out that the critic is being arbitrary.

(1) Mere opinion: This is where a person asserts his opinion without any justification and thinks that this settles the matter. But, a *rational* person should not base his beliefs on what he wants to be true, or what seems reasonable by mere intuition or opinion. Yet in my experience probably 90 percent of the arbitrary claims made by evolutionists (or

other Bible critics) fall under this category. The evolutionist will simply assert what seems reasonable to him without any justification, and will expect the creationist to agree. Such a procedure needs to be exposed as arbitrary and thus irrational.

As an example, some time ago an evolutionist reporter was interviewing me and asking about plate tectonics. He felt that the most popular creation-based model of tectonics was absurd, since it has the continents being pushed apart within a single year (at the time of the Genesis Flood.) However, he was not able to give a scientific or logical reason for his opinion. It just "seemed" to him that something so large could not move so fast!

I pointed out that the entire earth is much larger than its plates, yet earth orbits the sun at 67,000 miles per hour — so clearly, large things can move fast. Yet he still insisted that plates can't move fast, because it just didn't "seem" plausible to him. This of course was nothing more than a mere opinion. I knew that I needed to expose his thinking as irrational. So I very politely responded, "I'm sorry, did you have a *rational* or *scientific* objection?" This was my polite way of pointing out that he was not being rational or scientific, and that I wasn't going to try and give an answer according to his emotional, irrational standard (Prov. 26:4). Whenever someone asserts a mere opinion, simply ask him if he has a *rational* reason for that opinion.

(2) Relativism: A relativist asserts that there are no absolutes and that truth is subjective; "my truth is not your truth." However, all logical reasoning presupposes that there are absolutes and that truth is objective. The law of non-contradiction, for example, would be meaningless if truth varied from person to person. Relativists can be very irritating because they have essentially given up the laws of logic, yet they expect everyone else to abide by them.

This obvious inconsistency should be pointed out to the relativist. "If what you're saying is true, then why are you debating with me? How can you say that my position is *wrong* if truth is relative to the individual?" This inconsistency may not even bother the relativist since many of them feel no need to be consistent anyway. However, it should be pointed out that they are being unfair by *arbitrarily* expecting the biblical creationist to be consistent and logical if they are unwilling to do the same. It should also be pointed out that the relativist cannot possibly live according to his own professed worldview. He may profess a fairy-tale land where truth is subjective and contradictions are acceptable, but he must live in God's universe and must abide by God's absolute objective truth if he is to function. Remember, even the most ardent relativist looks both ways before he crosses the street. Moreover, he expects the motorist to abide by the same laws he does — to stop at the stop sign, for example. Just like all of us, the relativist knows in his heart of hearts the biblical God.

(3) Prejudicial conjecture: This is where a person substitutes an arbitrary conjecture for knowledge. He has failed to study the topic in question, and so he simply begins stating guesses based on nothing more than imagination. A prejudicial conjecture is *not* making a reasonable guess based on the best information available; this is perfectly acceptable. A prejudicial conjecture is where the information in question is publicly available, but the person has failed to do his homework. If he would have simply gone to a public library and done 30 minutes of research, he would know better than to make such an uneducated claim.

Since many people are ignorant of the history of the Bible, prejudicial conjectures abound. You may hear a claim such as this: "For all we know, the Bible was probably written by some monk during the dark ages. We don't know that any of the persons in the Bible even existed. And besides, it's been copied so many times it probably has lots and lots of errors." However, 30 minutes of actual research will refute all of these claims.

(4) Unargued philosophical bias. We all have a worldview — a philosophy that biases our interpretation of evidence for the better or for the worse. However, many people are unaware of their own worldview and do not understand that other people interpret evidence by a different standard. As such, many people do not realize that they need to argue for their worldview: they must show that their standard of interpreting evidence is the correct one, and not just assume this.

An unargued philosophical bias is (by definition) unargued. Therefore, we must learn to "read between the lines" — to understand the unstated presuppositions responsible for the erroneous conclusion of the evolutionist. For example, this statement contains an unargued philosophical bias: "Evolution must be true, because it is the only naturalistic way that life could come about." The bias here is that naturalism is true. We must expose this bias and force the evolutionist to (attempt to) defend it. We can use the "don't answer, answer" strategy to do this: "But, sir, I do not accept naturalism. In fact, if naturalism were true it would be impossible to prove anything since there would be no basis for laws of logic."

Another example is this: "There is no historical evidence that the events of the Bible ever happened." The person who makes this claim has an unargued bias: he is arbitrarily assuming that the Bible itself does not count as historical evidence. If we accept the Bible as it is written (as a history book) then *all* of the events it records have historical evidence — the Bible!

(I) Inconsistency Expanded

Just as there are four common types of arbitrariness, there are also four common types of inconsistency. These are (1) logical fallacies, (2) *reductio ad absurdum*, (3) behavioral inconsistency, and (4) presuppositional tensions. It may be useful to keep these four sub-categories in mind when conversing with a critic, but it is not essential. It is only necessary to point out that the unbeliever is being inconsistent, and it is not essential to name the type of inconsistency.

(1) Logical fallacies: Most evolutionists are just not good, clear, rational thinkers when it comes to worldview issues. Please do not misunderstand; I mean no disrespect here. I'm not saying that evolutionists are unintelligent or lack knowledge. On the contrary, I have worked with evolutionist scientists who are highly intelligent, skilled, and rigorously rational as it pertains to their research. However, when it comes to worldview issues or biblical issues, it just seems like logic goes out the window.

Creationists wanting to defend the faith well could greatly benefit from a study of logic and learning to spot logical fallacies. For this reason, I have chosen to dedicate two chapters of this book to this sub-category of inconsistency. For now, suffice it to say that we must watch for logical fallacies. In particular, watch for violations of the law of non-contradiction. Any self-contradictory worldview cannot be true.

(2) *Reductio ad absurdum*, "reducing to absurdity": In this type of inconsistency, a principle taken to its logical conclusion will yield an absurd result. Many evolutionists will want to take a philosophy only so far, and then inconsistently switch to another. Our refutation of

empiricism made use of this principle. Recall that empiricism teaches that all things are known through observation. But if we take this standard to its logical conclusion, we would eventually have to apply it to empiricism itself. If empiricism were true, we could never know that it was true since it has not been observed. Empiricism leads to the absurd conclusion that we cannot actually *know* anything.

(3) Behavioral inconsistency: This is the "actions speak louder than words" principle. A behavioral inconsistency shows that the evolutionist does not actually believe in his heart of hearts what he is saying. For example, consider the university professor who teaches that life is just a meaningless sequence of accidents, and that humans are just evolved animals — rearranged pond scum. But then he goes home and kisses his wife and kids, as if they were not just rearranged pond scum. Or consider the determinist who teaches that human beings have no choice in what they do; their actions are totally predetermined by the laws of chemistry in their brain. Yet he is outraged when someone steals his car. He insists that the thief be found and prosecuted. But why should a thief be punished if he had no choice?

In both cases, the behavior of the unbeliever is contrary to his words. This shows that he is *living* according to a different worldview than the one he *professes*. Non-biblical worldviews cannot account for those things we take for granted: morality, love, freedom, justice, and so on. Such deficiency is exposed by the behavior of the unbeliever. He cannot live according to his worldview. Note that this does not by itself disprove his worldview; that is done using the ultimate proof. But since his worldview is defective he cannot live according to its consequences, and his behavior shows that "deep down" he does not really believe it.

(4) Presuppositional tensions. We must be mindful of the presuppositions of the unbeliever. Secular presuppositions do not comport with each other. They are self-refuting, or make knowledge impossible. Watch for "stolen" presuppositions as well. The evolutionist will assume Christian presuppositions when they suit him (such as the idea of "right" and "wrong"), but will also assert secular presuppositions such as naturalism. These presuppositions do not comport. They are an irresolvable "tension" within his worldview. The evolutionist will not be able to account for such tensions, and thus his worldview is exposed as fallacious.

(P) Preconditions — Expanded

We have already covered three preconditions of intelligibility: (1) laws of logic, (2) uniformity of nature, and (3) morality. Without these, we could not really know anything since we would have no basis for rationality, science, or ethics. But there are many other things that we take for granted but without which we could not function. The list of preconditions could be expanded almost indefinitely, so let's look at just a few more: (4) the basic reliability of our senses, (5) the basic reliability of our memory, and (6) personal dignity and freedom.

(4) Reliability of our senses: We take for granted that what we see, hear, taste, smell, and touch really does exist and corresponds to what our senses tell us. We presuppose that our perceptions of the world are basically accurate. But how can we know this? If it is just an assumption, then we don't really *know* all the things we think we know. So we must have justification for the reliability of our sense perception if we are to know anything. Apart from the biblical worldview, this belief turns out to be very difficult to prove. We could do an experiment to "test" our senses. But since the results of any such experiment would have to be perceived through our senses, we could never know that we had accurately observed the results. Only the biblical creationist really has justification from his worldview.

Genesis chapter 1 indicates that God specially created human beings and gave them the responsibility of caring for His creation. Since our sensory organs were created by an all-knowing, all-powerful God (Prov. 20:12), we would expect them to work properly. After all, we would be unable to care for God's creation without sensory perception that is basically reliable. Of course, the Bible also indicates that the world was cursed as a result of man's rebellion against God (Gen. 3:17–19; Rom. 8:20–22). As such, the world is no longer perfect as it once was. Therefore, we would not expect that everyone's senses would work perfectly all the time (birth defects, accidents, and so on). However, since God never rescinded His command to care for the earth, it follows that our senses must still be basically reliable enough to accomplish this.[2]

In the evolutionary worldview, there is no justification at all for the reliability of our senses. Evolutionists do trust their senses, of course, but such a belief makes no sense if our sensory organs are merely the result of accidental mutations that conveyed some sort of survival value in the past. Evolutionists might argue that evolution can account for reliable senses because natural selection would preserve those things that have survival value. Since this is a very common response, it deserves some discussion.

First, having reliable senses (leading to accurate perceptions of the world) does not equate to survival value. Most of the organisms in the world (plants, bacteria, etc.) don't have "senses" or perceptions at all, let alone reliable ones. They survive quite well without them. In terms of population, bacteria are doing far better than we humans, despite their lack of sophisticated sensory organs or brains to interpret the sensations.

Second, apart from Scripture, there is no reason to think that our senses are reliable, even if they did convey survival value. Perhaps our perceptions of the world are totally fiction (i.e., a *matrix* world) — just the result of a complex chemical reaction that happens to have survival value in the real world. As an analogy, consider this: plants are green not because the color itself helps them survive, but because chlorophyll helps them survive, and chlorophyll happens to be green. Plants are green as a "side effect" of something that has genuine survival value. Could our perceptions of the world be similar? Perhaps our perceptions of the world are totally false but are just a side effect of the chemical reactions that help us survive. In the evolution worldview, there is no reason to assume that our mental picture of the world has any correspondence whatsoever to the real world. Apart from biblical creation, there just isn't any reason to think that our senses and perceptions of the world are reliable.

It is noteworthy that the reliability of our senses is a *presupposition*. It must be assumed *before* we begin to investigate anything else. Even before we can begin to read the Bible (which contains justification for this crucial presupposition), we must presuppose that our senses are reliable.[3] In the evolutionary worldview, the reliability of our senses must always remain an unjustified "blind" assumption. As such, if evolution were true, the reliability of our senses should be rejected as arbitrary (yet evolutionists are unwilling to do this — a behavioral inconsistency). But such an assumption can be justified (after the fact) in the biblical worldview. The biblical creation worldview gives us a good reason to trust that our senses are basically reliable. To put it another way, the belief that the Bible is true and the belief that our senses are reliable "go together."

However, the belief that evolution is true is *inconsistent* with the belief that our senses are reliable.

(5) Reliability of memory: We take it for granted that what we remember actually happened. But (as with the reliability of our senses) the reliability of memory is very difficult to prove apart from the Christian worldview. I could take a memory test, but in order to know how I did on it, I would have to already presuppose that my memory is basically reliable. Of course, the biblical creationist has justification for this claim. God made our minds so that we can remember the past (though not always perfectly because of the Curse).[4] In an evolutionary universe, why should we trust that our brains can reliably remember the past? According to evolutionists, the brain is simply the accidental result of random mutations that happened to somehow increase our ability to reproduce. There is no fundamental reason to think that we should be able to reliably remember the past in an evolutionary universe.

(6) Personal dignity and freedom: We all suppose that human beings deserve a certain level of respect, and that they have some degree of choice in what they do. For this reason, we will attend the funeral of a dear friend or relative. We expect everyone to abide by a certain code of behavior. We feel that people should be punished when they make choices that violate the rights of others. These things all presuppose the biblical worldview. According to Genesis, God made man in His own image (Gen. 1:26–27). As image-bearers of God, human beings are deserving of a certain level of respect and dignity. God gave Adam the power of choice (Gen. 2:16–17) and held him responsible for his actions (Gen. 3:17–19).

We take these creationist principles for granted. But they make no sense in an evolutionary universe. If human beings are just the accidental result of chemistry working over time, why would they be deserving of respect? Would we hold a funeral service if a few pounds of baking soda were destroyed by reacting with vinegar? Clearly, human beings are not just complex chemical reactions. If people are just chemistry, then they have no choice in what they do — just as vinegar has no choice but to react with baking soda. Therefore, why should we punish people who do evil if they have no choice? There could be no such thing as human freedom or dignity if evolution were true.

(7, 8, 9 . . .) There are many other things that we take for granted that only make sense in a biblical creation worldview. Why should there be laws of mathematics? Why should the universe be understandable? Why should music or art be beautiful? What worldview can make sense of joy, or for that matter pain? Simply pick any topic whatsoever and ask, "What worldview can make sense of this?" If an evolutionist is a strong advocate of animal conservation, ask him or her, "What worldview can make sense of the fact that we have a moral obligation to care for the creatures of the earth?" If an evolutionist is a mathematician, ask him or her, "What worldview can make sense of the laws of mathematics?" Ultimately, only a biblical creation worldview can make sense of all the things we take for granted.

(**A**) Arbitrariness: (1) Mere opinion (2) Relativism (3) Prejudicial conjectures (4) Unargued philosophical bias
(**I**) Inconsistency: (1) Logical fallacies (2) *Reductio ad absurdum* (3) Behavioral inconsistency (4) Presuppositional tensions
(**P**) Preconditions (1) Laws of logic (rationality) (2) Uniformity of nature (science and technology) (3) Absolute morality (ethics) (4) Reliability of senses (5) Reliability of memory (6) Personal dignity and freedom (7. . .) Many others

Conclusions

We have covered much ground so far. Although there are a few other tips and topics that we want to explore, we already have basically all that we need to refute any evolutionary argument that comes along. Using the ultimate proof, the "don't answer, answer" strategy, and the apologetic procedure outlined above, we are ready to give a powerful defense of biblical creation. In particular, we will keep in mind the "AIP" test as we critique the unbeliever's arguments.

In appendix B, we will apply what we have learned to actual letters written by people who are hostile toward biblical creation. This will give us a chance to practice what we have learned thus far. Readers who are anxious to begin using the ultimate proof may want to go ahead and read some of appendix B at this time before continuing on to the next chapter. Otherwise, we will continue with additional useful information to help refine our apologetic method in the next several chapters. These topics include the use of scientific evidence, spotting logical fallacies, biblical examples of apologetics, as well as additional topics that often come up in apologetic situations.

Endnotes

1. For this reason, presuppositions must be proved in a somewhat different way than are other truth claims. This topic is addressed in chapter 9.
2. Specifically, since this command was given to humanity as a whole, we expect that humanity as a whole has senses that are basically reliable. Obviously, the fact that some individuals in today's fallen world are blind or deaf does not prevent humanity as a whole from observing and caring for God's creation.
3. Some might object that this is a form of circular reasoning. We will deal with this charge in chapter 9.
4. It is doubtful that our minds were designed to remember every single thing even before sin and the Curse; God's perfect plan is that we are finite creatures with limitations. Such a discussion is beyond the scope of this book. But it is safe to conclude that diseases such as Alzheimer's or false memory syndrome would not have been an issue before the Fall of man.

CHAPTER 6

THE PLACE OF EVIDENCE

In chapter 1 we asked the seemingly innocuous question, "What is the place of scientific evidence in the debate over origins?" Through careful reasoning, we came to the surprising yet inevitable conclusion that scientific evidence *by itself* cannot possibly resolve the debate over origins. Scientific evidence can be very useful in debates when everyone involved agrees on how the evidence should be interpreted. It would be perfectly appropriate for a creationist to argue with another creationist that certain evidence supports a particular scientific model. When both persons agree on the "rules of interpretation," then they should draw the same conclusions when exposed to the same evidence.[1]

The problem with the origins debate is that creationists and evolutionists have a different opinion on what the rules of interpretation should be. They each interpret scientific facts in light of their respective worldviews. Both sides are always permitted to invent a "rescuing device" to explain seemingly contrary evidence. Therefore, we must use a different approach to ultimately settle the origins debate.

We have found that the debate can be resolved by using the

ultimate proof: by showing that the biblical creation worldview alone provides the preconditions of intelligibility in a way that is consistent and non-arbitrary. But we didn't really use any scientific evidence in our procedure. This may leave some readers wondering if evidence has a place in apologetics. It does. Scientific and historical evidence is very useful in apologetics — if used properly. In this chapter we will explore rational ways to use scientific evidence.

1. Confirming Biblical Creation

One perfectly appropriate use of scientific and historical evidence is to *confirm* biblical creation. The word "confirm" can be used in more than one way, so allow me to clarify. When we say evidence confirms creation we mean that it is consistent with creation — it coincides and shows agreement. Many Christians have been taught that the scientific evidence points to evolution and have erroneously concluded that they must have a "blind" faith. Many evolutionists conflate "science" with "evolution," hoping that they can convince people that we must accept evolution if we are going to accept science. Such erroneous teachings must be challenged, and scientific evidence is very useful in accomplishing this.

Science is perfectly consistent with biblical creation. Many examples can be given. Genetics confirms that organisms reproduce "after their kinds" — exactly what we would expect from Genesis. The fossil record indicates a global catastrophe: that animals and plants were killed and buried by flood waters. This is exactly what creationists would expect to find from the global Flood described in Genesis. C-14 in diamonds and other materials is exactly what the biblical creationist would expect to find, since the earth is thousands of years old. These scientific facts challenge the absurd notion that "all of science is on the side of evolution."

Moreover, these evidences are faith affirming. Christians need to understand that their worldview is not merely hypothetical. The real universe is the biblical universe. Since the Bible is true, it can be used to explain and make successful predictions about what we find in the physical universe. Genetics, geology, astronomy, paleontology, archaeology, and many other sciences all show facts that are what we would expect, given the truth of the Bible.[2] It is encouraging for Christians to learn about these facts.

The methods of science cannot serve as a foundation for the Bible, because they depend upon biblical presuppositions. The Bible is the ultimate standard. Science is secondary.

The Bible is the ultimate standard and the foundation of science. Therefore, scientific evidence, when properly interpreted, will always coincide with the Bible.

2. An Introduction to Worldviews

In any debate over origins, it is crucially important to understand the nature of worldviews and how worldviews control our interpretation of evidence. Without this understanding, the persons debating will merely be "talking past each other" and will never get to the real issue. Most people do not even realize that they have a worldview, and thus have not given any real thought to what their own worldview is. They are under the impression that "evidence speaks for itself." This error must be addressed and refuted if the debate is to be resolved. Evidence can be used to accomplish this.

We could take a particular scientific fact and then show how creationists and evolutionists draw different conclusions from this fact because they have different worldviews. For example, consider the fact that some apes and human beings have similar DNA. An evolutionist would conclude that this is because apes and humans are descended from a common ancestor. But a creationist would conclude that this is because apes and humans are made by the same God and have somewhat similar physiology, which would require similar genetic instructions. Each position can account for the facts, but the interpretation is different.

Another example would be fossils. The evolutionist believes that fossils have been deposited over millions of years as local floods and other small-scale catastrophes have killed and buried organisms. But a creationist believes that most of the fossils were deposited in the Genesis Flood, when the waters covered the entire globe, killing and burying millions of living creatures. Each position is able to account for the same facts in different ways.

Our goal at this point is *not* to argue that the creationist has a better interpretation of the evidence (this step will come later). Rather, our modest goal here is twofold.

First, we show that there exists a creationist interpretation of the data. This may seem trivial, but most people have been so inundated with evolution that they are unaware that a creation-based interpretation of the data is even possible. People are unable to accept a biblical interpretation of data if they are unaware of the existence of such a view.

Second, we help our opponent to become aware of his own worldview. The observable facts are not in dispute; rather it is the conclusions that we draw from such facts that differ. We show that creationists and evolutionists interpret the same facts differently — and that they *must* do so because they have different worldviews. The goal is to educate our opponent on the nature of worldviews, how worldviews affect interpretation of facts, to introduce him to our worldview, and to get him to realize that he, too, has a worldview.

3. Showing Inconsistency and Arbitrariness

When performing our internal critique of the unbelieving worldview, we must always look for "AIP": arbitrariness, inconsistency, and the preconditions of intelligibility. Scientific and historical evidence can help us accomplish this. For the moment, consider just the first two: arbitrariness and inconsistency. The way that evolutionists deal with scientific and historical evidence is often very inconsistent and arbitrary. Such "intellectual sins" must be exposed.

It is often alleged that since the Bible has been copied so many times, what we have today cannot be historically reliable.[3] Yet historical research confirms the reliability of the Bible. The number of ancient manuscripts is large, and the time scale between when the originals were written and the oldest extant copies is small,[4] which minimizes the possibility of transmission errors. By these criteria, the Bible is one of the most historically reliable manuscripts from the ancient world.

Contrast this with the works of Plato. Ancient copies of Plato are far fewer in number and the time span of transmission is much greater,[5] yet virtually everyone accepts them as authentic. If people want to deny that the Bible has been accurately transmitted, that's their choice, but then how can they go on to accept other *less reliable* manuscripts like Plato? It is *inconsistent* for someone to deny the historical reliability of the Bible, while embracing the historical reliability of Plato, or for that matter, any other ancient document.

Thus, we do *not* use manuscript evidence or archeology in an attempt to prove that the Bible is true — as if these lines of evidence were more authoritative than Scripture. Rather, we use such evidence to show that the secularist's position is inconsistent with itself and is therefore false.

Consider SETI — the search for extraterrestrial intelligence. People in this research program hope to detect radio signals from alien civilizations. But many things in space produce radio waves — stars, quasars, pulsars, etc. How would we distinguish an intelligent signal from a "natural" one? One criterion that would certainly do the job is to find information in the radio signal. Clearly, if we received a radio signal that contained instructions on how to build a complex machine, no one would doubt that the transmission came from an intelligent source. Of course, DNA has just such encoded information: instructions on how to build a complex machine. Yet those same researchers will deny that DNA has an intelligent source. It is *inconsistent* for unbelievers to accept coded information as an indication of intelligence in space, while denying that very same principle in the DNA of living organisms.

Arguments based upon interpretation of scientific evidence (such as those we discussed in chapter 1) can be a great way to point out the arbitrariness of secular thinking. We can show that the theorems of information theory indicate that the information in DNA must have originally come from a mind. Therefore, DNA cannot be the result of chemical evolution. Evolutionists might object that there is some unknown mechanism that generates information in DNA; "we just haven't discovered it yet." But this explanation is *arbitrary*. It is simply a rescuing device.

Many lines of evidence at least appear to confirm creation and a "young" universe.[6] Evolutionists tend to be very arbitrary when dealing with these. For example, spiral galaxies wind up too quickly to last billions of years, so secular astronomers have proposed a hypothetical mechanism to create new spiral arms.[7] C-14 in diamonds certainly challenges the evolutionary claim that diamonds are more than a billion years old; C-14 just cannot last that long. So evolutionists propose that the system has been contaminated or that there is some sort of "recharging mechanism." But such claims are totally *arbitrary*; the evolutionist does not have a reason for them. So evolution turns out to be the "evil twin" of what evolutionists accuse creation of being: a blind faith.

Is there a way out? Recall that a rescuing device is not *necessarily* arbitrary. We can always appeal to our worldview as the reason for our rescuing device. So the evolutionist could respond that he has a good reason for his many rescuing devices; he could say, "These explanations are required by my worldview, and I am certain that my worldview is correct." But then the evolutionist must be prepared to defend his worldview — and this he will not be able to do. Few evolutionists would take this path anyway; most evolutionists believe that their beliefs are the result of objective evidence, not a worldview that guides their interpretation of evidence.

4. Introducing the Ultimate Proof

In addition to exposing arbitrariness and inconsistency in evolutionary worldviews, scientific evidence can be used as a way of introducing the preconditions of intelligibility, and can lead us to the ultimate proof of creation. We might say, "We've been talking about scientific evidence, but which worldview can make sense of the fact that science is actually possible? Which of our worldviews can account for the fact that the universe is logical and understandable by the human mind? Which worldview can make sense of laws of logic by which we reason and the uniformity of nature by which we do science?"

Unbelievers will take it for granted that scientific evidence is meaningful and useful in helping us to understand the universe. But such a belief presupposes the biblical worldview. Evolutionary worldviews cannot account for the preconditions of intelligibility that make science possible. Scientific evidence can be used to help make this very point. In fact, absolutely any piece of scientific information can be used as an illustration of the ultimate proof.

Applying the Four Uses of Evidence

These four uses of evidence in apologetics may not come up in every debate. Every situation is different. In fact, it is possible to argue for the biblical worldview without explicitly presenting any scientific evidence at all (we might use the morality illustration for example). But often enough, the above steps will occur in just the order they were presented here.

For example, an evolutionist might claim, "There is no evidence whatsoever for the creationist position." We could use the evidence in way #1 and say, "Actually, there are many lines of evidence that confirm biblical creation. Consider the information in DNA . . ." and so on. The evolutionist might respond, "But these other evidences (fossils, etc.) support evolution, not creation." Then we would use evidence in way #2 and say, "Actually, creationists interpret those same fossils differently than you do. Here is how we understand the evidence." (We then present our interpretation.) "So you see, we all have the same facts, but we interpret them differently because we have a different worldview."

An evolutionist may then try to argue that his interpretation of the evidence is better than ours. We could then point out that his interpretations are arbitrary and inconsistent by using evidence in way #3. We could use the arguments presented in chapter 1 to expose the fact that the evolutionist must constantly invoke rescuing devises to explain away contrary evidence — this is totally arbitrary.

A *clever* evolutionist will at this point either appeal to his own worldview (as the reason for his rescuing devices), or (more likely) will point out that creationists also have rescuing devices. (If he fails to realize these things, then we should help him out by suggesting them ourselves.) Now the evolutionist has enough education to begin to properly understand the true nature of the origins debate — it's a debate over worldviews. As such, we move to the fourth use of evidence and ask, "Which worldview can make sense of science anyway? For that matter, which worldview can make sense of any of the things we take for granted — personal dignity and freedom, rationality, morality, and so on?"

The Misuse of Evidence

There may be other appropriate ways to use scientific evidence as well. I don't claim that the above four are exhaustive. Science might be used to dispel the myth that "creationists don't believe science." It might be used to generate interest in the topic. On some occasions, I have found that merely discussing scientific information will awaken an unbeliever's suppressed knowledge of God. These are all appropriate uses of evidence, and there may be others.

But there is one way of using evidence that is *not* appropriate, and yet it is a way that Christians commonly use. This is the treatment of scientific evidence, and humanity's understanding of it, as *superior* to the Word of God. That is, Christians will sometimes argue that a neutral and objective evaluation of evidence — apart from any biblical presuppositions — will prove that the Bible is true or at least *probably* true. They imply, without directly saying so, that the mind of sinful man is capable of objectively evaluating scientific evidence apart from the biblical worldview, and drawing the correct conclusions, thereby judging the Bible to be true. The goal of this approach is commendable, but the method is not.

We saw previously that there is no neutral ground when it comes to an issue of one's ultimate authority. Moreover, evidence cannot be correctly evaluated apart from biblical presuppositions. The preconditions of intelligibility that we all use of necessity are only justified within the biblical worldview. The Bible, being the inerrant revelation of the God of truth, is necessarily true (even though unbelievers deny this). So it is irrational to attempt to judge an infallible standard by fallible standards.

And it is also immoral. God commands us not to put Him to the test (Matt. 4:7). Our finite and fallible minds are not in a position to judge God's Holy Word, because it is God's Word that will judge our minds (Heb. 4:12). God is the judge of us. For us to attempt to judge Him and His Word is an absurd and disrespectful role reversal. Let God be found true, though every man be found a liar (Rom. 3:4; NASB). We should, of course, use our minds, in a God-honoring way, to reason and to realize that the Bible is true. But if we are to be rational and moral, we are to do so using the standards that God has prescribed, not those of sinful man.

So how do we discern whether we are using scientific evidence rightly, or wrongly? We must ask ourselves, "Does this use of scientific evidence treat the Bible as *less* authoritative than the evidence?" If so, then it is putting God to the test and is unbiblical. But if not, and if the evidence is used to challenge unbiblical claims and to glorify God, then it is probably a perfectly good use. Science is the servant of Scripture, not its master.

Some may then ask, "How much scientific evidence should I use in a conversation with an unbeliever? Should I focus more on the preconditions of intelligibility, or focus more on scientific details? What is the proper balance?" I would suggest that it really depends on the conversation. Some discussions will naturally lend themselves to scientific details, others will not. Some unbelievers couldn't care less about the science, but to others it is critically important. I try to meet the unbeliever where he or she is at, to the best of my ability.

Also, consider that God gives different interests to different people, and we are free to direct the conversation into areas of interest. I have a strong background in science, and so I am comfortable talking about such details. I therefore tend to use a lot of science in my conversations with unbelievers. But others may not have such an interest, and may use less. That's fine. I will suggest though that it is highly useful for all Christians to know *at least the basics* of creation science since this is such an important and criticized aspect of Christianity.

Some may also ask, "If the scientific details are so important, then why does *The Ultimate Proof of Creation* list only a few, and only in chapter 1?" The reason is simple: there are already many excellent books that show how science confirms biblical creation. There was no need repeat what has already been written. But I would suggest that Christians should read at least a few creation science books, such as the *Answers Books*, or *Creation Basics and Beyond*. The purpose of this book is to show readers how to *use* the information given in those other books properly and effectively.

David and Goliath

In a way, scientific and historical lines of evidence are like the five stones David used to kill Goliath (1 Sam. 17:40). Winning the battle is not about the size or number of the stones. What's much more important is how you use them. It really doesn't take a lot of knowledge of science to refute evolution, but some knowledge of science can be very helpful if used properly. David knew how to use a slingshot properly; he had practiced. More importantly, he knew that mere weapons were not what would ultimately decide the fate of a battle; the victory would belong to God alone (1 Sam. 17:47). There is a lesson here for the modern apologist.

God has called *everyone* to be ready to give a defense of the Christian faith (1 Pet. 3:15). Not everyone can or should go on to get a PhD in science, but almost everyone can learn two or three scientific facts that can be used in apologetics in one of the four ways listed above.

Remember, David had only five stones — and he ended up needing only one. But we should also remember that David was very familiar with the weapon he chose. It would have been presumptuous of him to expect God to give him victory if David had not taken the time to learn his skill. Likewise, if we are going to use scientific facts in defense of the Christian faith (and we should be prepared to do so), we must take the time to understand them well, and use them in a way that is correct and faithful to the text of Scripture.

Endnotes
1. Even among creationists, there are some differences of opinion on the rules of interpretation. Therefore, even creationists may draw different conclusions when examining the same evidence. The same is true of evolutionists as well.
2. For more information and specific examples from these fields of science, see *The New Answers Books*, Volumes 1 through 4 (Green Forest, AR: Master Books).
3. The claim is a prejudicial conjecture — one of the forms of arbitrariness.
4. The earliest fragments of the New Testament date to less than 50 years after they were written. The bulk of the important biblical manuscripts dates to 200–300 years after the texts were first written.
5. The earliest extant manuscripts of Plato date to around A.D. 900, yet Plato wrote the originals around 350 B.C.
6. See www.answersingenesis.org.
7. The "spiral density wave" hypothesis is challenged by the fact that magnetic fields run parallel to the spiral arms. If the spiral arms became wrapped after billions of years, the magnetic field lines would cancel, and any new spiral arms created by hypothetical density waves would not have such a magnetic field.

Chapter 7

LOGICAL FALLACIES — PART I

Most of apologetics comes down to good, clear, logical (and therefore *biblical*) thinking. Unbelievers are often arbitrary and inconsistent in their reasoning. And their worldview cannot account for the preconditions of intelligibility, leading to the bizarre conclusion that they couldn't really know anything at all if their worldview were true. We have now learned a procedure for exposing erroneous reasoning, and in appendix B we show that this method is very effective on several real-world examples. We are now going to explore in greater detail one of the specific types of inconsistency we listed in chapter 5 — logical fallacies.

Introduction to Logical Reasoning

First, we need to define a few terms. A *proposition* is a statement that can be designated as either "true" or "false." So "all mammals have kidneys" is a proposition and it happens to be true.[1] The statement "no mammals have kidneys" is also a proposition, and it happens to be false. In logic, an *argument* is defined as two or more propositions, where the truth of one is claimed to follow from the truth of the other(s). So, if I said, "(1)

All mammals have kidneys. (2) All dogs are mammals. (3) Therefore, all dogs have kidneys," this constitutes an argument[2] because the third proposition is asserted to be true on the basis of the other two. The statement being asserted (3) is called the *conclusion,* and the other propositions (1 and 2) are called *premises.* The conclusion is sometimes preceded by the word "therefore," which makes it easy to recognize.

In an argument, the premises are taken for granted; it is assumed that they are true. It is usually further assumed that both parties agree that the premises are all true. (This may turn out not to be the case, but it is nonetheless assumed by the person making the argument.) Then from these premises, we draw a conclusion. If an argument is to be a good one, all of its premises must be true, and its conclusion must rationally follow from them. So in a good argument, the conclusion will be true as well, or at least very likely (depending on the type of argument). The laws of logic tell us what conclusions we may legitimately draw from any given premises. In a sense, the laws of logic describe the correct "chain of reasoning" from premises to conclusion.

Proposition — a statement that can be assigned a truth value. Propositions are either true or false.	**Argument** — a sequence of propositions where the truth of one is asserted to follow from the truth of the other(s).
Conclusion — the proposition in an argument that is asserted on the basis of the other propositions	**Premise** — a proposition in an argument that is said to support the conclusion. The premises are assumed to be true.

A *logical fallacy* is a common error in reasoning. Sometimes people will make a mistake in their "chain of reasoning" from premises to conclusion. That is, even though their premises may be perfectly true, they have drawn an incorrect conclusion from them. As an example: "(1) Some mammals are cats. (2) All dogs are mammals. (3) Therefore, some dogs are cats." The premises (1 and 2) are perfectly true, but the conclusion (3) is obviously false and does not really follow from the premises. This argument is a fallacy.[3] The thing that makes fallacies so seductive is that they often sound reasonable on the surface. This is why it is so important to be familiar with the most common fallacies.

Not all mistakes in reasoning are logical fallacies. Often the "chain of reasoning" is perfectly legitimate, but the person has started from a false premise and has reached a false conclusion. Consider the following argument: "(1) All dogs are mammals. (2) All mammals are reptiles. (3) Therefore, all dogs are reptiles." This argument is bad, but it does *not* commit a *logical fallacy*. If the premises were true, the conclusion would legitimately follow from them. But the second premise is false, and thus the conclusion is unreliable. So when people draw an incorrect conclusion, we cannot immediately assume that they have committed a logical fallacy; it may instead be the case that one of their premises is false. A good way to respond to the above argument is: "Although your chain of reasoning is correct, your second premise (that all mammals are reptiles) is false, and thus your conclusion is unreliable."

So there are two ways an argument can be faulty. (1) It may contain a logical fallacy — an error in the "chain of reasoning." (2) It may have a false premise. In this book, we have already learned how to deal with false premises. Secular presuppositions (like naturalism, empiricism, and relativism) are false, yet non-Christians often assume that such things are true. They end up reaching false conclusions. This is not a logical fallacy, but it is still bad reasoning since their premises (their presuppositions) are false. We can expose faulty presuppositions using the methods we've developed. So it is now time to deal with logical fallacies — errors in the reasoning process itself.

Kinds of Logic

There are two basic categories of logic: inductive and deductive. An inductive argument is one in which it is claimed that the conclusion is *likely* to be true if the premises are. A deductive argument is one in which it is claimed that the conclusion is *definitely* true if the premises are. The previous examples were all of the deductive variety. Of course, a deductive argument may turn out to be a bad one. Nonetheless, if it is *claimed* that the conclusion necessarily follows from the premises, then the argument is of the deductive variety. If it is claimed that the conclusion is only very likely to be true, then the argument is inductive.

Inductive arguments are classified as either "strong" or "weak." They are "strong" if the conclusion really is very likely to be true given the premises, and "weak" if that is not the case. An example of an inductive argument is: "I just phoned Dr. Lisle and he did not answer. Therefore, he is probably out of his office." The conclusion does seem to be supported by the premise. So this is a strong argument. However, with an inductive argument, additional information can alter the conclusion. Suppose we added one more premise: "Dr. Lisle never picks up his phone even when he is in the office." Now the conclusion that "Dr. Lisle is probably out of his office" is not so likely. Additional information can change a strong argument into a weak one.

Deductive arguments are classified as either "valid" or "invalid." If the conclusion does indeed follow from the premises, the argument is valid; otherwise it is invalid. No additional premises can change a valid argument into an invalid one. Consider our opening argument: "(1) All mammals have kidneys. (2) All dogs are mammals. (3) Therefore, all dogs have kidneys." No additional information will change the validity of this argument. It does not matter what else we know about dogs, kidneys, mammals, or anything in the universe. If (1) and (2) are true, then so must (3) be true. So, this argument is valid. The argument is also "sound." A "sound" argument is a valid argument that has true premises (and thus the conclusion must also be true).

Textbooks on logic will also divide the topic according to "formal" and "informal" logic. Formal logic is that which can be put into a type of symbolic notation and examined for validity without knowing the meaning of the propositions. Formal logic can look a lot like algebra; it will contain expressions like "(1) if **p** then **q** (2) **p** (3) therefore **q**." The symbols "**p**" and "**q**" stand for propositions, but the validity of the argument does not depend on what propositions they are! It depends solely on the "form" of the argument — hence "formal logic." Deductive logic can be expressed in such forms. We will deal with formal logical fallacies in the next chapter.

Informal logic does not use symbols; it uses ordinary language and is therefore very intuitive and easy to learn. So we will begin by studying the fallacies associated with informal logic. These are also called "ordinary language fallacies." There are many such fallacies, but we will only address the ones that are commonly committed in apologetic situations.

Informal Logical Fallacies

There are three broad categories of fallacies associated with ordinary language. These are fallacies of ambiguity, fallacies of presumption, and fallacies of relevance. Evolutionary arguments abound with fallacies from all three categories, and so do other non-biblical positions. But since this book specializes in dealing with the evolutionary worldview, we will provide examples of evolutionary arguments containing these fallacies. I believe it will be extremely helpful for biblical creationists to be able to recognize such fallacies when they occur. Regrettably, Christians are not immune from committing logical fallacies either. Therefore, common fallacies committed by Christians will also be explored. We want to make sure that we use only good argumentation when defending the faith; anything less would not be honoring to the Lord that we serve.

1. Fallacies of Ambiguity

Fallacies of ambiguity are arguments that are faulty because they use words or phrases that are unclear or have more than one meaning. There are six common fallacies that are usually listed under this category: equivocation, amphiboly, accent, reification, composition, and division. Two of these occur frequently in apologetic situations.

The **fallacy of equivocation** occurs when the meaning of a word is shifted in the course of an argument. For example: "Practice makes perfect. Doctors practice medicine. Therefore, doctors must be perfect." Here the word "practice" is used in two different ways, and so the argument is fallacious. One of the most common informal fallacies committed by evolutionists is the fallacy of equivocation on the word "evolution." Evolution can simply mean "change" in a general sense, or it can refer to the idea that all life is descended from a common ancestor. Either meaning is legitimate, but the two should not be conflated within an argument as follows.

The fallacy of equivocation. The word "evolution" is used in two different senses.

"Creationists do not believe in evolution. But evolution happens — every day things *change*. So, it is absurd for creationists to deny evolution." The first and third sentences in this argument use the term "evolution" in the sense of common descent. But the argument hinges on the second sentence where the word "evolution" is used simply to mean "change." So, the argument commits the fallacy of equivocation. Clearly, there is nothing contradictory about denying some kinds of alleged change (common descent) while accepting other kinds of change.

Another example is, "Science is a very powerful and reliable tool; it has allowed us to develop technology, and even to put men on the moon. So why would people deny the science of evolution?" This argument equivocates on the word "science," which can either mean operational science or origins science. Operational science is the reliable, trustworthy tool that is responsible for technology. Origins science is an attempt to understand past events in light of present evidence; it is much more easily tainted by historical bias than operational science and is not directly testable or repeatable. The two types of science should not be conflated within an argument.

The concept of evidence does not actually speak. This is the fallacy of reification.

The fallacy of reification is committed when a person attributes a concrete and often personal characteristic to a conceptual abstraction. A classic example is: "It's not nice to fool Mother Nature." Nature is a concept, a name we give to the sum total of the sequence of events in the universe. Nature cannot be "fooled" as if it had a mind. Another example is, "Even while Joe was home, his job was calling him, luring him back to the office." Reification is perfectly acceptable in poetry, but should not be used in logical argumentation because it is ambiguous and can obscure important issues. Evolutionists frequently commit this fallacy, particularly with the concepts of nature, evolution, evidence, and science.

For example, "Nature selects those individuals who are most fit." But nature has neither mind nor choice and thus cannot literally *select* anything. "Evolution figured out how to get around these problems." But evolution cannot think. "Natural selection guided the development of all the species we see on earth." Natural selection is a concept; it cannot literally *guide* anything. "Science is atheistic in its outlook and procedures." But science has no beliefs about God, or anything else! "The evidence speaks for itself." Evidence does not actually speak, only people do.

2. Fallacies of Presumption

Some arguments might *become* good ones if additional information were available. But when such information is missing, the argument is fallacious. A fallacy of presumption is an argument that is faulty because it contains one or more unproven or unfounded assumptions. In some cases, the argument can be corrected by supplying additional information to bolster the assumptions within. But when the person supplying the argument is unable to justify internal assumptions, the argument is fallacious. There are many fallacies in this category.

Fallacies of presumption include sweeping generalization, hasty generalization, bifurcation, begging the question, question-begging epithet, complex question, "no true Scotsman," special pleading, false analogy, false cause, and slippery slope. I've seen every one of these fallacies used in defense of evolution. So we will cover all the fallacies in this category.

A **hasty generalization** is when someone draws a general inference from too few specific instances. Suppose we traveled to Florida for several days, and the weather was unusually chilly. After returning home, we erroneously conclude that the climate of Florida is quite cold. This is a hasty generalization. The weather we experienced during our brief stay was *atypical*. So to generalize from such little experience is fallacious.

"Joe is a creationist, and his research is very sloppy and poorly documented. Therefore, creationists must be very bad researchers." The fact that one creationist may have been less than thorough in his research does not imply that creationists are generally so sloppy.

A **sweeping generalization** is when someone applies a generalization to a situation where it does not apply. Many generalizations are not universal; they have exceptions. To ignore this fact is to commit the fallacy of a sweeping generalization. For example, "Jogging is good for the heart. Tim has a heart condition, so he really should go jogging more often." Although jogging is *generally* good for the heart, there may be cases when it is not advisable — especially for someone with a particular heart condition.

"Nothing is true just because someone says it is. Therefore, we shouldn't just accept everything God has said." This is fallacious because although it is *generally* true that people don't speak only the truth, God is an exception; He never lies and He knows everything, therefore we should always take Him at His word.

A sweeping generalization can be thought of as the opposite of a hasty generalization. In a hasty generalization, the argument goes (too rapidly) from a specific instance to a generalization, whereas with a sweeping generalization the argument begins with a generalization and goes to a specific instance. Remember that with a sweeping generalization, the generalization itself is *true* but has been applied to an exception, resulting in an absurd conclusion. With a hasty generalization, the generalization is *false* (potentially), because it has been derived from exceptional instances.

The **fallacy of bifurcation** is committed when two propositions are presented as if they were mutually exclusive and the only two possibilities, when in fact they are not. It could be that other options exist. For example, "Either the traffic light is red or it is green" commits the fallacy of bifurcation because a third possibility exists: the light may be yellow. Red and green are *contrary* but not contradictory positions.[4] Alternatively, it may be that the two positions are fully compatible — they can both be true. "Either Bob will go into the ministry or he will move to Kansas." Since it is perfectly possible for Bob to do both of these things, the argument commits the fallacy of bifurcation. This fallacy is also called a "false dilemma" and "the either-or fallacy."

For example, "Either you live by faith, or you are a rational thinker." But one can live by faith in the biblical God *and* be a rational thinker; in fact, we've seen that rational thought *requires* faith in the biblical God. "I cannot accept the Bible because I believe in science." There is no contradiction between these two positions, so the fallacy of bifurcation is committed. "Either the universe operates in a law-like fashion or God is constantly performing miracles." But a third possibility exists; the universe normally operates in a law-like fashion and God occasionally does a miracle.[5]

Begging the question is when the conclusion of an argument is incorporated into one of its premises — or when the truth of a premise depends upon the conclusion. This fallacy is also called *circular reasoning.* "How do I know evolution is true? Because it is a fact!" This argument is asserting (A) that evolution is true on the basis of (B) that it is a fact. But (A) is merely a restatement of (B). A person arguing this way has merely assumed what he is trying to prove. And merely assuming something is no proof at all. This is one of the most common fallacies committed by evolutionists and old-earth creationists. It is therefore very important to give special attention to this fallacy.

The fallacy of begging the question. The assumption that miracles are impossible presupposes that the Bible is not true. Thus, this person is reasoning in a vicious circle.

For example, "Miracles are impossible because they cannot happen." The conclusion is merely a restatement of the premise, so the argument is faulty. Many examples of begging the question are subtle. For example, "young-earth creationists are wrong because radiometric dating shows that rocks are billions of years old." The problem with this argument is that young-earth creationists do not accept the assumptions that have gone into radiometric dating.[6] So by accepting that radiometric dating is reliable, the arguer has already assumed that young-earth creationists are wrong, and has then concluded that young-earth creationists are wrong. This begs the question. *Every old-earth argument I have ever seen commits the fallacy of begging the question.* Old-earth creationists (and evolutionists) subtly assume as part of their premises what they are trying to prove.

We mentioned earlier the importance of an *internal critique* of the unbeliever's worldview. Recall, that this is step 2 of our apologetic procedure. We can now see why an internal critique is necessary. If we merely argued that the unbeliever is wrong based on our own worldview, we would be begging the question. That is, we would essentially be arguing "your position is wrong because my (opposing) position is right." Whenever an evolutionist attempts to refute creation by any method other than an internal critique, he is begging the question. It is important to realize this, and to point out that by making certain assumptions the evolutionist has already presupposed that creation is false.

Unfortunately, Christians sometimes commit this fallacy as well. "(A) The Bible must be the Word of God because it says it is. (B) What the Bible says must be true since it is the Word of God." Note that both (A) and (B) are true; nonetheless, this argument is fallacious because it begs the question. Since (A) is only *guaranteed* to be true if (B) is true, and since (B) is only *guaranteed* to be true if (A) is, the argument is a vicious circle and does not really prove anything. It's perfectly consistent to assume both (A) and (B), but we cannot use merely one of these as proof of the other. After all, the argument would have the same weight when applied to any other book that claims to be inspired by God.

Begging the question is a very strange and unique fallacy. With all the other fallacies, even when the premises are true the conclusion can be false. So we say "the conclusion does not follow from the premises." But this is not the case with begging the question; the conclusion necessarily does follow from the premise. Therefore, by definition, begging the question is actually *valid!* This may cause us to stop and ask whether it is truly a fallacy since no error in logic is committed.

But recall that when we make an argument, we take for granted that the premises are true, and that the person with whom we are arguing also takes them as true. The idea is to convince our opponent of a new conclusion. But when we beg the question, if our opponent already accepts the premises then he already accepts the conclusion too. So there would be no reason to make an argument. And if our opponent does not accept the conclusion, then he will necessarily reject the premise as well. So while valid, a simple circular argument is not *useful*. It does not prove anything new.

It would seem that begging the question is not legitimate because it is *arbitrary*. We cannot merely assume as a premise what we are trying to prove.[7] So when someone begs the question, we might respond: "You have simply assumed what you are trying to prove. This is arbitrary. Do you have a *reason* for your conclusion, or have you simply arbitrarily asserted it?"

A **question-begging epithet** is when someone imports biased (and often emotional) language to support a conclusion that is logically unproved. The idea is to persuade someone using biased language rather than logic. If a reporter stated, "This criminal is charged with the vicious murder of the innocent victim," this is a question-begging epithet because he could have use less-biased language: "This suspect is charged with killing the other person." That the other person is an innocent victim and that the first is a criminal are not yet established. The use of the word "vicious" is also unproved and further biases that conclusion. Emotions can distract; they can prevent people from drawing logical conclusions. When people use this principle to persuade others to draw a faulty conclusion, they have committed the fallacy of the question-begging epithet.

The first several examples in appendix B contain a number of question-begging epithets. In example #2, the critic says, "I pray you'll have an epiphany and stop misleading people to believe in nonsense and lies." Rather than making a logical argument that our position is wrong, the critic has simply assumed this and used emotional language to reinforce that assertion. Watch for words like "ignorant," "dishonest," "stupid," "gullible," and other disparaging remarks. When such claims are merely asserted without evidence, the argument is fallacious.

A **complex question** is the interrogative form of begging the question. This is when a question contains an unproved assumption. As such, any answer seems to affirm that the question is legitimate, when in fact it is not. The classic example is, "Do you still beat your wife?" Either a yes or no answer would seem to imply that you once did beat your wife, when in fact that may not be the case. A complex question should really be divided into separate questions: "(1) Did you ever beat your wife? (2) If so, do you still continue to do so?" This is why the question is *complex*. Watch for such questions in evolutionary arguments: "Why are you creationists against science?" But creationists are not against science, so the question is fallacious. It should have been divided into two questions: "(1) Are you creationists against science? (2) If so, why?" Another example is, "Which of the two contradictory stories of creation in Genesis do you accept?" But there is only one account of creation in Genesis, and there are no contradictions within it.[8] So the critic has committed the fallacy of a complex question. He should have divided the question: "(1) Are there two contradictory stories in Genesis? (2) If so, which do you accept?"

Note that what you consider to be a complex question depends greatly on your worldview. "Have you repented of your sins?" would not be considered fallacious to a Christian (since we know that all have sinned). But the non-Christian might take issue with this and would want the question to be divided: "(1) Have you sinned? (2) If so, have you repented?"

The **"no true Scotsman fallacy"** could be considered a sub-category of begging the question. The fallacy is committed when someone attempts to protect his claim from a counter-argument by defining a term in a biased way (which begs the question). The example from which the name is derived is something like this: Person A asserts that no Scotsman puts sugar on his porridge. Person B attempts to counter this claim by pointing out that Angus is a Scotsman who puts sugar on his porridge. Then person A responds, "Ah, but no *true* Scotsman puts sugar on his porridge."

The fallacy begs the question by simply defining a *true* Scotsman in such a way that the claim is assumed to be true. It amounts to saying, "A true Scotsman does not put sugar on his porridge, because otherwise, he wouldn't be a *true* Scotsman." Since the premise and conclusion are equivalent, the argument begs the question.

Consider these claims made by an evolutionist (E) and how he would respond when presented with counter-evidence by a creationist (C):

E: "No scientist believes that God created in six days."

C: "The scientists at Answers in Genesis believe God created in six days."

E: "Well, no *real* scientist believes that God created in six days."

E: "No peer-reviewed science journal would accept a creationist paper."

C: "The *Answers Research Journal* accepts creation papers all the time."

E: "Well, no *reputable* journal would accept a creationist paper."

Both of the above arguments commit the "no true Scotsman fallacy." Since they define "reputable journal" and "real scientist" in an arbitrary way, the claims are reversible. We could equally well say, "Actually, no *real* scientist believes in evolution. And no *reputable* journal would publish an evolutionary paper." I would never actually claim these things, of course, but it would be perfectly acceptable to point out that we *could hypothetically* make these equally arbitrary claims whenever an evolutionist commits the "no true Scotsman fallacy."

Special pleading is the fallacy of applying a double standard. That is, the arguer has applied a standard to his opponent that he does not apply to himself. The duplicity may be subtle and due only to a choice of words: "I'm firm, but you are just stubborn." Or it may be more obvious. "You can't tell other people what not to do!" is a clear case of special pleading since the arguer obviously does not apply this standard to himself.

"You can't just assume that the Bible is true; you must have proof of something before you believe it." Yet this critic does not have proof that his position is true; he is applying a double standard. "You can only use papers submitted in secular journals; creationist journals don't count." This is an arbitrary double standard. We could equally well argue that only creation-based journals count, and secular ones do not.

A **false analogy** is when a comparison is made between two things that are alike in only trivial ways that are not relevant to the conclusion. "Why should you complain about having to work 12 hours a day? After all, our computers are working 24 hours a day with no breaks at all." But of course, people are different than computers, which require no rest. So the analogy is faulty.

One of the most common false analogies committed by evolutionists is seen in example #1 of appendix B. "Your message is akin to asking us to believe the world is flat or that the sun revolves about the earth despite overwhelming empirical evidence to the contrary." Here the critic compares the beliefs of a flat earth and geocentric solar system to creation. But the notions of a flat earth and geocentric solar system can be falsified by operational science in the present, and so it would be absurd to embrace such ideas. But biblical creation is about the past; it is not falsified by observations in the present (in fact, it is consistent with them). So the analogy fails.

The **fallacy of false cause** is committed when someone concludes an incorrect cause-and-effect relationship between two events. Sometimes two events are genuinely correlated — there is a connection between them. But that doesn't mean that one caused the other. For example, suppose someone did a research project and found that on days when tar is sticky, there are more heart attacks than on other days. He then erroneously concludes that sticky tar causes heart attacks. In reality, the higher temperatures are what have caused the tar to be sticky and have contributed to an increased number of heart attacks.

Alternatively, there may be no strong connection at all between two events. Any similarity in time may simply be a coincidence. Superstitions fall under this fallacy. The idea that walking under a ladder, encountering the number 13, or a black cat crossing your path have somehow caused subsequent misfortune is the fallacy of false cause.

"Fossils can be arranged in a sequence from simpler to more complex. It is therefore clear that the more complex forms evolved from the simpler forms." The fact that some fossils come before others in a sequence does not imply that they have *caused* the others. After all, the different models of cars in existence today could be lined up in a sequence, but this doesn't mean that they are biologically descended from a common ancestor.

"Creation is becoming more popular in the United States, and test scores are dropping dramatically. Clearly, creationism is destructive to education!" The notion that the first event caused the second does not follow, and so the argument is a false-cause fallacy.

The **slippery slope** fallacy is the argument that a particular course of action will set off a chain reaction, inevitably leading to an undesirable result, while overlooking other factors that would prevent such a result. "If we allow them to increase the speed limit on this road to 45, then eventually that won't seem fast enough and they'll increase it again and again until it is absolutely unsafe to drive on it." But the desire to preserve human life makes it unlikely that it would ever be allowed to reach an unsafe limit. By overlooking this factor, the arguer has committed the slippery slope fallacy. There are of course genuine slippery slopes that are not fallacies — where a given action really will generate a chain reaction. But when other factors are likely to prevent the chain reaction, the argument is a fallacy.

"If we allow for the possibility of miracles, then science would come to a halt. We'd never know if we're observing the laws of nature or a miracle." But this overlooks the fact that miracles are rare (and not necessarily a suspension of the laws of nature anyway). Clearly, if God occasionally suspended the laws of nature in order to accomplish an extraordinary purpose, this would not in any way prevent us from studying the laws of nature as they normally are. Another example: "If children are taught that God created everything, then they will not search for the real explanation. They will lose their sense of curiosity, will understand nothing of science, and will not be able to function in the real world." But there is no rational reason to connect the teaching of creation with the chain of events that are alleged to follow.

3. Fallacies of Relevance

An argument whose conclusion is simply not relevant to its premise is called a fallacy of relevance. In the Christian worldview, everything relates to God (and therefore to each other) in some way; but some things are more closely connected than others. So this type of fallacy is a question of degree. If the conclusion is not strongly relevant to the premises, then a fallacy of relevance has been committed. Such fallacies include the genetic fallacy, the ad hominem fallacy, irrelevant thesis, straw-man, and several types of faulty appeals.

The **genetic fallacy** is where an argument is claimed to be false based on its origin rather than for logical reasons. "You learned that argument from the *National Enquirer*, so it really can't be true." Granted, it is perfectly relevant to point out that if a claim comes from a typically unreliable source (for example, a tabloid newspaper), then this casts doubt on its truthfulness. But it has no bearing on the validity of an argument. It would be legitimate to question a claim (not an argument) based on its source, but only if that source has been established to be unreliable. An argument should be evaluated on its merit, not on how it came to be.

"The Bible was written thousands of years ago by people who knew nothing about modern science. So why should we trust any of its claims?" The fact that the Bible is very ancient and that its authors did not know modern science is irrelevant to its *truth*. Also, this argument (like many attacks on Scripture) ignores the special status of the Bible. That is, the Bible claims to be the inspired Word of God and is thus quite different from many other historic documents. Granted, critics may reject this claim, but if they then conclude that the Bible is false we should remind them that they have started with this very assumption; they have begged the question.

The ***ad hominem* fallacy** is committed when an argument is directed against a person rather than his or her position. The phrase *ad hominem* is Latin and means "to the man." The tactic is fallacious since the validity of an argument does not depend on the person who is making it.

There are two types of the ad hominem fallacy: abusive *ad hominem* and circumstantial *ad hominem*.

When someone commits the abusive *ad hominem*, he attacks the character of his opponent, rather than dealing with the issue at hand. "Christians have been responsible for some horrible atrocities; just think of the crusades. So how can you possibly believe that Christianity is true?" The fact that sometimes Christians have acted sinfully is not relevant to the position the Christian advocates (the Christian worldview). "Creationists are just dishonest; you can't possibly believe their theories." Even if a particular creationist has lied about something (which does happen sometimes, unfortunately), it does not necessarily mean that the position he is advocating is false.

In some cases, the abusive *ad hominem* is offered to dissuade onlookers from accepting any possible counter-response from the opponent. This fallacy is often used in formal debates and is called "poisoning the well." For example, "My opponent in tonight's debate has been divorced three times. Given his lack of character, I don't think we can really trust anything he has to say." Of course, the marital problems are not really relevant to the point of the debate (unless the debate was about marriage, and even then it would not necessarily mean the opponent's position is wrong). So the attack is fallacious. Nonetheless, some people might be tempted to treat any counter-response with inappropriate suspicion.

The circumstantial *ad hominem* is committed when it is alleged that a person only makes a claim due to his circumstances, rather than for logical reasons. "You're only for higher gasoline prices because you work at a gas station." However, even though the circumstances may motivate someone to argue for a certain position, this does not by itself mean that the position is wrong or that his argument is bad. The argument should be evaluated on its own merits, not on the circumstances of the person making the claim.

For example, "You're just a Christian because you were raised in a Christian family." No doubt, people who are reared in a Christian home are more likely to become Christians. But this does not mean that they do not also have good independent reasons for holding to the Christian worldview. "You are just arguing for creation because you read a book on it." It may be true that reading a book on creation has motivated us to better defend the position. But this has no bearing on whether or not creation is true. After all, one could equally well say, "You just believe in the multiplication table because your teacher taught it to you." This may be true, but it certainly does not mean that the multiplication table is false.

Fallacies of faulty appeal are committed when a person appeals to something or someone that is not really relevant to the claim under investigation. Several fallacies fall under this general category. One can appeal to emotion, as in the case of appeal to pity, fear, or "mob." One can appeal to an authority of some kind. Or one can appeal to ignorance.

The **faulty appeal to pity** occurs when we argue for a position on the basis of pity. "Professor, please give me an A for the class. My parents promised to help me buy a car if I get all As." In the case of evolution, a proponent of the position may attempt to persuade his audience by talking about all the persecution he has endured from creationists. Even if that were so, it would not give any support to his claim.

The **faulty appeal to fear** occurs when someone argues for a position on the basis that harm will come to you if you are not convinced. For example, imagine a lawyer arguing, "Ladies and gentlemen of the jury, you must find the defendant guilty of murder. Otherwise, you may be his next victim!" Of course this threat is not relevant to whether the defendant is actually guilty, so the argument is fallacious. Likewise, students are often pressured to believe in evolution on the basis that if they don't they will not be accepted to a good college, or will be denied a university position upon graduation. Professors are pressured to teach evolution only, lest they be denied tenure. High school teachers are forbidden to discuss creation and are threatened with legal action. All of these follow the same fallacious strategy: "You must believe my claim, or there will be consequences!"

The **fallacy of mob appeal** is an attempt to persuade people (usually a large group of people) by using powerful feelings, rather than logic. This fallacy is often used in a formal debate or presentation. Imagine an evolutionist responding to the Christian's claim that God is the basis for morality by saying, "I say we don't need God to know right from wrong. You have every right to follow your own standard! Don't let others tell you what to do. It is your right as an American to think for yourself!" Such a speech might be followed by thunderous applause — even though it is logically absurd and self-refuting. (How could we possibly obey the instruction to not let others tell us what to do?) But by invoking powerful emotions like patriotism and the desire to feel autonomous, the arguer may sway many people with this fallacious speech.

The **faulty appeal to authority** is when someone argues that a claim must be true simply because someone (or a group of people) says so. There are two sub-categories that we will address here: appeal to the one, and appeal to the many. Both types are sometimes used by evolutionists, and are even combined in some cases.

The **appeal to the one** is the fallacy of saying that something must be true simply because an expert says it is. As with many fallacies, this one is a question of degree. Clearly, the opinion of an expert on a topic should not be dismissed arbitrarily. However, even experts are occasionally mistaken, so their opinions should not be taken as unquestionable. This is especially evident in cases where other experts in the field disagree. Clearly, two contrary positions cannot both be true. When someone cites an expert as definitive *proof* of a position, we would do well to remember this humorous variation of Newton's third law: "For every expert, there is an equal and opposite expert." Now, if almost all experts (regardless of their worldview) agreed on a particular claim in their area of research, it would *not* be fallacious to accept their opinion as at least very likely. In fact, it would probably be fallacious (arbitrary) to *not* do so.

Also, we should always consider the biases of the individual, and how such biases have affected his or her conclusions. Yes, an evolutionist expert on radiometric dating might think that such methods support millions of years; but his biases should be considered before we accept his conclusion.[9] No mere human knows everything, and therefore we should never simply accept a claim as infallibly true if it is simply the opinion of a fallible expert. Another way in which this fallacy is committed is when someone gives an opinion outside his or her area of expertise. Such an opinion has little value unless it is backed by additional evidence.

The **appeal to the many** is the other subclass of the faulty appeal to authority. It is also called an **appeal to the majority**. This fallacy is committed when someone argues that a position must be true because a majority of people believe it. It seems strange that people would fall for such an obvious error. Yet, they do. "After all, how could all those people be wrong?" The appeal to the majority is often combined with the appeal to the one; this is when someone appeals to a *majority* of *experts*. "How could all those scientists be wrong about evolution?" The Bible gives the answer to this in Romans 1:18–23. The thing to remember about all

Little Johnny has committed the fallacy of appeal to ignorance. Just because a claim cannot be disproved does not mean that the claim is true.

appeals to authority is that an argument should really be evaluated on its internal merit, not on the person making it.

An **appeal to ignorance** is when a position is claimed to be true simply because it has not been proven false. "There must be life in outer space. No one has ever proven that there isn't." But just because no one has been able to disprove a claim does not mean the claim is true. An appeal to ignorance can always be rebutted by an appeal to ignorance. We could show the absurdity of the above argument by asserting, "There *cannot* be life in outer space since no one has ever proved that there *is*." Appeals to ignorance are fallacious because a lack of evidence against a position is not the same as evidence *for* a position.

As with many other fallacies, the appeal to ignorance is a matter of degree. Suppose someone argued, "No one has ever been able to create energy from nothing despite many thousands of experiments on the subject. So, it is reasonable to conclude that such a thing is not possible." This argument commits no fallacy since many experiments have been involved, under very different conditions. The conclusion is likely

It is easy for an evolutionist to refute a weak argument of his own invention. But the actual creationist position might pose more of a challenge.

(but not proved) from the premise.

The **fallacy of irrelevant thesis** occurs when someone attempts to prove a conclusion that is not at issue. The arguer's reasons may very well be true, but they do not answer the question that is at issue. "The people who want to reduce the amount of nuclear weapons are mistaken. After all, such an action will not solve all the world's problems." The second sentence is true, of course, but it is not relevant to the first. That is, no one has suggested that a reduction of nuclear weapons will solve *all* the world's problems, only that it is good in some ways. Evolutionists frequently commit the fallacy of irrelevant thesis. Consider the following arguments.

"Why is the universe ideally suited for life? Because otherwise we wouldn't be here to observe it." It is true that if the universe were not suited for life we wouldn't be here to observe it. But this does not actually answer the question of *why* the universe is suited for life — it only tells us why we are able to observe the universe. By analogy, imagine that I was the only survivor of a plane crash. When asked why I alone survived, it would be absurd to say, "Because if I hadn't lived, I wouldn't be here to answer your question."

A common old-earth creationist example is: "The days of creation cannot be ordinary days. After all, the sun wasn't created until the fourth day." The length of a day is controlled primarily by earth's rotation.[10] So the fact that the sun was not created until the fourth day is totally irrelevant.

Another example is, "Why do living creatures have complex parts that function together so perfectly? Because if they didn't they would have died off." The second sentence is true, but does not really answer the question. "You don't need Christianity to explain morality. After all, I'm an atheist, and I am very moral." The second sentence may be true, but it is not relevant to the issue of explaining how morality can exist apart from Christianity. All fallacies of irrelevant thesis can be answered with this simple rebuttal: "True perhaps, but irrelevant."

The **straw man fallacy** could be considered a sub-class of irrelevant thesis. In a straw-man argument, a person misrepresents the position of his opponent, and then argues against this counterfeit ("straw man") position. His argument may be a very good one, but since he is not arguing against that actual point at issue, it is irrelevant. Straw man arguments are very common in the origins debate since evolutionists are often not familiar with what creationists actually teach.

For example, "Creationists believe that God created all the animals as we see them today. But some breeds of dogs are known to be quite recent." This argument misrepresents what biblical creationists teach. God did *not* create the animals as we see them today, rather He created the basic kinds (dogs, cats, etc.) and some diversification has happened since. "Creationists claim that you must believe in creation in six days in order to be saved. But the Bible teaches nothing of the kind." Again, this argument might be a good one against someone who actually held the position. But I'm not aware of any biblical creationist that holds that belief in a six-day creation is a salvation requirement. So the argument is a straw man fallacy.

Summary

We have explored informal logical fallacies, those types of fallacies committed in ordinary language. Generally, these can be broken down into three major categories: fallacies of ambiguity, fallacies of presumption, and fallacies of relevance. All of the fallacies we discussed have appeared in evolutionary literature, and examples of each type were included above. In my experience, the most common informal fallacies committed by evolutionists are equivocation (on the word "evolution"), reification (of nature, evolution, science, or evidence), begging the question (criticizing creation on the basis of evolution), irrelevant thesis (a variety), and straw man arguments (misrepresenting what creationists teach, perhaps unintentionally). A familiarity with the above fallacies will drastically improve the ability of a creationist to pick up on evolutionary inconsistency.

Endnotes

1. To be precise, the proposition is the meaning of the statement. So, "All mammals have kidneys," and "All things that are mammals are things that have kidneys" are the same proposition, even though the statements are worded differently.
2. This type of argument is called a standard form categorical syllogism.
3. This argument commits the "fallacy of the undistributed middle."
4. When two propositions are contradictory, one must be true and the other must be false. On the other hand, contrary propositions cannot both be true, but both can be false. "The traffic light is red" and "The traffic light is green" are contraries. "The traffic light is red" and "The traffic light is not red" are contradictories; one must be true, the other false.
5. In addition, a miracle is not *necessarily* a departure from the law-like operation of the universe. Sometime God acts in an extraordinary way that is nonetheless "within" the laws of nature. This is addressed in chapter 9.
6. Specifically, the assumption that the decay rate has always been constant is rejected by most biblical creationists. The RATE research group has uncovered compelling evidence that such rates have been drastically accelerated in the past. That decay rates are generally constant is the assumption of uniformitarianism. Essentially, all old-earth arguments presupposed uniformitarianism and (to some extent) naturalism; however, these assumptions are rejected by biblical creationists. By embracing such assumptions, the old-earth supporter has arbitrarily prejudged the biblical position to be false.
7. In some cases (as when dealing with certain presuppositions) it is absolutely unavoidable to exclude the conclusion as part of the premises. For example, we could prove that laws of logic exist, but not without first assuming that they exist (otherwise we could not begin to construct an argument at all). However, in a good argument we cannot *merely* assume what we are trying to prove. Additional premises must be imported if the argument is to be considered sound. So there are actually correct forms of circular reasoning. But vicious circles (ones that merely assume what they try to prove) are unacceptable. We will learn to distinguish different types of circles in chapter 9.
8. Genesis 2 is a detailed description of the events of day 6. It is fully compatible with Genesis 1 when the context is understood.
9. This doesn't mean we simply dismiss his conclusions either. That would be a circumstantial *ad hominem* fallacy. But we must always be mindful of how a person's worldview will influence his interpretation of the facts.
10. The earth's motion around the sun accounts for only about 4 minutes of a solar day. The other 23 hours and 56 minutes are due entirely to earth's rotation in space, and have nothing to do with the sun. As long as there is a source of light (which there was for the first three days) and a rotating planet, there will be ordinary day and night.

Chapter 8

Logical Fallacies — Part II

Now that we have an understanding of informal logic and have covered the most common informal fallacies committed by evolutionists, it is time to begin our discussion of *formal* deductive logic and the corresponding formal logical fallacies. In this chapter, we will briefly cover the different types of formal deductive logic, and show how to refute invalid arguments by logical analogy. We will then move onto specific fallacies. In my experience, there are only two *formal* logical fallacies that are frequently committed by evolutionists: "affirming the consequent" and "denying the antecedent." (These will be the only two fallacies covered by name in this chapter.) They are quite common in evolutionary (and old-earth creationist) arguments. So it is very useful to understand them and be able to spot them. Finally, we will discuss the importance of consistency in logical reasoning.

I find formal logic very interesting, and rather intuitive. It has a mathematical quality to it that I, as a scientist, really appreciate. Of course, God has given each of us different interests and different strengths. Some people find formal logic very difficult and abstract, perhaps due to the use of symbols. On the one hand, I wouldn't want this chapter to discourage someone from reading the rest of the book. So if any readers find this chapter overly cumbersome — just skip it. (I won't tell anyone.) On the other hand, there is apologetic value in studying formal logic. The two fallacies we cover in this chapter are very, very common. Please consider this chapter to be the "icing on the cake" of apologetics. It's nice to know formal logic when defending the faith, but you can live without it.

Types of Formal Deductive Logic

Recall that formal logic is that which can be represented with symbols such as "if **p** then **q**" where **p** and **q** represent any generic propositions. Formal logic is deductive in nature — which means the conclusion definitely follows from the premises (if the argument is valid). An example of a valid deductive argument is: "(1) If **p** is true, then **q** is true. (2) **p** is true. (3) Therefore, **q** is true." You can substitute absolutely any proposition for **p** and **q** and you will always find that if the premises (1 and 2) are true, then so is the conclusion (3). So, the argument is valid. An even shorter way of writing this argument is "(1) if **p** then **q**, (2) **p**, (3) therefore **q**." This means exactly the same thing as the longer version.

> *Categorical logic deals with classes and uses words like "all, some, no, and not."*

Formal deductive logic is normally divided into two classes: categorical logic and propositional logic.[1] Categorical logic deals with the nature of classes, and class inclusion and exclusion. Categorical arguments use words such as "*all, some, no,* and *not.*" The argument "(1) All dogs are mammals, (2) no mammals are reptiles, (3) therefore no dogs are reptiles" is a categorical syllogism. A *syllogism* is an argument that has exactly two premises

> *Syllogism: an argument that has two premises and one conclusion*

and one conclusion. We will deal primarily with arguments that are syllogisms in this chapter.

Propositional logic deals with the way propositions are connected. Propositional

> *Propositional logic deals with the connections between propositions and uses words like "if-then, and, or, and not."*

arguments use words such as "*If-then, and, or,* and *not.*" The argument "(1) If it is snowing, then it must be cold outside. (2) It is snowing. (3) Therefore it is cold outside" is a propositional syllogism. In fact, it is an instance of the first argument introduced in this section. Simply substitute "**p**" for "it is snowing" and substitute "**q**" for "it is cold outside" and we get "(1) if **p** then **q** (2) **p** (3) therefore **q**."

Refutation by Logical Analogy

The fallacies that we will focus on in this chapter are part of the propositional type of logic. But I want to briefly address how to identify and refute other types of formal fallacies as well. Refutation by logical analogy is a powerful way to refute an invalid argument without actually having to know the specific reason why the argument is fallacious. This method will work on *any* invalid argument, though it is more difficult to use on some than on others. Let's consider the following categorical syllogism:

> Argument A:
> 1. Some men are cowards.   (premise)
> 2. All daredevils are men.   (premise)
> 3. Therefore, some daredevils are cowards.   (conclusion)

This same argument can be rewritten using symbols: M for "men," D for "daredevils," and C for "cowards":

> Argument A (rewritten with symbols):
> 1. Some M are C.
> 2. All D are M.
> 3. Therefore, some D are C.

It may not be immediately obvious whether this argument is valid or not. But one simple way to prove that it is not valid is to give another argument that has the *same form* (it "looks" the same when reduced to symbols) that is clearly invalid. That is, we construct an argument of the same form that has true premises and a false conclusion:

> Argument B:
> 1. Some mammals are cats.   (true)
> 2. All dogs are mammals.   (true)
> 3. Therefore some dogs are cats. (false)

Using this way of thinking, Rich could also argue against the existence of painters, architects, builders, his own parents. . . . This is a refutation by (informal) logical analogy. It would be absurd for Rich to argue against the existence of other people in this way. So, the analogous argument against God is refuted.

But Argument B has exactly the same form as Argument A. It can also be rewritten using symbols (C for "cats," D for "dogs," and M for "mammals") and will look identical to Argument A (rewritten with symbols). But Argument B is clearly invalid because it is obvious that the premises are true, and yet the conclusion that "some dogs are cats" is clearly false. Therefore, Argument A is also invalid because it has the same form as an argument that is clearly invalid.

So without knowing exactly what fallacy is committed,[2] it is always possible to refute an invalid argument by logical analogy. If someone stated Argument A, we could respond, "Actually, your argument (A) is invalid. It would be just like saying this: (we state Argument B) — which is clearly absurd." Refutation by analogy can also be used on informal fallacies. In such cases, we invent an argument that is similar in essence to the fallacy, and yet has a conclusion that is obviously false. To refute an informal fallacy, the analogous argument must be sufficiently similar; otherwise the opponent can accuse us of committing the *fallacy of false analogy*.[3]

The only drawback of using refutation by logical analogy is that the analogies can be cumbersome, and can be rather difficult to "think up" on the spot. Remember, the key is to create an argument that has (1) the same form as the original, (2) has both true premises, and (3) has a clearly false conclusion. It can be quite a challenge to create a new argument that meets all three criteria, especially if you have to do it quickly. Therefore, it is helpful to know some specific formal fallacies. In categorical logic, there are actually six formal fallacies,[4] but these are beyond the scope of this book, and are far less common than the two propositional logical fallacies that follow. So we now turn to propositional logic.

Propositional Logic

One type of propositional argument is called a disjunctive syllogism. It looks like this:

1. **p** or **q**	(premise)
2. Not **p**	(premise)
3. Therefore **q**	(conclusion)

This is a valid argument. So we can substitute any propositions for **p** and **q**, and if the premises are true, then so is the conclusion. For example:

1. Either Dr. Lisle is in the office or he is working from home.
2. Dr. Lisle is not in the office.
3. Therefore, Dr. Lisle is working from home.

Clearly, if the premises are true, then the conclusion is as well. So this argument is valid.

This now brings us to the kind of argument we want to focus on in this chapter: a mixed hypothetical syllogism. Since it is a syllogism, we already know that it will have two premises and one conclusion. One of these two premises will be a hypothetical proposition: an "if-then" statement. The other one is not, so the argument is "mixed." There are only two valid mixed hypothetical syllogisms, and we've already seen an example of the first:

Modus Ponens:

1. if **p** then **q**	(premise)
2. **p**	(premise)
3. therefore **q**	(conclusion)

Recall that this can also be stated: "If **p** is true then **q** is true. (2) **p** is true. (3) Therefore **q** is true." Whenever we have a hypothetical premise ("if **p** then **q**"), the first proposition (**p**) is called the "antecedent" and the second proposition (**q**) is called the "consequent." This argument is called *Modus Ponens* — which means the "method of affirming." The second premise *affirms* that **p** (the antecedent) is true. So *Modus Ponens* is also called "affirming the antecedent." Let's see how the argument works when we substitute propositions for the symbols:

1. If it is snowing, then it must be cold outside. (if **p** then **q**)
2. It is snowing. (**p**)
3. Therefore, it must be cold outside. (therefore **q**)

We now consider the other valid type of mixed hypothetical syllogism:

Modus Tollens:
1. if **p** then **q**   (premise)
2. not **q**   (premise)
3. therefore, not **p**   (conclusion)

The second premise asserts that the consequent (**q**) is *not* true. Therefore, neither can the antecedent be true, since if it were, the consequent would also be true. This type of argument is called *Modus Tollens* — meaning the "method of denying." In this argument, the second premise *denies* that the consequent is true. So this type of argument is also called "denying the consequent" and is perfectly valid. Here is an example of *Modus Tollens*:

1. If it is snowing, then it must be cold outside. (if **p** then **q**)
2. It is not cold outside. (not **q**)
3. Therefore, it is not snowing. (therefore, not **p**)

Affirming the Consequent

We now consider an *invalid* mixed hypothetical syllogism:

Argument C:
1. if **p** then **q**
2. **q**
3. Therefore, **p**

This argument is fallacious. Although the truth of **p** guarantees the truth of **q** (according to the first premise), the reverse is not necessarily so. The proposition **q** could be true even if **p** is false, so the argument is a fallacy. Let's substitute some propositions for the symbols **p** and **q** to see why Argument C fails:

> 1. If it is snowing, then it must be cold outside. (if **p** then **q**)
> 2. It is cold outside. (**q**)
> 3. Therefore, it must be snowing. (therefore **p**)

But clearly, just because it is cold outside does not *necessarily* mean it will be snowing. It might be the case by accident, but since it is not always the case, the argument is invalid: even if the premises are true, the conclusion can still be false. This is called the "fallacy of affirming the consequent" because the consequent (**q**) is affirmed in the second premise, yet this does not guarantee that the conclusion will be true. Let's consider some evolutionary examples of this fallacy:

1. If evolution were true, we'd expect that organisms would share some similarity in their DNA.

2. Organisms do share some similarity in their DNA.

3. Therefore, evolution is true.

But there could be many reasons why organisms have similarities in their DNA. For example, they all have the same Creator, or they all have some similarities in their biochemistry.

1. If the big bang were true, we'd expect to see a cosmic microwave background.

2. We do see a cosmic microwave background.

3. Therefore, the big bang is true.

Again, this commits the fallacy of affirming the consequent. There are many possible explanations for the cosmic microwave background that have nothing to do with a big bang.

1. If evolution were true, we would expect to find a logical sequence of fossils in the rock layers.

2. We do find a logical sequence of fossils in the rock layers.

3. Therefore, evolution is true.

But based on flood models, creationists also expect a sequence of fossils in the rock layers. So creation would also have to be true by the same reasoning. Clearly, the premises do not prove the conclusion.

Denying the Antecedent

We now consider the other type of invalid mixed hypothetical syllogism:

> Argument D:
> 1. if **p** then **q**   (premise)
> 2. not **p**   (premise)
> 3. therefore, not **q**   (conclusion)

This argument denies that **p** is true, and then concludes that **q** must also be false. But this need not be so. The proposition **q** might be true even when **p** is false, so the argument is invalid. This is called the "fallacy of denying the antecedent" because the second premise denies the antecedent, yet this does not guarantee the conclusion. Let's substitute some propositions for the symbols **p** and **q** to illustrate why this argument fails.

> 1. If it is snowing, then it must be cold outside. (if **p** then **q**)
> 2. It is not snowing. (not **p**)
> 3. Therefore, it is not cold outside. (therefore, not **q**)

But clearly, just because it is not snowing does not mean that it must not be cold outside. The argument is fallacious because it can have true premises and a false conclusion. Let's consider an evolutionary example of denying the antecedent:

1. If we found dinosaur fossils and human fossils in the same rock formation, this would indicate that they lived at the same time.

2. We do not find dinosaur fossils and human fossils in the same rock formation.

3. Therefore, they did not live at the same time.

This argument commits the fallacy of denying the antecedent. There are a number of reasons why we would not expect dinosaur fossils and human fossils together (for example, if they typically did not live in the same regions).

1. If they found Noah's ark, then that would show that Genesis is true.

2. But they haven't found Noah's ark.

3. Therefore, Genesis is not true.

Just because an ancient artifact cannot be located does not mean it did not exist. So the argument is fallacious.

If **p** then **q** **p** Therefore **q**	*Modus Ponens* (Affirming the Antecedent)	AA ✓
If **p** then **q** **q** Therefore **p**	FALLACY (Affirming the Consequent)	AC ✗
If **p** then **q** Not **q** Therefore not **p**	*Modus Tollens* (Denying the Consequent)	DC ✓
If **p** then **q** Not **p** Therefore not **q**	FALLACY (Denying the Antecedent)	DA ✗

For those new to formal logic, it may be difficult to quickly recall which forms of reasoning are valid and which are fallacies. Here's a "trick": First, we abbreviate the four mixed hypothetical syllogisms by the first letter in each (as in the third column of the table): AA = Affirming the Antecedent, DC = Denying the Consequent, AC = Affirming the Consequent, DA = Denying the Antecedent. The ones that have only one A in their abbreviation are fallacies; the others are not. So AC and DA are fallacies, whereas AA and DC are valid.

Sound versus Valid

Not all mistakes in reasoning are logical fallacies. Consider the following argument:

1. If the sun is hot, then Martians will invade the earth.
2. The sun is hot.
3. Therefore, Martians will invade the earth.

Is this argument valid? The answer is yes. It is a *Modus Ponens* (affirming the antecedent), which we have already established is perfectly valid. No logical fallacy has been committed. Remember, "valid" simply means that the conclusion follows from the premises. But the above argument has a false premise. Therefore the conclusion is not necessarily true even though the form is valid. So this argument is *unsound*. A sound argument is one that is valid *and* has true premises. In response to the above argument we might say, "Although your argument is valid, it is not sound. Your first premise is absurd, and thus your conclusion is not reliable." It is very common for people to erroneously claim that an argument is invalid, when in fact the argument is valid but unsound.

Enthymemes

In everyday argumentation, people rarely use arguments as clearly spelled out as the above examples. They will state things in a less-than-precise way and will assume that certain facts are understood. This is fine, but it is also acceptable for us to "translate" the argument into a more standard form — providing we preserve the meaning of the argument.

In many cases, people will not explicitly state one of the premises (or perhaps the conclusion) in their argument. They take it for granted that the missing proposition is understood by all. An argument with an unstated proposition is called an "enthymeme." Enthymemes are perfectly acceptable, but it is also acceptable for us to fill in and explicitly state the missing premise, to show why the argument is faulty.

I once debated an evolutionist (Jim) who argued this: "Dinosaurs clearly did not live at the same time as people. After all, we don't find their fossils in the same rock layers." To show why this enthymeme is faulty, we must "translate" it into a full syllogism[5] and supply the missing premise:

1. If dinosaur fossils were found in the same rock layers as human fossils, then they lived at the same time. (This is the missing line.)

2. They are not found in the same rock layers.

3. Therefore they did not live at the same time.

It is now clear that this argument commits the fallacy of denying the antecedent. Since the argument is invalid, the conclusion is unreliable. Of course, we could also refute this argument by logical analogy. I could have said, "Jim's argument is invalid. By his reasoning, Jim and I do not live at the same time. After all, our fossilized bodies are not found in the same rock layers!"

Sometimes when the enthymeme is converted into a standard syllogism, it turns out to be valid but unsound. More often than not, the false premise is precisely the premise that was left unstated. For example: "There cannot be proof of God's existence. After all, there are many atheists in the world today." By supplying the missing premise (1) we end up with this syllogism:

1. If there was a proof of God's existence, then there would not be any atheists.

2. There are atheists.

3. Therefore, it is not the case that there is proof of God's existence.

The argument is a perfectly valid *Modus Tollens* (denying the consequent),[6] but it is unsound because the first premise (the very one left unstated by the critic) is false. Just because there is proof of something doesn't mean that everyone will accept it.

The Necessity of Consistency

We've already touched upon the importance of having a consistent worldview. Recall that testing a worldview for inconsistency is the second step of the "AIP" test. Now that we have had an introduction to formal logic, we are in a position to ask, "Why? Why is it so important that our worldview must be fully consistent with no contradictions?" Aside from the obvious fact that contradictions are not true, there are severe consequences for a worldview that contains even one contradiction.

Two propositions are said to be contradictories if one is the negation of the other. So (**A**) and (not **A**) are contradictory propositions. In English, we turn a proposition into its contradictory proposition by adding the prefix "it is not the case that." So the propositions "Dr. Lisle is at work today" and "It is not the case that Dr. Lisle is at work today" are contradictory propositions. When two propositions are contradictory, it is always the case that one of them is true and the other one is false.

What happens when we assume that two contradictory propositions are both true? It turns out that in such a case, we can *validly* conclude absolutely anything! It is literally possible to reach *any* conclusion whatsoever using correct logic starting from two contradictory premises. (This is why it is so important that our worldview must contain no contradictions.) Here is an example of this:

Let's start with a proposition (**p),** which states, "Dr. Lisle is the author of this book." This is a true proposition of course, which means its negation (not **p**) — "It is not the case that Dr. Lisle is the author of this book" — is necessarily false. But suppose you allow me to assume that both (**p**) and (not **p**) are true. I can then validly conclude any ridiculous proposition I want; let's suppose I want to conclude **q**, which states "the moon is made of green cheese."

Now, if (**p**) is true, then the compound proposition (**p** or **q**) is also true. This is because I can add anything to a true statement by connecting it with an "or" and the compound statement will also be true.[7] So the phrase "Dr. Lisle is the author of this book *or* the moon is made of green cheese" is a true proposition. But I've also been allowed to assume that (not **p**) is true. "It is not the case that Dr. Lisle is the author of this book." So I can construct the following syllogism:

1. Dr. Lisle is the author of this book *or* the moon is made of green cheese. (**p** or **q**)

2. It is not the case that Dr. Lisle is the author of this book. (not **p**)

3. Therefore, the moon is made of green cheese. (therefore **q**)

This is a disjunctive syllogism — the first propositional syllogism we covered in this chapter. It is a valid argument. Since I could have used any proposition for **p**, and any proposition for **q**, the above argument shows that I can validly conclude absolutely anything from any contradiction.

You may wonder sometimes why people come to such absurd conclusions, and we now have a possible answer. It may be that their logic is perfectly valid, but that their worldview contains a contradiction. With even one seemingly insignificant contradiction, we can validly conclude absolutely anything, no matter how ridiculous. The contradiction may not be as obvious as the example above. But whether subtle or obvious, we can validly conclude anything at all from just one contradiction. This is why it is essential to be able to spot inconsistencies in the evolutionary worldview.

Summary and Conclusions

The two formal logical fallacies (affirming the consequent and denying the antecedent) are some of the most common fallacious arguments offered by evolutionists. They are often stated as enthymemes but can always be translated into standard form by correctly supplying the missing premise. The biblical creationist should always be ready to expose these fallacies, along with the informal fallacies studied in the previous chapter.

However, we should also remember that not all false conclusions are the result of logical fallacies. An argument may be perfectly valid, but nonetheless unsound due to a false premise. In fact, from contradictory premises, we found that one can validly conclude absolutely anything. The ability to recognize and expose fallacies and false premises is a crucial but often overlooked part of Christian apologetics.

Endnotes

1. There is also a way of combining categorical logic and propositional logic; this is called "quantified logic" and is beyond the scope of this book.
2. For the curious reader, this fallacy is called the "fallacy of the undistributed middle." This is because the middle term, M, is not used in a way that refers to ("distributes") all of its members. In other words, only *some* M are C and only *some* M are D. The middle term must be distributed in at least one premise for any categorical syllogism to be valid.
3. See chapter 7.
4. There may be a few more or a few less, depending on how they are counted.
5. It is also possible to translate this enthymeme into a valid Modus Ponens argument by substituting a different missing line: "If dinosaur and human fossils are not found in the same rock layers, then they did not live at the same time." But the argument would still be unsound since the missing premise would be false. An unsound argument can never be translated into a sound one.
6. It denies the consequent because it *denies* that there are *not* any atheists. The double negative means that there *are* atheists.
7. In logic, this is called the "law of addition." (1) **p** (2) therefore, **p** or **q**.

CHAPTER 9

CLOSING THE LOOPHOLES

We now have a very powerful procedure for defending the Christian faith. But when people are first introduced to this method, there are some common misconceptions. In fact, the method I have been defending throughout this book has been criticized by some Christians on the basis of what often turns out to be a simple misunderstanding. In the remaining cases, the critic has not carefully considered the philosophical implications of his criticism (such as the claim that there really is a *neutral* worldview position). Since we now have some experience in dealing with things like worldviews, presuppositions, arguments, fallacies, and so on, we are in a position to answer these criticisms, and to close some "loopholes" that were left open in the previous chapters.

Is it really necessary to have an ultimate standard, or is it possible to evaluate evidence in a neutral and objective way? If we use the Bible in our defense of the Bible, doesn't this constitute circular reasoning? How would people have defended the biblical worldview before the Bible was written? Is there a place for faith in apologetics, or is it all about reason? If there is uniformity in nature, doesn't that imply that the present really is the key to the past (i.e., uniformitarianism)? If miracles can happen, then how would science be possible? Questions like these are easily answered now that we have the appropriate tools and background.

The Necessity of an Ultimate Standard

There is a story about a little old lady who challenged a scientist on the nature of the earth.[1] The scientist had just given a lecture on astronomy, talking about the roundness of the earth and how it orbits the sun and so on. The lady came up to him after the lecture and said, "What you have told us is rubbish. The world is really a flat plate supported on the back of a giant tortoise."

The scientist smiled and replied, "What is the tortoise standing on?" Obviously, it would have to rest upon something — another turtle perhaps? And that would have to rest upon another. He had her.

But the little old lady would not be swayed. She replied, "You're very clever, young man, very clever. But it's no use. It's turtles all the way down!"

Beliefs are much like the turtles in the little old lady's view of the earth. Our beliefs are supported by other beliefs, which are supported by still others. Is there an ultimate standard — a belief that is the foundation of all others? Or is it just "turtles all the way down"? Some have supposed that an ultimate standard is only for the "religiously minded." Many people feel that they themselves do not have an ultimate authority, or a faith commitment of any kind. Rather, they believe that their perceptions of the world

Everyone has an ultimate standard, whether he realizes it or not. If it is not the Bible, it will be something else.

are objective, neutral, and not dependent on any ultimate standard. Of course, this idea is itself a belief about the world through which all other observations are interpreted. So the belief that there is no ultimate standard turns out to be an ultimate standard itself. In chapter 2 we gave some reasons why such a "neutral" position is not possible. Now that we have a better understanding of presuppositions and arguments, we can demonstrate this more rigorously.

For any belief that a person has (p), we can always ask, "How do you know that to be true?" The person will then supply an argument (either an inductive or deductive one) that supports his belief. In his argument, the person will appeal to another proposition (q) that he believes supports his conclusion (p). But since he has appealed to another proposition (q), we now must ask the question, "Okay, but how do you know q is true?" In his defense of q, the person will appeal to yet another proposition (r), which we can again question, leading him to suggest another proposition (s), and so on. Ultimately, any such chain of reasoning must come to an end. It must terminate in an ultimate standard — let's call it (t).

Why must the chain end? If it doesn't end then it goes on forever. And if it goes on forever, then the argument could never be completed. But an incomplete argument doesn't prove anything at all. Moreover, we cannot know an infinite number of things anyway. So all of our chains of reasoning must be *finite*. Therefore, everyone must have an ultimate standard: a proposition (upon which all others depend) that cannot be proved from a more foundational proposition. This must be the case for all people, whether they realize it or not.

But now we must ask the "killer" question: "How do you know that your ultimate standard (t) is true?" There are three bad answers to this question, and one good one. One bad response would be, "I know t is true because it follows logically from u." But if that is so, then t really isn't the ultimate standard — it's not the most foundational proposition if it follows from something else. Any person responding in this way has not understood the nature of an *ultimate* standard.

If a person understands that he cannot appeal to a greater standard, he may try appealing to a lesser standard. He may say that t must be true because it implies s (where s is claimed to be true because it follows from t). But this is a bad argument for a couple of reasons. It commits the fallacy of begging the question. Since s is only necessarily true if

t is, the person is essentially arguing that **t** is true because **t** is true. When restated, the argument clearly commits the fallacy of affirming the consequent. (1. If **t** then **s**. 2. **s**. 3. Therefore **t**). One cannot prove an ultimate standard in this way. So this response also fails. We again ask, "How do you know that your ultimate standard (**t**) is true?"

Some people might say, "I guess I can't actually prove my ultimate standard. I accept it as a presupposition." Granted, by their very nature, presuppositions must be accepted before they can be proved. But if they cannot (eventually) be proved, then they are *arbitrary* and thus irrational. In fact, if a person's ultimate standard cannot be proved, then that person does not actually *know anything*! Here's why.

We argue that we know **p** is true because it follows from **q**, which follows from **r**, and so on, all the way back to our ultimate standard (**t**). So, all these propositions (**p**, **q**, **r**, and **s**) depend upon the truth of **t**. Therefore, if **t** is not known to be true, then neither can we know that **p**, **q**, **r**, and **s** are true. Remember that in order to know something, we must have a reason for it. But if there is no good reason to believe **t**, then there is no good reason to believe **p**, **q**, **r**, or **s** since these all depend upon **t**. Since *all* beliefs are dependent through a chain of reasoning upon a person's ultimate standard, if the ultimate standard is not known to be true (i.e., provable), then one cannot actually know anything whatsoever. Of course, some of the person's beliefs might happen to be true, but they cannot be *known* to be true.

So we have established the following: (1) Everyone must have an ultimate standard (there is no "neutrality"). (2) An ultimate standard cannot be proved from another standard (since there is no greater standard, and appealing to a lesser standard is fallacious). (3) An ultimate standard cannot be merely assumed (otherwise, we couldn't know anything at all). This leaves only one possible answer to the question of how an ultimate standard is proved. An ultimate standard *must prove itself*. It must be self-attesting. It must provide criteria for what is to be considered true, and by which all claims are judged — including the ultimate standard itself.

This immediately invites a crucial objection: If an ultimate standard is used to prove itself, aren't we simply arguing in a circle? We have already shown that it is fallacious to merely assume what we are trying to prove — this is the fallacy of begging the question. We cannot merely say that "**t** is true because **t** is true." And yet we are forced into the seemingly strange yet inevitable conclusion that we must somehow use our ultimate standard to prove our ultimate standard.

Circular Reasoning

There are two things to remember about circular reasoning when it comes to an ultimate commitment. 1. It is absolutely unavoidable. 2. It is not *necessarily* fallacious. First, some degree of circular reasoning is unavoidable when proving an ultimate standard. This follows from what we have already established: an ultimate standard cannot be proved from anything else, otherwise it wouldn't be *ultimate*. Therefore, if it is to be proved, it must use itself as the criterion.

Notice that God Himself uses a type of circular reasoning when He makes an oath. Human beings appeal to a greater authority as confirmation of an oath (Heb. 6:16). But since God is ultimate, He can only use Himself as the authority. Hebrews 6:13 states, "When God made His promise to Abraham, since there was no one greater for him to swear by, he swore by himself." Clearly, some degree of circular reasoning is inevitable when it comes to proving an ultimate authority.

Second, not all circles are fallacious. Remember that begging the question is not actually invalid, but it is normally considered a fallacy because it is arbitrary. But what if it were not arbitrary? What if the argument went "out of its plane," going beyond a mere simple circle, and used other additional information to support the conclusion? What if we found *after* making an assumption that we had good reasons for it? This would be perfectly legitimate.

In fact, any true presupposition must use itself as part of its own proof. So some degree of circular reasoning is involved, but it cannot be a simple "vicious" circle. It must go beyond its own "plane." Consider this proof that there are laws of logic:

1. If there were no laws of logic, we could not make an argument.

2. We can make an argument.

3. Therefore, there must be laws of logic.

This argument is perfectly valid. It is a *modus tollens* syllogism (denying the consequent).[2] And the premises are true. So this is a good argument. Yet it is subtly circular. We have assumed in this proof that there are laws of logic; *modus tollens* is a law of logic and we have used it as part of the proof that there are laws of logic. In this case we had no choice; in order to get anywhere in an argument we must presuppose that there are laws of logic. However, this argument does not *merely* assume what it is trying to prove; it imports additional information to support its conclusion. But what makes this a really good argument is that any possible rebuttal would also have to use laws of logic; therefore, any potential rebuttal would be self-refuting. A great way to show that a particular presupposition must be true is to show that one would have to assume that the presupposition is true even to argue against it! An argument that proves a precondition of intelligibility in this way is called a *transcendental argument*.[3]

The Christian's ultimate standard is much like this; any attempt to refute the Bible must assume that the Bible is true in order to get started. The Bible not only provides criteria for itself, but does so for *all other facts*. It gives us a foundation (the biblical God) for rational reasoning (including laws of logic), science, morality, reliability of our senses and memory, and so on. It even gives us a foundation for why we should not be inconsistent or arbitrary (because God isn't, and we are to imitate Him — Eph. 5:1). The Bible passes its own criteria for truth (it is consistent, non-arbitrary, etc.) and provides criteria for everything else. The Christian circle is not a vicious circle, but one that can account for all human experience and reasoning. As with the argument for laws of logic, any attempted rebuttal would be self-refuting, because it would have to use things (laws of logic, the charge to be consistent, and so on) that *presuppose* the Christian worldview.

Proverbs 1:7 states, "The fear of the LORD is the beginning of knowledge, but fools despise wisdom and discipline." So we can either begin with God and His presuppositions (as revealed in His Word), or we can reject them and be reduced to foolishness. The Christian claim is therefore not a vicious circle. I'm not merely arguing, "The Bible must be the Word of God because it says it is." Rather, I'm arguing, "The Bible must be the Word of God because it says it is **and** if you reject this claim you are reduced to foolishness." This moves beyond a simple vicious circle of reasoning. Like laws of logic, the Bible must be true because if it were not, we could not prove anything.

Non-Christian Circles

An ultimate standard must do more than simply prove itself. It must provide a basis for proving absolutely everything that is knowable. And this is quite a challenge. The Christian's ultimate standard is able to do this. But no non-Christian standard is up to the challenge. Non-Christian circles turn out to be self-refuting, rather than self-attesting, and they cannot account for the preconditions of intelligibility.

Non-Christian circles of reasoning are ultimately self-defeating. They do not pass their own test.

Consider empiricism — the belief that all knowledge is gained by observation. Is empiricism self-attesting? Is it able to prove itself by its own standard? No. If all knowledge is gained by observation then we could never know that empiricism is true. If empiricism could be shown to be true, then it would be false. It is self-defeating.[4] Consider materialism — the belief that all that exists is matter in motion. Does materialism pass its own standard for truth? Not at all. We could never prove that materialism is true by its own standard, because we would need laws of logic (in order to prove anything), which are non-material and thus cannot exist in a materialistic universe.

So the question is *not*, "Which worldview uses some degree of circular reasoning?" They all do. The question is, "Which worldview is actually able to do this *successfully*?" The Christian worldview is the only one that is actually able to authorize itself — to pass its own criteria while simultaneously providing criteria for everything else. Remember, a circular argument is not invalid but is normally fallacious because it's arbitrary. But in the case of biblical creation it's *not* arbitrary. The reason for our circle is that it is the only one that makes knowledge possible.

Notice that even the standards by which all worldviews are judged are actually biblical standards. We have insisted all along that a worldview should be self-consistent. But why? The reason is that God is self-consistent, and thus all truth is. A clever unbeliever should have responded, "No, no. I'm not going to be *consistent*. That's a *biblical* standard." We have insisted that a worldview should be non-arbitrary since God has logical reasons for what He does. A clever unbeliever should have responded, "No, no. I'm not going to have *reasons* for what I believe. That's a biblical concept." And yet, virtually no one thinks to argue this way. Why?

All unbelievers are made in God's image. As such, they know in their heart of hearts the biblical God. God has built into them the knowledge that they should be consistent, non-arbitrary, rational, moral persons. And try as they might, they cannot completely escape this principle. The unbeliever must live in God's universe, and therefore must accept God's presuppositions in order to function. The unbeliever might deny being made in God's image, but he cannot escape it.

Defending the Bible — Before the Bible Was Written?

What about those people who lived before the Bible was written? Would they have been able to have a rational worldview? How could believers defend the biblical worldview before the Bible was written? First, remember that the ultimate proof of creation is not that people must profess the Bible — or even read the Bible to be rational. The argument is that the Bible must be *true* in order for rationality to be possible. Only the biblical worldview can make sense of rationality, morality, and science. And the biblical worldview has always been true, even before the Bible that articulates this view was inscribed.

Second, although people have not always had the complete Bible as we have it today, they have always had special revelation from God. God talked with Adam directly (e.g., Gen. 2:16–17), and no doubt Adam passed on what he had learned about God to his children and grandchildren (Gen. 4:26). In fact, Adam lived for many years and could have passed on his firsthand knowledge of God to his descendents for many generations. It also seems likely that much of the early knowledge of God was written down (Gen. 5:1). So people have had knowledge of the biblical God and biblical creation right from the beginning. And throughout time, God continued to reveal Himself through the prophets (2 Pet. 1:21).

People have always had access to God's special revelation, even long before the Bible was completed. Therefore, people have always had a foundation for rationality, science, and morality. At any point in history, people could have used the *ultimate proof of creation*, though they would have undoubtedly picked illustrations of it that were suitable to their culture. Of course, now that the Bible is completed, it may be *easier* to defend the faith. We have a more complete revelation from God than our ancient ancestors. Therefore, it is all the more indicting for us today when we fail to obey God's command to give an answer to those who ask a reason for the hope within us.

The Place of Faith

What is the place of faith in apologetics? Since we have a proof of the Christian worldview, do we really need faith? What is the relationship between faith and reason? In this section, we will explore these questions and will find that faith is absolutely essential to our apologetic. It is the prerequisite for logical reasoning.

Critics of Christianity often have a misconception of what faith is. They think that Christians live in two "worlds": the world of faith and the world of reason. Many critics believe that Christians use the world of faith when making moral decisions, or when talking about religion, but that we live in the world of reason when it comes to practical matters. They consider faith to be *contrary* to reason. Understandably, they consider such a dichotomy to be irrational. Moreover, some critics believe that Christians actually take pride in our alleged irrationality: that we believe in absurd things for the very sake of their absurdity, as if it were a "religious" badge of honor.

But such a conception of faith is not biblical. According to Hebrews 11:1, faith involves a confidence in things that are unseen. Therefore, when anyone believes in something that they have not perceived with their senses, they are acting on a type of faith. But everyone believes in some things that they have not perceived with their senses. Laws of logic cannot be perceived by the senses, and so faith is involved whenever someone trusts in laws of logic. Therefore, all logical reasoning presupposes some type of faith. But not all faiths are equal. Only faith in the Bible as our ultimate standard will result in a coherent worldview that can make sense of human experience and reasoning.

Faith is not antagonistic to reason. On the contrary, biblical faith is *required* for reasoning. One must believe in order to understand. Faith must come first; we need certain presuppositions in order to even begin to reason. For example, we must first believe that there are laws of logic before we can argue for them logically. We must first have faith that our senses are reliable before we can even begin to read the Bible. But when we do read the Bible, we will find that our faith is justified. Biblical presuppositions such as logic, uniformity, reliability of senses, and memory all make sense in the biblical worldview. The Bible provides the justification for these things.

So we find that we have a good *reason* for our faith. One great reason for the Christian faith is that without it, we couldn't reason. If we really understand this principle and are able to patiently and graciously explain it to others, then we have fulfilled 1 Peter 3:15. By setting apart Christ as Lord of our mind, we are able to give an answer when someone asks us for a reason for the hope within us.

Uniformity and Uniformitarianism

The biblical creation worldview stands alone in that it guarantees a certain degree of uniformity in nature. Other worldviews might allow for uniformity of course, but they are unable to provide a cogent reason for it. But the biblical creationist believes in a God who is beyond time, who has revealed Himself to man, and who has promised a certain degree of consistency in the future (Gen. 8:22). As such, nobody besides the biblical creationist can actually *know* that the future will resemble the past.[5] Therefore, only the biblical creationist has a logical foundation for science.

But some questions remain. To what extent is nature uniform? Does God's upholding power imply a constancy of conditions and rates? Can God alter the way He upholds the universe? If God did alter the way He upholds the universe, would this destroy the possibility of science and technology? To answer these questions, we must look to our ultimate standard: the Bible.

Hebrews 1:3 tells us that Christ upholds "all things by his powerful word." It is therefore by the direct power of God that the universe continues to exist and function. Colossians 1:17 tells us that in Christ "all things hold together." This means that planets, stars, and even atoms are held together by God's power.

Secularists might complain about this. They might say, "Don't you know that planets and stars are held together by gravity, and atoms are held together by electromagnetic forces?" This is true, of course, but it commits the fallacy of bifurcation (a false dilemma). Gravity and electromagnetic forces are descriptions of the way in which God holds the universe together. The laws of physics are not a replacement for God's power; they are an example of God's power. The fact that many such laws can be written with simple mathematical equations tells us something about how God thinks and acts.

The fact that God is beyond time and space, along with His promise to continue to provide certain things in the future (Gen. 8:22), tells us that we can expect the laws of nature to be constant over both time and space. As a biblical creationist, I expect that the laws of nature will be the same in the core of Jupiter as they are here on Earth, and that they will be the same on Friday as they were on Monday. The Bible teaches uniformity. But this does not mean that *conditions* in the core of Jupiter will be the same as on Earth, nor does it mean conditions (weather conditions, for example) on Friday will be identical to those on Monday. The Bible does not teach *uniformitarianism* — the notion that present rates and processes are constant over time or space.

God's consistent power does not imply that conditions or rates have always been identical. In fact, the Bible specifically denies this. Genesis 1:31 teaches that the world was once very good, but now it is under a bondage of corruption due to Adam's sin (Rom. 8:20–22). The world was once totally under water (Gen. 7:19–23), but now it isn't. Things have certainly changed. God has made a universe in which conditions and rates can change quite drastically, and yet God Himself does not change. He upholds the universe in a consistent way. So the Bible teaches uniformity but denies uniformitarianism.

Although uniformity does not in any way require uniformitarianism, uniformitarianism does indeed require uniformity. Hypothetically, if conditions (rates and processes) were basically the same throughout time, then that would certainly require that the laws of nature were constant throughout time. Clearly, conditions could not be consistent if the laws of physics and chemistry were constantly changing. But apart from the Bible, there would be no basis for uniformity. And yet the Bible specifically denies uniformitarianism. Thus, those who believe in uniformitarianism are in the rather embarrassing position of having to rely on the Bible (to have uniformity) while simultaneously denying it (to have uniformitarianism). Uniformitarianism is inherently irrational.

Miracles

If nature is rigidly law-like, then does this mean that miracles are impossible? First, we need to decide what constitutes a miracle. The Greek word that is often translated "miracle" in some Bible translations is *semeion* (σημειον) and is more formally translated as "sign" as in "signs and wonders" (e.g., John 4:48). Jesus performed many miracles: He turned water into wine, healed the sick, gave sight to the blind, and even raised the dead. These were all accomplished by God's sovereign power. But we have already pointed out that the entire universe is governed and upheld by God's power (Heb. 1:3). So what makes a miracle different than anything else?

All of Christ's miracles were beyond our ordinary, everyday experiences. They were unusual and were designed to accomplish a specific purpose. Christ healed the sick because He had compassion on them, but these miracles also confirmed Christ's deity. This is what makes a miracle different from ordinary providence. A miracle is an extraordinary and unusual manifestation of God's power to accomplish a specific purpose.

Based on the above definition, do miracles violate the laws of nature? The answer is: not necessarily. Many of the amazing things God has done have made use of natural law and are not necessarily violations thereof. Consider the parting of the Red Sea (Exod. 14:21–22, 29). This was certainly an unusual manifestation of God's power and made possible the flight of the Hebrews. It fits our definition of a miracle, yet God used wind to drive back the water (Exod. 14:21). Wind is a natural force, and so the parting of the Red Sea does not violate any obvious physics principles.

Some people might argue that miracles are necessarily violations of natural law. "(1) Natural law is the normal (*usual*) way God accomplishes His will. (2) Miracles are *unusual* manifestations of God's power. (3) Therefore, miracles cannot be described by natural law." But this argument commits the fallacy of equivocation[6] on the word "usual." There are degrees of what is to be considered usual. Something can be unusual in the sense of having extraordinary timing, and yet usual in the sense of being described by natural law. So miracles are not necessarily exceptions to natural law.

On the other hand, some miracles really could be beyond natural law. God is under no obligation to uphold the universe in a perfectly rigid uniform way (providing any exceptions are not so severe as to cause God to break His promise to provide some degree of uniformity). Miracles such as Joshua's long day (Josh. 10:12–14) and Jesus walking on water (Matt. 14:25) may indeed have involved a temporary suspension of the laws of nature.

Technically, it is impossible to prove that any miracle violates natural law. The reason is that we do not know all the laws of nature. Therefore, any given miracle might simply be a manifestation of an undiscovered principle of physics, or a manifestation of known principles acting in ways that we do not presently understand.[7] But let's suppose for the sake of argument that some miracles are indeed beyond natural law. Is this a problem for the Christian worldview? Would it make science impossible?

Some critics have argued that any violation of the laws of physics by God would bring science to a crashing halt. Therefore, they argue that we ought to reject the possibility of miracles — or at least those miracles that seem to violate the laws of nature. But is such a position rational? Science does require a certain degree of uniformity in nature. But there is no reason to suppose that science requires that the universe is perfectly uniform at all times. As long as miracles are rare (which they are by definition), science can proceed. The notion that miracles would make science impossible is nothing more than a slippery slope fallacy.

So the Christian worldview can account for the law-like properties of the universe. And if there are rare exceptions, the Christian worldview can account for this as well. But the secular worldview cannot account for either of these things. In the secular worldview, there is no reason at all to expect the universe to be law-like. There is no reason to believe that the universe will continue to behave in the future as it has in the past. Ironically, in the secular worldview, every time we are able to make a successful prediction about the future (the position of the planets and so on), it is a sort of "miracle" because the secular worldview has absolutely no logical reason whatsoever for the uniformity of nature, and thus the success of science.

Endnotes

1. I first read about this story in Hawking's book *A Brief History of Time*. There are several versions of the story, but all are similar in essence.
2. See chapter 8.

3. A transcendental argument is the type of argument that Dr. Bahnsen used in his debates when he argued for the existence of the biblical God. Dr. Bahnsen did a lecture series along with Michael Butler on transcendental arguments. CDs of the series are available from the Covenant Media Foundation (www.cmfnow.com).

4. Many empiricists try to get around this by essentially asking for just one exception to their own philosophy in order for it to "get started." If the view of empiricism is exempted from its own criteria, then they believe it will work for all other truth claims. But this is inconsistent and is the fallacy of special pleading. It is also arbitrary — why exempt one claim from the standard and not others?

5. The creationist can do this consistently. He knows based on his own worldview. The evolutionist can only know about uniformity by inconsistently appealing to biblical creation.

6. Equivocation is called the "fallacy of four terms" if it is used in a formal deductive syllogism.

7. Some atheists have argued that they would believe in God if only they were to see a miracle with their own eyes. However, if such a thing happened, the atheist would almost certainly invoke a rescuing device; he or she would argue that the apparent miracle is the manifestation of an unknown law of nature, or an undiscovered application of an existing law. I suggest that such a rescuing device is perfectly justified, since past experience has shown us that many things once thought mystical are now understood in terms of natural laws. Therefore, miracles will not convince someone who has decided already that he or she will not believe in God.

CHAPTER 10

APOLOGETICS IN THE BIBLE

There are a number of different views on how the Christian faith should be defended; but not all are *good* views. Some people believe that faith is a matter of belief only, and that there is no need to defend it at all. Others believe that we should not assume the truth of the Bible until *after* we have persuaded the unbeliever that the Bible is true. Strangely, few people think to actually consult the Bible to see what *it* says about how we should defend the faith. And that is very unfortunate, because the Bible actually has quite a lot to say about apologetics. The way in which we defend the faith needs to be faithful to the Bible.

First, we must deal with those who claim that the Christian faith needs no defense. Although this position may sound very bold, it is not consistent with Scripture. First Peter 3:15 tells us that we need to always be ready to give a defense of the faith. Those who ask us if we have a reason for our faith are to be given an answer. This indicates that we should indeed have a *reason* for our faith. As we have demonstrated in this book, the Christian does indeed have a very good reason for his or her faith. Without the biblical God, we could know absolutely

167

nothing. Our reasoning presupposes biblical faith. So the notion that Christianity cannot be proved or does not need to be proved is not consistent with the teaching of the Bible, nor is it a rational position.

Evidential Authority versus Biblical Authority

The Christian must be ready to give an answer — a reason for the faith. But what kind of reason should we give? Broadly speaking, there are two positions on the issue. There is the "evidential authority" approach, and there is the "biblical authority" approach. The "evidential authority" supporters attempt to show that objective ("neutral") evaluation of evidence will necessarily lead to the conclusion that the Bible (or creation specifically) must be true. The "biblical authority" supporters take Scripture to be their ultimate standard, even when defending it. They point out that without first presupposing the Bible, we could not make sense of any evidence anyway.

We've already seen that an "evidential authority" approach will not rationally resolve worldview disputes. Evidence is very useful when we agree on how it should be interpreted. But when the rules of interpretation are the very thing being disputed (as is the case with the origins debate), evidence by itself will not settle things. So when people say that they believe that a sufficient amount of scientific evidence is the way to prove creation or evolution, this shows that they really do not understand what is going on.

People will always interpret the evidence in light of their worldview. Therefore, evidence by itself will not cause a rational person to reconsider his or her worldview. The evidential authority position also commits the pretended neutrality fallacy. There is no "neutral" evaluation of evidence. All facts are interpreted through a person's worldview — there are no exceptions. An evidential authority approach is simply not rational because it does not deal with the real issue: competing worldviews.

On the other hand, the biblical authority approach is what we've been using throughout this book. We could restate the ultimate proof of the Bible as: "The Bible must be the ultimate standard because no other standard can make knowledge possible." The Bible must come first; it must be presupposed before we can properly evaluate evidence. Notice that the biblical authority approach does make use of evidence. But since all evidence must be interpreted through an ultimate standard, we must always start with the Bible (the only possible consistent and self-attesting ultimate standard) when we interpret any evidence.

A biblical authority position doesn't necessarily mean that the Bible is *chronologically* first in terms of when we come to believe things. Clearly, we must trust our senses before we can read the Bible, which provides the justification for reliability of senses. Rather, the biblical authority approach simply means that the Bible is foundational — it is the ultimate standard. It means that when we argue for the truth of the Bible, we must begin our argument by presupposing the Bible as our supreme criterion for evaluating all facts. Critics will accuse us of circular reasoning, but we have already shown in the previous chapter that such reasoning is logically necessary and not fallacious if done properly. Remember, all people must appeal to their ultimate standard even when defending it. But according to Scripture, only the Bible can do this successfully; only the biblical God can be the foundation for knowledge (Prov. 1:7; Col. 2:3). No one has ever been able to come up with another ultimate standard that can account for rationality, science, and morality.

The Bible's Standard for Reasoning

The evidential authority approach simply does not stand up to rational scrutiny. On the other hand, the biblical authority approach has given us an ultimate proof of the biblical worldview. Most importantly, we find that the Bible itself endorses a biblical authority approach. The idea that we cannot know anything apart from the biblical God is not a modern claim; it is contained within the pages of Scripture. As discussed earlier, Proverbs 1:7 states, "The fear of the LORD is the beginning of knowledge, but fools despise wisdom and instruction." We must begin with a reverential submission to God as revealed in the Bible in order to have knowledge. This proverb also shows what happens when one rejects the instruction and wisdom of God's Word: he is reduced to foolishness.

The idea that all knowledge begins with the biblical God is found throughout the Bible. In Romans 1:18–23 we see a wonderful illustration of the ultimate proof. These verses tell us that everyone has innate knowledge of God (verses 19–20); this is why everyone knows about laws of logic, uniformity, and morality. But people suppress that truth (verse 18). They do not acknowledge God as the foundation of knowledge, and as a result, their thoughts are reduced to foolishness (verses 21–22).

Colossians 2:3 tells us that "all the treasures of wisdom and knowledge" are deposited in Christ. Thus, we cannot have genuine knowledge apart from Christ. Colossians 2:8 warns us about being robbed of these very treasures by accepting secular standards — worldly philosophy. It states, "See to it that no one takes you captive through hollow and deceptive philosophy, which depends on human tradition and the basic principles of this world rather than on Christ." So our way of thinking, our philosophy, must be according to Christ and therefore according to His revealed Word. Any other standard is merely "empty deception."

The evidential authority position is really a secular position. It asserts that man is able to come to correct conclusions about evidence without the presuppositions of Scripture. But God says that secular "wisdom" is foolish, useless, futile, and ignorant. First Corinthians 3:19 tells us that "the wisdom of this world is foolishness in God's sight." First Corinthians 3:20 states that "The Lord knows that the thoughts of the wise are futile." Ephesians 4:17–18 says this about secular thinking: "So I tell you this, and insist on it in the Lord, that you must no longer live as the Gentiles do, in the futility of their thinking. They are darkened in their understanding and separated from the life of God because of the ignorance that is in them due to the hardening of their hearts."

Notice the last phrase of this verse; it tells us the source of secular foolishness — a hardened heart. It's not merely a matter of different presuppositions — as important as that is. The unbeliever has a spiritual problem. He is in rebellion against God and does not want to accept God's standards. First Corinthians 2:14 states, "But a natural man does not accept the things of the Spirit of God, for they are foolishness to him; and he cannot understand them, because they are spiritually appraised" (NASB). Without the help of the Holy Spirit, the unbeliever cannot even understand the things of God. This may be the most important overlooked fact in all of apologetics. This is one reason why we cannot "argue someone into heaven." The Lord must grant repentance (2 Tim. 2:25; Acts 5:31; Rom. 2:4).

The evidential authority approach would have us attempt to show that the Bible is true by starting from another (neutral) standard. But the Bible clearly teaches that there is no other standard for knowledge than God's (Prov. 1:7; Col. 2:3). So if it were possible to prove the Bible from another standard, then the Bible couldn't be true! The Bible affirms that people do not come to God through secular reasoning: 1 Corinthians 1:21 states, "For since in the wisdom of God the world through its wisdom did not come to know God, God was well-pleased through the foolishness of the message preached to save those who believe" (NASB). Ironically, only by embracing what the world considers foolishness (God's Word) can we escape the foolishness of the world.

First Corinthians 2:5 tells us that our faith should not rest on the "wisdom" of men but on the power of God. Here Paul is not condemning wisdom — only secular "wisdom." He indicates in the next three verses that we should have a wisdom that is from God: a wisdom that the secular world does not understand. All the treasures of wisdom and knowledge are in Christ (Col. 2:3) and therefore we must "surrender" our thinking to Him in order to really have wisdom and knowledge. Second Corinthians 10:5 tells us that we must "take captive every thought to make it obedient to Christ." If we are to have knowledge, we must not conform our thinking to the world (Rom. 12:2) but to Christ.

Does Evidence Convince People?

Evidence can certainly be used to convince people of a point if they already have a correct worldview — a correct framework for interpreting the evidence. But if their worldview is faulty, there is no guarantee that they will be convinced. So we must always guard ourselves against an evidential authority approach. It is very tempting to think that there are some lines of evidence that are absolutely not open to interpretation: facts that prove the Bible is true. But such a "magic bullet" approach just will not work. There is always a rescuing device to explain away contrary evidence. If people have faulty presuppositions, they may not be convinced no matter how good the evidence may seem.

Jesus understood the necessity of taking a biblical authority approach. He illustrated this principle with the story of Lazarus and the rich man (Luke 16:19–31). The rich man in this story had rejected the gospel, and so he died and went to hell. Calling from hell, he begged father Abraham to send Lazarus to go and preach to his five brothers, lest they also end up in hell. But Abraham's response was that the brothers have the Scriptures: "They have Moses and the Prophets; let them listen to them." The rich man responded, "No, father Abraham, but if someone from the dead goes to them, they will repent!" But Abraham's response was "If they do not listen to Moses and the Prophets, they will not be convinced even if someone rises from the dead." It's an amazing response: those who do not accept the Scriptures will also not be convinced by a resurrection!

The rich man had an evidential authority mindset. He believed that seeing someone being raised from the dead would be such spectacular evidence that his brothers would certainly change their worldview. But Jesus (speaking as Abraham) tells us that is not the case. Yes, resurrection from the dead is spectacular evidence — but will only be interpreted as a proof of Christianity by someone who *already* accepts biblical presuppositions. Therefore, if people do not accept the Scriptures ("Moses and the Prophets"), they will not accept the evidence of resurrection.

"But surely this is a special case," some might argue. Yet we see this very principle played out in Christ's Resurrection. Matthew 28:17 tells us that Christ was seen by His followers after the Resurrection: "When they saw him, they worshiped him. . . ." Yes, many of His followers accepted biblical presuppositions, and worshiped the resurrected Christ — no surprise there. But the last three words of Matthew 28:17 are very interesting: ". . . but some doubted." In the very presence of the resurrected Lord, there were some who doubted! The Resurrection of Christ is one of the most spectacular evidences of His deity. Yet it did not convince everyone, even those who saw Him with their own eyes. So much for "seeing is believing"!

There are those who say, "If I only saw a miracle, then I'd believe. If God would show me a spectacular sign, then I'd become a Christian." Nonsense. There were those who witnessed miracles and yet didn't believe. Think of all the masses who witnessed the miracles of Christ; did all of them bow and worship Him as Lord? No, they crucified Him. The problem is *not* that people don't have enough evidence. The problem is that they suppress what they know to be true (Rom. 1:18). The key, therefore, is not merely to throw evidences at the unbeliever, but to expose his suppressed knowledge of God.

Possible Counter-Examples?

Some people might object to the biblical authority approach and think that they have a clear counter-example: "But so-and-so was convinced that the Bible must be true because of the scientific evidence." What are we to make of those people who convert to Christianity apparently having been convinced by scientific evidence? Do such counter-examples mean that an evidential authority approach is acceptable and effective in some instances?

First of all, we need to remember something that was stated in the introduction of this book. People are sometimes convinced by *bad arguments*. Most people are not good, clear thinkers. As such, they sometimes are persuaded by fallacies. The fact that a Christian may see someone convert to Christianity after using an evidential authority approach does not mean that his approach was logically cogent or ethical! The argument we have made in this chapter is that only the biblical authority approach is faithful to the Scriptures and that an evidential authority approach is ultimately irrational because evidence can only be properly interpreted in light of Scripture. So the fact that people are occasionally apparently persuaded by an evidential authority approach is utterly *irrelevant* to the claim that such an approach is irrational and unbiblical.[1]

Second, even in those cases where people seem to be persuaded by evidence, we must understand that it was not a "neutral" evaluation of the evidence. Evidence can be used to expose the unbeliever's suppressed knowledge of God; this is a perfectly appropriate use of evidence. Remember, all unbelievers do know God in their heart of hearts. They do rely on His presuppositions (inconsistently), and as such, they sometimes do correctly interpret evidence. Whenever an unbeliever correctly interprets evidence, it is because he is not being true to his professed secular worldview. Therefore, we cannot *count* on unbelievers to consistently interpret the evidence correctly, but they occasionally will due to their inconsistency.

Third, if we argue that the Bible is true on the basis of some piece of scientific evidence, then we are teaching people that the Bible is less foundational than human understanding of scientific evidence. That is, we would essentially be teaching that man's ability to understand the evidence is the ultimate standard — not God's Word. Since most (well-meaning) Christian apologists today use an evidential authority approach, we are raising up a generation of Christians who do not accept the Bible as their ultimate standard. Yes, they believe the Bible, but only insomuch as it fits in with their personal evaluation of the evidence. And if their interpretation of some evidence doesn't fit the Bible, they feel that it is the Bible that must be reinterpreted. As such, we have Christians who believe in things like millions of years, "day-age" creation, theistic evolution, and so on. We have a generation of Christians who are "carried about with every wind of doctrine" (Eph. 4:14; KJV) because they are not firmly rooted in the Word of God as their ultimate standard.

Finally, I feel it necessary to again point out that it is perfectly appropriate to use scientific and historical evidence as *part* of our apologetic — but not as the *foundation* of our apologetic. In chapter 6 we saw that there are a number of good ways to use evidence in our defense of the faith — showing internal inconsistencies in the secular view, for example. So, by all means, we can and should use various evidences as part of our apologetic — providing we do it in the appropriate way. And there are (unfortunately) some situations where we cannot legally explicitly mention the Bible, yet we can still use evidence to accomplish *part* of our apologetic. There are perfectly appropriate uses of evidence. The error is in thinking that we could somehow prove the Bible from a *neutral*, objective evaluation of evidence. We must constantly keep in our mind that the only reason that evidence makes any sense at all is because the Bible is true.

Biblical Examples

The Bible gives us many examples of the fallacious, evidential authority approach: people that decided to put more confidence in their own interpretation of evidence than in God's revealed Word. One of the first examples is Eve (Gen. 2–3). God had told Adam that He was not to eat from the tree of knowledge of good and evil, and this instruction was passed on to Eve as well.[2] But when the serpent (Satan) challenged God's command, Eve responded with an evidential authority approach. She decided to treat God's Word as one hypothesis, and Satan's claim as another. She decided that she would be the one to judge between the two positions. She then did what any true empiricist would do; she performed an experiment to see which claim was correct.

Her actions were not only immoral, but irrational as well. Think about it: Eve was relying on her senses and on her mind to judge whether or not God was honest. But God had created Eve's mind and senses. So if God were dishonest, then there would be no reason for Eve to trust her senses or her mind in the first place. What could Eve hope to gain from such an experiment? Her response to Satan should have been: "God's Word is true. Therefore, you are a liar. Get behind me, Satan!" But instead she decided that she should be her own ultimate standard. And then Adam followed suit.

On the other hand, Christ, the Last Adam, was consistently biblical in His approach to all things. Consider Christ's temptation in the wilderness (Matt. 4:1–11). Satan tempted Jesus by saying, "If you are the Son of God, tell these stones to become bread." It wasn't that Satan really doubted, of course; he knew who Christ was. But Satan was suggesting an evidential authority approach to evaluate the claim: an evidence that would appeal to the flesh. But Christ responded with Scripture: "It is written: 'Man does not live on bread alone, but on every word that comes from the mouth of God.'" Not only did Jesus respond with a biblical authority approach, but the very Scripture He quoted indicates a biblical authority approach — that we should live by the Word of God.

Far too many Christians put more confidence in their personal assessment of evidence than they do in the infallible Word of God. They think that they must first establish the truth of the Bible by unbiased evaluation of evidence; only then do they bow the knee to Christ. Only after they have been satisfied by their own autonomous standard do they acknowledge the kingship and sovereignty of Christ. But such an attitude is irrational and unbiblical. We have demonstrated that we must in fact *begin* our apologetic by bowing the knee to Christ. We must start by acknowledging the sovereignty of Christ and His Word as our ultimate standard if we are to come to any rational conclusions whatsoever.

In fact, this is the key to success in apologetics. First Peter 3:15 does not start with "be ready always." It starts with "but sanctify Christ as Lord in your hearts" (NASB). The first part of 1 Peter 3:15 is the prerequisite for accomplishing the rest of the verse. We must begin our apologetic by setting apart Christ as Lord in the core of our being (our "heart"). We start with Christ's presuppositions as revealed in His Word. We learn to see how people rely on their suppressed knowledge of Him. *Then* we will always be ready to give a defense of the confidence within us.

The Apologetics of Christ

Christ and the Apostles consistently used a biblical authority approach to apologetics. Not only that, they used the very procedure that has been outlined in this book. They applied the "don't answer, answer" strategy when responding to foolish claims. They presented the Christian worldview and did an internal critique of the non-Christian worldview. In their critique of unbelieving thought, they pointed out arbitrariness, inconsistency, and even the preconditions of intelligibility. Of course they didn't use these modern terms, but the concepts are there. Let's consider a few examples.

We begin with Jesus. Christ's responses to His critics were truly brilliant. He was never stumped but was always ready to give a defense. Consider Matthew 12:24–29. Here the Pharisees asserted that Jesus was only able to cast out demons because He Himself was using the power of Satan ("Beelzebul") — not God. Jesus responded using the "don't answer, answer" strategy. He did not accept their foolish standard ("don't answer"), but then He showed how silly their position was by showing what would hypothetically happen if it were true ("answer").

Christ pointed out that a kingdom or city that is divided against itself will not stand. So it wouldn't make sense for Satan to cast out his own demons, for then he would be divided against himself. Moreover, Jesus asked them, "And if I drive out demons by Beelzebul, by whom do your people drive them out?" He was pointing out that they could not condemn Him without condemning themselves. They were guilty of the fallacy of special pleading. Christ brilliantly showed the inconsistency and arbitrariness of the Pharisees' position.

Another example is found in Matthew 21:23–27. Here the chief priests asked who gave Christ the authority to teach the things He was saying. But Jesus knew that they had a foolish standard (otherwise they would have already known the answer). So He didn't answer them according to their standard, but then showed the inconsistency of their position by asking them a question: by what authority did John baptize? This put the critics on the "horns of a dilemma." For if they answered correctly ("from heaven"), then Jesus could simply ask them why they didn't believe what John was saying about Him. And if they said anything else, they feared the reaction of the people who accepted John as a prophet of God. Christ neutralized their objection, and they were unable to answer Him.

Several more examples are found in Matthew 22:15–46. Christ patiently answered the objections of His critics. But then He exposed the foolishness of their thinking by asking them questions — by making them defend their position. Remember, the non-Christian does not have an apologetic; he cannot defend his view rationally. It's important to remember that in our defense of the faith we can ask the critic to defend his or her faith as well. Christ's critics were not able to defend their position. "No one could say a word in reply, and from that day on no one dared to ask him any more questions" (Matt. 22:46).

The Apologetics of Paul

The Apostle Paul also used the Bible as his ultimate standard. He presented the Christian worldview, he internally critiqued the secular worldview using the "AIP" test, and he used the "don't answer, answer" strategy in his responses. A great example of Paul's defense of the faith is found in Acts 17:16–34. Here, we find Paul in Athens — a city full of idol worship. He was reasoning in the synagogue and in the market place every day with those who happened to be present. Paul was not employing an emotional "pull at the heartstrings" approach to evangelism; he was *reasoning* with people. The philosophers there were very hostile to Christianity and they began mocking him. They then brought him before the Areopagus (a council of justice) to ask him about what he was teaching. Verses 22–31 record the essential points of Paul's defense of the faith.

Paul begins by analyzing the worldview of his critics (Acts 17:22–23). This is always an important step if we are to perform an internal critique. Paul notes that the Athenians were very religious — in the sense that they worshiped idols. One of their altars had the inscription "to an unknown god." Paul uses this concession of ignorance as a springboard to begin presenting the Christian worldview. This he does beginning in verse 24 by going back to Genesis — explaining that God is the Creator of the world and everything in it. He corrects his critics' erroneous view of deity by pointing out that the Creator God would not dwell in temples nor would He need to be served by human hands since it is God who gives life and breath to all (verse 25).

In verses 26–27 Paul continues presenting the Christian worldview by showing that we are all descended from Adam. He indicates that God has been sovereign in human history and that God is not far from us. In verse 28 Paul moves back to an internal critique — pointing out that in God we live and move and exist; a fact that the Athenians apparently already knew. But which worldview can makes sense of this fact? Certainly not a worldview in which the gods are made of gold or stone, but rather the Christian worldview makes intelligible this fact. The Christian God is all-powerful, and thus certainly able to sustain man's existence.

Paul continues his internal critique by pointing out that even his critics' own poets confirm what he is saying. He is showing that the Athenians did indeed know the biblical God in their heart of hearts.

The poets had stated that we are God's offspring — which (in a sense) we are since we are made in God's image. In verse 29 Paul is pointing out that only the Christian worldview can make this intelligible. The Christian view states that God made man in His own image. But the Athenian gods were made of gold, silver, and stone — and they were created by man; how could we be their offspring? Paul is showing a devastating inconsistency in his critics' worldview.

Having laid waste his opponents' position, Paul goes back to his presentation of the Christian worldview in verses 30–31. He teaches that all should repent and turn back to the biblical God, because God is going to judge the world through Christ. He ends by speaking of the Resurrection of Christ. Notice that Paul does use the Resurrection as evidence of Christ's deity — but only *after* he had given his listeners the proper framework in which to interpret that evidence. He had already destroyed the Athenian worldview and showed that the Christian worldview provides the preconditions of intelligibility for what the Greeks knew to be true.

Moreover, Paul had provided the biblical background to understand the theological implications of the Resurrection. By going back to Genesis, Paul showed that God is the sovereign Creator and thus has the right to set the rules. But mankind has rebelled against God and deserves judgment. God calls us to repent — to receive Christ as Lord and Savior. Christ's resurrection demonstrated (within the biblical worldview) that He was who He claimed to be — the Son of God. Many Christians today start with Christ's crucifixion and Resurrection in their evangelism; but this is not effective if the unbeliever does not have the proper interpretive framework. We must do as Paul did; we must go back to Genesis and explain Christianity from its beginning.

Paul's Success

Paul had a threefold response. (1) Some people mocked (Acts 17:32), (2) others wanted to hear more (verse 32), and (3) some joined him and believed (verse 34). We can expect one of those three basic types of response as well. Strangely, some Christians have claimed that Paul really wasn't very successful in his defense of the faith in Athens. They compare his results with the three thousand people (Acts 2:41) who were saved when Peter preached to the Jews in Jerusalem (Acts 2:14–36). Some have even suggested that Peter's approach to evangelism was much better than Paul's since many more were saved in Jerusalem than in Athens. But such a notion fails for a number of reasons.

First, Peter and Paul were using the *same basic* approach. Both used the biblical authority method as their apologetic, and both preached the Resurrection of Christ. There is an important distinction in the details, however, since Paul's audience was much different than Peter's. This brings us to the second point.

We must consider that Peter's sermon was to a Bible-believing audience (the Jews), whereas Paul's sermon was to a secular audience (the Greeks). Surely Paul had the more hostile crowd, and so we would hardly expect as many Greeks to convert as Jews. The Jews already had a biblical worldview; they believed the Old Testament and were expecting a Savior. They understood the problem of sin because they understood Genesis. They already knew the biblical God and so Peter had no need to explain such things. He simply had to help them overcome a "stumbling block" (1 Cor. 1:23) — the fact that Jesus is the Messiah that they were expecting.

Paul was preaching to a group of people who had a totally different way of thinking — a secular worldview. If he had started his defense with the Resurrection of Christ, it would have made no sense. The Greeks would have considered it "foolishness" (1 Cor. 1:23). Paul had to critique their secular way of thinking and present the Christian worldview from its beginning in Genesis. Only then would his audience have the correct framework in which to interpret Christ's Resurrection. Paul's critics were completely antagonistic to his worldview, yet some converted after his presentation. He was very successful indeed!

But ultimately, "success" in apologetics really should not be measured by whether the critic comes to receive Christ. God has not called us to convert people into Christians; this is beyond our power. He has called us to give a defense of the faith. Whether a person ultimately receives Christ is between the person and God. But God will often use us as part of the process; we are to give an answer. So our responsibility is to make sure we give a faithful defense of the biblical worldview. Paul did just that. He was successful because he was obedient to God. And God blessed his endeavors and a number of people were saved. The fact that two of these people are mentioned by name (Acts 17:34) suggests that they may have been persons of high social standing. Who knows what influence they had in spreading the gospel to others?

Both Peter and Paul used a cogent biblical authority approach in their defense of the faith. But each adapted the details to his particular audience. Paul was right to spend more time demolishing the secular worldview of his audience and presenting the foundational aspects of the Christian worldview starting from Genesis. And Peter was right to skip these steps since his audience already knew this. This is why it is so important to understand the worldview of our critics when we defend the faith.

Today our culture is much more like the Greeks' than the Jews'. Most people today do not claim to believe in biblical creation. As such, they do not really understand the concept of sin, the righteousness and justice of God, and the need for repentance. They do not have the theological framework to correctly interpret the death and Resurrection of Christ. Therefore, with most people today, we will need to evangelize much as Paul did. We need to learn to critique the secular worldview and present the Christian worldview from the beginning in Genesis.

Being Christ-Minded

The biblical worldview provides the preconditions that are essential for knowledge. It is a rationally defensible position. On the other hand, non-biblical worldviews are nothing more than speculations of men, created so that unbelievers will not have to submit to the authority of God. By aligning our thinking with God's Word, we can learn to refute non-biblical conjectures. Second Corinthians 10:5 states, "We are destroying speculations and every lofty thing raised up against the knowledge of God, and we are taking every thought captive to the obedience of Christ" (NASB). Our defense of the Christian faith should not simply end with submitting our thinking to Christ, it must begin there.

Endnotes
1. It's the fallacy of irrelevant thesis.
2. We know that Eve knew about God's command since she was able to quote it to the serpent in Genesis 3:2–3. Whether God had told her directly, or whether Adam had passed this on to her, the Scriptures do not say.

CONCLUSION

There is an old story about a man with a very strange problem: he was convinced that he was dead. His doctor tried to assure him that he was *not* dead, and was in fact perfectly healthy. "After all," argued the doctor, "you're able to walk and talk." But the man remained convinced that he was dead. He pointed out that muscle spasms can occur after clinical death, and this could explain his ability to walk and talk. The doctor presented medical charts and tables. But the man wouldn't budge; he pointed out that charts can be falsified, and that the doctor probably wasn't reading them correctly anyway.

Finally, the doctor had an idea — a way he could *prove* that the man was alive. The doctor asked, "Do dead men bleed?" The man responded, "Well, no. Dead men don't bleed." The doctor then took a small needle and pricked the man's arm. Sure enough, a small droplet of blood emerged. "See," said the doctor. The man responded, "Well how about that! *I guess dead men* **do** *bleed!*"

Did the doctor have evidence to support his position? Of course he did. But the man was not convinced of this evidence because he had erroneous presuppositions. He was able to invent a rescuing device to explain the evidence within his own worldview. The doctor's approach was ineffective because he failed to appreciate the power of a worldview. Mere evidence is not enough. The doctor *should* have challenged the man's worldview. He should have asked, "*Why* do you think you are dead?" The doctor needed to have a better understanding of the man's worldview so that he could do an internal critique, rather than just throwing particular lines of scientific evidence at him.

The debate over origins is analogous to this story. Creationists and evolutionists often "talk past each other" because they fail to recognize the importance of presuppositions. Rather than just throwing evidences at their opponents, creationists and evolutionists must learn to deal on the level of worldviews. We creationists must challenge non-biblical worldviews, critiquing them from within. We must expose their arbitrariness, inconsistency, and failure to provide a rational basis for knowledge. Only a worldview based on God's revelation can stand up to rational scrutiny.

Those who reverentially submit to God and His Word will be wise; but those who reject God are reduced to foolishness (Prov. 1:7). Jesus affirmed this crucial principle in Matthew 7:24–27.

> Therefore everyone who hears these words of Mine and acts on them, may be compared to a wise man, who built his house on the rock. And the rain fell and the floods came, and the winds blew and slammed against that house; and yet it did not fall, for it had been founded on the rock. Everyone who hears these words of Mine and does not act on them, will be like a foolish man who built his house on the sand. The rain fell, and the floods came, and the winds blew and slammed against that house; and it fell — and great was its fall (NASB).

Only a worldview based on the rock of God's Word will stand.

War of the Worldviews

There is a kind of war that is taking place in the world today — a war of ideas. It's a battle of competing authorities. One side argues that only the biblical God can provide a foundation for truth and reasoning. The other argues that human beings independent of God's revelation are able to determine truth. The problem with all worldviews that are based on autonomous human reasoning is that the human mind just isn't quite up to the job. Human beings have limited experience and we don't always think properly; so, apart from God, how can we be absolutely certain about anything? With finite knowledge, how could we ever know for certain that there is not some undiscovered fact that refutes what we think we know? If we invent our own ultimate standard for truth, how can we ever know that it is correct?

But God's nature is quite different from ours. He does not observe and learn about the universe the way we do because He does not have our limitations. God (by virtue of His nature) already knows everything (Col. 2:3), and thus only He is in a position to be absolutely certain about anything on His own authority. However, God has revealed some of His knowledge to us by His Word. We must therefore learn to base our thinking on God's revelation, and refute those who would challenge their Maker.

Second Corinthians 10:3–5 says this about the war of the world-views: "For though we walk in the flesh, we do not war according to the flesh, for the weapons of our warfare are not of the flesh, but divinely powerful for the destruction of fortresses. We are destroying specula-tions and every lofty thing raised up against the knowledge of God, and we are taking every thought captive to the obedience of Christ" (NASB). The key to victory is to submit our thinking to Christ. Ro-mans 12:2 tells us that we should not be conformed to the ways of this world, but that we should be transformed by the renewing of our mind in Christ.

Our apologetic is not merely a defense of the biblical worldview, but an application of it. Knowing that a reverential submission to God is the beginning of knowledge, we can expose the absurdity of rejecting the biblical God and reduce the critic to foolishness (Prov. 1:7). This should never be done in a harsh or mocking way, but always with a rev-erential respect for our critic. After all, the critic is also made in God's image and therefore deserves to be treated with dignity. We should also remember that we, too, have been the critic.

Those who argue against the biblical God are battling against the One who can save them from what we all deserve — an eternity in hell. Moreover, the critic must use biblical principles in order to ar-gue against the Bible. The critic is actually opposing himself. We must gently correct and instruct the critic, praying that the Lord will grant repentance. Second Timothy 2:24–25 states, "And the servant of the Lord must not contend; but be gentle to all men, apt to teach, patient, in meekness instructing those that oppose themselves; if God perhaps will give them repentance to the acknowledging of the truth" (Webster translation). We refute evolutionists for their own good. It is not an academic "game." We want people to be saved.

Many Christians would like to have a piece of scientific evidence that absolutely proves the Christian worldview — a "magic bullet" that cannot be interpreted any other way. But all people think in terms of a worldview. They will always interpret scientific or historical evidence in light of their own ultimate standard. For this reason, a "magic bullet" (evidential authority) approach is not logically sound. Yes, people are occasionally persuaded by a bad argument. But the Christian is under a moral obligation to argue truthfully. And if we're honest, the Bible cannot be proved by an evidential authority approach since the Bible must be presupposed in order to have a rational foundation for interpreting evidence.

We must use a biblical authority approach to defend the Christian faith. When we do this, we find that there is indeed an ultimate proof of biblical creation and the Christian worldview in general. No refutation of the ultimate proof is possible, since any critic would have to borrow biblical principles like laws of logic in order to construct his argument. Like the critic of air, the evolutionist must use principles that are contrary to his worldview in order to argue *for* his worldview. In order for his argument to be meaningful, it would have to be wrong. All arguments against biblical creation presuppose biblical creation!

The Debater of this Age

No one can stand against God. First Corinthians 1:20 states, "Where is the wise man? Where is the scribe? Where is the debater of this age? Has not God made foolish the wisdom of the world?" (NASB). Most of apologetics is simply good, logical, biblical thinking. As we learn to "think God's thoughts after Him" we will become better at defending the faith and better thinkers in general. This is a lifelong process. But it begins with submission to God's standard.

This is the ultimate proof of creation. The Bible is not proved externally by some greater standard of knowledge. In a sense, it proves itself. Only the biblical worldview is able to provide a rational foundation for all human experience and reasoning while passing its own criteria. Other worldviews turn out to be mere idols, failing to provide a basis for knowledge and refuting themselves in the process. Biblical creation is proved by the fact that if it were not true, we couldn't prove anything at all.

Critics will not like this argument, of course. They will want to simply dismiss it as "too philosophical" or "just not a good argument." But they will not be able to refute it. And that is the key. Remember it's not the Christian's job to "open their heart." Only the Holy Spirit can do that. It's the Christian's job to "close their mouth" — to give a good defense of the faith. The ultimate proof is an irrefutable argument for the Christian worldview.

I pray that this book is helpful to Christians in defending the faith. I have intentionally emphasized the defense of Genesis since it is foundational to the other books of the Bible; all major Christian doctrines depend on a literal Genesis either directly or indirectly. Also, Genesis has become one of the most attacked books of the Bible. It is therefore very important to be able to defend Genesis, as well as the other 65 books of the Bible.

Our defense of the faith does not come from knowing more scientific facts than other people. I am convinced, however, that it is a good idea to know *some* science, and to show how such evidence (properly understood) agrees with Genesis. Answers in Genesis and other apologetics ministries have produced a number of resources to that end. But science is not the foundation of our defense, nor does our defense of the faith rest on our formal education or academic credentials. Certainly it is useful to have a PhD in science, philosophy, or theology. But it is not required. The command to be always ready to defend the faith comes from the Apostle Peter (1 Pet. 3:15). Peter was a fisherman (Matt. 4:18): a perfectly noble career, but not one that we would normally consider to be highly academic.

Our defense of the faith comes from learning to think and to argue in a biblical way. God is logical, and we should be too. God tells us that all knowledge is in Him (Col. 2:2–3), so we should train ourselves to recognize this fact. Therefore, we should learn to see how the preconditions of intelligibility are all found in the biblical God. We must learn to spot arbitrariness and inconsistency in the secular worldview. We must learn to see the logical fallacies and false premises of evolutionary arguments. We do this not merely to win arguments, but to win people. Our goal should never be one of personal pride — trying to appear more intellectual than those who oppose us. Our goal should be to glorify God by giving a defense of the faith that is faithful to Him.

APPENDIX A

RIGHTLY DIVIDING THE WORD OF TRUTH

Throughout this book we have presupposed that the Bible is to be read in a natural, straightforward manner: that it really means what it says. But there are professing Christians who challenge this way of thinking. There are those who say that the Bible is not meant to be taken as history, but as a metaphor. Then again, there are others who say that the Bible is indeed a history book, but that the words don't really mean what they say; for example, people claim that the word "day" in Genesis 1 isn't really a true day, but is instead a vast period of time. Still others say that only parts of the Bible are true. In this appendix, we will address these questions: How should we read the Bible? How are we to interpret the meaning of the words?

Although there are a number of different views on how the Bible should be read, only one will turn out to be rationally defensible: what we might call a "natural" or "straightforward" reading. This is why we have taken the natural reading position in this book. Before we defend this view, it is useful to describe what a "natural reading" means. At Answers in Genesis, we use the "grammatical historical approach" to interpret Scripture.

187

The approach is so named because we use grammar and history to understand the meaning of the text. We are convinced that we should interpret the text according to the author's intention. By understanding the history of the time and the grammar of the language, we can consistently arrive at the author's intention. Grammar and history help us to understand the type of literature so that we can ascertain the meaning of the words.

Much of the Bible is written in the historical narrative style. It's basically a history book. Therefore we should read it as we would read a history book — as literal history. The books of Moses and the Gospels, for example, are historical in style, and so we take them literally. The Bible also contains doctrinal teaching — books that elaborate and clarify Christian doctrines. The epistles such as the Book of Romans are written in this style. Their message is clear and literal. So we take historical sections of the Bible and the epistles literally. Note, however, that even in primarily literal language there are occasional figures of speech that are clearly not meant to be taken in a wooden literal fashion. This is no different from our ordinary everyday speech, which is essentially (but not entirely) literal.

But not all sections of the Bible are written this way. The Bible also contains poetic literature. The Book of Psalms is an obvious example. Poems should not be read in a strictly literal fashion. Poetic sections of the Bible are perfectly true and inspired by God, but they use a number of metaphors, similes, and other non-literal figures of speech. The Bible also contains prophetic literature. For example, sections of the Book of Daniel and much of Revelation are written in this style. Such literature makes heavy use of symbols and makes many allusions to other sections of Scripture. Prophetic literature is not meant to be read in a wooden literal fashion, though, in some cases, the literal interpretation of the symbols is also provided. In poetic and symbolic sections of the Bible, we use the clear literal teachings contained in the historical sections to help us understand the meaning. We interpret the unclear in light of the clear.

Each style of literature can be identified by the grammar used. Often it is helpful to go back and look at the original language as well: looking for use of the Hebrew waw-consecutive as an indicator of historical narrative, and synonymous or antithetical parallelism as an indicator of poetic sections.[1] Even the form of verbs used will indicate the type of literature as documented by Hebrew scholar Dr. Steven Boyd.[2]

The details go beyond the scope of this book. Suffice it to say that it is relatively easy to identify the type of literature, and we read the text in a way that is consistent with the type of literature. In summary, we read the Bible in a *natural* manner, just as we do with other books. In all cases, we use grammatical and historical context, interpreting Scripture in light of Scripture to help us understand the author's intention.

This really is the same basic approach we take to all language. We would not read a textbook on American history as a poem, nor would we take an Edgar Allan Poe poem literally. Every type of literature is taken in a natural sense. Yet many people are not consistent when it comes to the Bible. They do not interpret sections of the Bible in the same way as we would modern literature of the same type. We will see that such an unnatural reading of the Bible leads to insurmountable problems, and ultimately destroys the possibility of knowledge. This is why we must read the Bible in a natural sense if we are going to be rational. Any alternative will lead to absurdity. Let's explore this idea.

Alternative Views

When we read the Bible in a natural way, we find that we can account for the preconditions of intelligibility. Human reasoning and experience make sense in light of the natural reading of Scripture. Of course, not every one believes that the Bible should be read in such a straightforward way. There are those who reject portions of the Bible, or who take historical sections (such as Genesis) as non-literal. For example, many professing Christians do not believe that God created in six days, yet they still claim to believe in the Bible. Some claim that God created through evolution and insist that this is perfectly compatible with the Bible. Obviously, such people are not reading the Bible in a natural way. What are we to make of non-natural readings of the Bible?

Upon inspection, we will find that worldviews based on *non*-natural readings of the Bible have the same defects as secular worldviews. Therefore, we can use the same apologetic procedure and methods developed in this book to refute non-straightforward approaches to Scripture. When we apply the "AIP" test to non-natural approaches to Scripture, we will find that such views do not pass the test. They are arbitrary, inconsistent, and fail to provide the preconditions of intelligibility. Obviously, we cannot cover all such views, but it is instructive to very briefly refute a few of the more common ones.

The Scriptures Bow to "Science" View

One very common view today is the idea that we must interpret Scripture in light of what "science says." Such a view commits the fallacy of reification; science is a conceptual tool and doesn't actually *say* anything. Advocates of this view might avoid the fallacy of reification by restating their position: "Scripture must be interpreted to match the opinion of the majority of scientists." But this replaces one fallacy with another — it's now the fallacy of appeal to majority/authority. The faulty appeal is often disguised by its wording; some might say, "We must interpret Scripture in light of scientific knowledge." But what is considered "knowledge" differs from person to person. So they really mean "what is considered scientific knowledge by the majority of scientists."

However it is worded, this type of view holds that a certain level of scientific understanding is necessary in order to correctly understand the Bible. One of the most common forms of this view is that

"Tell me again why I should trust scientists' ability to be accurate about life on Earth **millions of years ago**..."

we should interpret the words of Genesis to be compatible with the big bang and the notion that the earth is billions of years old. From this idea we get the "day age" and "progressive creation" interpretations of Genesis.

According to these views, the days of Genesis 1 should be interpreted as long ages, not ordinary days. Supporters believe that God created over billions of years so as to match the time scale of life on earth that is assumed by evolutionists. Such views have many internal inconsistencies. As one example, the order in which life is created in Genesis does not match the evolutionary order — so making the days into ages really doesn't solve the perceived problem. For a more thorough refutation of the details of these views, see *Old Earth Creationism on Trial*.[3]

The ideas of a big bang and the earth being billions of years old are relatively modern ideas. Certainly the majority of scientists did not believe in a big bang until the middle of the 20th century. This is part of the inconsistency of the "Scripture below science" view. The "correct" interpretation of Scripture is never constant in this view; it changes as the majority opinion of the scientists change. Are we to believe that people misinterpreted Genesis for thousands of years, until modern scientists finally figured out the "truth"?

If a certain level of scientific knowledge is necessary to understand the Bible, then how can we ever know that we've reached that level? Surely our present understanding of the universe will be considered primitive 500 years from now. Since our understanding of science is constantly improving, *we could never know for sure that our understanding of Scripture is correct.* And if our understanding of the Bible is not certain, then we really cannot know anything, because the biblical worldview alone provides the preconditions of intelligibility. Thus, the position that the Bible must be interpreted

The changing nature of what is considered "scientific knowledge" makes it untenable as an ultimate standard.

"... and this new discovery completely changes everything you were ever taught about the origin of life. Oh, wait! A new discovery totally changes what I just reported. ..."

to fit the majority opinion of scientists is self-defeating. People who hold such a view do not have the Bible as their ultimate standard. But knowledge must begin with God (Prov. 1:7), not man. The "Scripture below science" view is reduced to absurdity.

Here is another way to think about this. We have already established several things in this book. (1) Everyone needs an ultimate standard (chapter 9). (2) Only the special revelation of God (the Bible) can rationally serve as an ultimate standard since it alone provides a rational basis for the preconditions of intelligibility (chapters 1–3). (3) Therefore, those who do not have the Bible as their ultimate standard are irrational. But we now add an additional bit of information to our chain of reasoning. (4) Those who interpret the Bible to match the claims of scientists do not have the Bible as their ultimate standard. This should be clear; if we adjust our understanding of the Bible to match another claim, then that other claim is more foundational in our thinking than the Bible. An ultimate standard cannot be modified by an outside claim, otherwise it wouldn't be *ultimate*. Therefore, (5) those who interpret the Bible to match the claims of scientists are irrational. The compromised views of Scripture have given up biblical authority and are reduced to foolishness alongside the secular worldviews.

Revelation through Nature

Often the view that we must adjust our interpretation of the Bible to the majority opinion of scientists is defended under the argument that "God has also revealed Himself in nature. Since God cannot lie, the Bible and nature must agree." Such statements are common among theistic evolutionists and old-earth creationists. Once again we see the fallacy of reification — nature treated as if it were a person that could have a position on a topic. Another problem with this view is a category mismatch: nature is not propositional truth — it's not made up of statements. Nature cannot literally *agree* with the Bible. It's really "what the majority of scientists say about nature" that old-earth creationists and theistic evolutionists believe we should interpret the Scriptures to match. And we've already seen the problems with this view.

But perhaps the most intriguing thing about this claim is that it is self-refuting. Suppose we asked an advocate of this view, "How do you know that God has revealed Himself in nature? And how do you know God is self-consistent?" The only rationally objective response he could give is, "Well, the Bible says as much. Romans 1 teaches that God has revealed Himself to everyone." But now he is in quite a bind, because only if we take the Bible in a natural way would we conclude that God has revealed Himself in nature. If Romans 1 were not literally true, then there would be no reason to believe that God has actually (literally) revealed Himself in nature. So the view that we should reject a natural reading of the Bible in light of natural revelation *presupposes* a natural reading of the Bible! It is self-refuting.

Metaphorical Views

There are those who teach that the Bible is just a book of spiritual truths and morality and that it is not to be taken literally. But the Bible presents its morality in the context of history. All Christian doctrines presuppose the literal history of the Bible. It is because God literally created human beings that we are responsible to Him for our actions. It is because God literally made Eve from Adam's side and brought her to him that we have a basis for marriage. Moreover, only if the history recorded in the Bible is literally true would we have a basis for the preconditions of intelligibility.

It is only if the biblical God literally created as He says He did that we should believe that human beings are made in His image and are thus deserving of dignity. Only if Genesis 8:22 is literally true can we have a basis for the uniformity of nature upon which all science depends. So those who reject the history of the Bible while attempting to hold onto its morality are in the same position as those who reject the Bible outright; such positions fail the "AIP" test. They are inherently irrational views.

The Eclectic View

There are those who claim that only portions of the Bible are true. Advocates accept some portions of Scripture but dismiss those portions that are less palatable. Such a view is inevitably arbitrary; how are we to decide what sections to embrace and what sections to reject? Whatever the reason is, advocates of this position *must* have some greater authority by which they judge which sections of the Bible they will accept. Like Eve, they have decided that they will judge God's Word according to their own arbitrarily chosen standard. But ultimately, only the Bible can serve as a non-arbitrary ultimate standard. Advocates of the eclectic view erroneously attempt to judge an ultimate standard by a lesser one.

Those who don't take the Bible in a natural way are inconsistent, since they expect to be taken in a natural way.

"To begin our debate, each of you will have one hour to present his point of view. That is a LITERAL hour, just in case one of you would want to interpret it into a longer period of time!"

The Bible is not truly their ultimate standard, and thus their position is reduced to absurdity.

The Double Standard

Many people have written books that promote a non-natural reading of the Bible. But there is something very ironic about all these authors; they all expect us to read their books in a natural way! Just imagine if we did to an old-earth creationist what he does to the Bible — reinterpret his words to match our beliefs. He would be outraged. So all people who hold to a non-natural reading of Scripture commit the fallacy of special pleading; they apply a different standard to themselves than they do to the Bible. If the non-natural views are applied *consistently*, all of them are self-refuting since we would not take the views themselves in a natural way.

Self-Refutation

That all language should be taken in a natural way is actually a precondition of intelligibility. Rational debate would be impossible if all parties did not presuppose that they are speaking in a natural, straightforward way. Therefore, anyone who argues against the position that language must be taken in a natural way must first assume that language should be taken in a natural way. In order for his argument to make sense, it would have to be wrong!

Yes, the biblical God is the foundation for things like logic, uniformity, and morality — but only if the Bible is taken in a straightforward, natural way. If sections of the Bible are rejected, or if the literal history is taken metaphorically, then we would lose the foundation for all reasoning and experience. There would be no reason to trust that our senses are basically reliable or that human beings have dignity if the sections of the Bible that touch on such things were not literally true.

If the Bible is truly our ultimate standard, then (1) it must be entirely true, and (2) it must be read in a straightforward, natural fashion. Otherwise, we would need a *greater standard* to (1) judge which sections of the Bible are true, or (2) to tell us how we should interpret the various verses. Therefore, any proponents of a non-natural reading of the Bible, be they old-earth creationist, theistic evolutionists, or whatever, do not have the Bible as their ultimate standard. And we have already shown what happens when people give up the Bible as their ultimate authority: they are reduced to foolishness. Only a natural, straightforward reading of the Bible will result in a worldview that is logical, consistent, non-arbitrary, and in which science, technology, and knowledge are possible.

Endnotes

1. See Tim Chaffey and Jason Lisle, *Old-Earth Creationism on Trial* (Green Forest, AR: Master Books, 2008).
2. See the RATE book volume 2, available through the online bookstore at www.answersingenesis.org.
3. By Tim Chaffey and Jason Lisle, available through the online bookstore at www.answersingenesis.org

ANSWERING THE CRITICS — PART I

I t is now time to apply what we have learned. We have seen that the ultimate proof provides an irrefutable argument for biblical creation, and that non-biblical worldviews can be exposed as fallacious using the "AIP" test, following the "don't answer, answer" strategy. We have provided many examples throughout, but these have been hypothetical, "chemically pure" examples geared specifically for the topic under discussion. In this appendix we will examine actual letters written by evolutionists (and other Bible skeptics). We will see that evolutionary arguments are easy to refute using the information we now know. This appendix is provided to hone the skills and techniques developed primarily in the first five chapters of this book.

All of the letters included in this appendix are actual e-mails that have been submitted to the Answers in Genesis website. Because it is not our intention to embarrass anyone, the names of the authors will be replaced with the initial of their first name. After the critic's message will appear my analysis of it, and then an example of how we might respond. Some of these letters (along with my reply) have been posted on the Answers in Genesis website under the feedback section. However, most have not been posted, since we receive far too many to publish them all.

If you are a creationist wanting to hone your apologetic skills, this appendix is a chance to practice. In each case, I suggest that you read the critic's message, and then think about how you would reply to it before you read my analysis or my reply. I would recommend that you actually write out a response to at least a few of these, just for practice. See if you are able to spot arbitrariness and inconsistency in the critic's letter. Try to determine what his or her worldview is, and think about how it fails to meet the preconditions of intelligibility. Always use the "don't answer, answer" strategy in your reply. Always answer with gentleness and respect, but never at the expense of truth.

After you have pondered a response, compare it to the analysis and response that I gave. Please don't think of my response as the best one possible; in some cases you may have thought of a better way of answering the critic. Perhaps you caught something that I missed. That would be great! But you may find that I caught something you missed as well, and so this is a great way to learn by example. One other tip: usually a shorter response is better than a long one. The critic is more likely to read a short rebuttal than a lengthy counter-response (although the latter is sometimes necessary). So do not feel the need to point out every mistake in the critic's thinking; I try to hit only the main points.

1. "Follow the evidence"

G. of Edmunston, NB, Canada, writes:

> Your denial of basic science will in the long run discredit you and your cause. The empirical evidence is available for all to consider. Your message is akin to asking us to believe the world is flat or that the sun revolves about the earth despite overwhelming empirical evidence to the contrary.

Analysis:

Before responding to G's letter, it is important to understand his worldview. He is obviously not a biblical creationist, since he is writing against the Answers in Genesis position. He is likely an evolutionist, or possibly an old-earth creationist; in any case, he has rejected the Genesis account of creation. He mentions the term "empirical evidence" twice in his short message. This suggests the G. may be an empiricist —

he believes that all knowledge is gained through objective observation. However, this position destroys the possibility of knowledge, as we have repeatedly shown.

Notice that G. seems to have a high regard for science; yet, since he is not a biblical creationist, he has no rational foundation for the uniformity of nature upon which all science depends. This is an inconsistency that we must point out in our reply: why should he trust in science, given his worldview? Also, G. believes that the origins debate can be settled merely by "neutral" investigation of the "evidence." But this commits the pretended neutrality fallacy. This shows that G. does not understand the nature of worldviews; the origins debate is really a question of how empirical evidence should be interpreted.

The fact that G. believes that Answers in Genesis, as a ministry, "denies science" shows that he is not familiar with what we teach. This is common among evolutionists; you must be ready to patiently educate them about the biblical creation worldview, and about the shortcomings of their own worldview.

Possible Response:

Dear G.,

With respect, you seem to be very misinformed on our position. We do not deny science, we embrace it! In fact, as creationists we expect that the universe would be understandable, and operate in a uniform, logical fashion since it was created by a logical God who constantly upholds it. But, on your belief system, why would you expect that the universe should be understandable? If biblical creation were not true, how would science be possible?

I would also suggest that you read some of our articles on worldviews and presuppositions. We embrace the same empirical evidence you do; the issue is not the evidence *per se*, but rather how such evidence should be interpreted. We interpret evidence in light of biblical history, which you seem to arbitrarily dismiss. When understood, the evidence is very consistent with biblical creation; see some of our articles on information science and irreducible complexity.

— Dr. L.

2. "Stop lying to people!"

R. from San Francisco, California, writes:

> *How can you honestly deny science and be so ignorant to the obvious truth about our beginnings? I pray that you'll have an epiphany and stop misleading people to believe in nonsense and lies. You're ultimately going to turn people off to God. If anyone has half a brain they're going to look to science for truth, not 4,000-year-old stories written by goat herders.*

Tommy was stunned as he looked through his multifocal lenses at the email on his 2.7 gigahertz computer with wireless high-speed digital Internet hookup, in his air conditioned office with LED lighting and surround sound. . . .

Analysis:

This person seems to hold to a theistic evolution position; he or she believes in God but rejects the Bible. But apart from God's revelation, how can we know anything about God? The first two sentences of this letter contain a "straw man argument" — a misrepresentation of our position. That is, the critic indicates that we "deny science" and teach "nonsense and lies." This is untrue, and is also a *reversible* claim: we could make these exact same statements about an evolutionist (though we should not, since it would be impolite).

Perhaps most significantly, this critic is very concerned that we should not teach "nonsense and lies." Thus, he or she believes that we have violated the moral code. But an absolute moral code is inconsistent with an evolutionary position. This critic also implies that the Bible is just a collection of "stories," rather than recorded history. But he or she presents no evidence to support this claim. Recall, this is a prejudicial conjecture — one of the types of arbitrariness.

Possible response:

Dear R.,

I really appreciate that you are very concerned that people should not lie or mislead others. We certainly agree — that's why we teach *creation*. After all, since God made human beings in His image (according to Genesis), we are responsible to Him for our actions. And God has told us in the Bible that lying is contrary to His nature (Num. 23:19), and that we are not to engage in it (Exod. 20:16). But you seem to arbitrarily dismiss the history recorded in the Bible, so I do not understand why (on your belief system) it would be wrong to lie. If humans are just evolved animals, why should we be so concerned if they lie to, or even kill another one? After all, we wouldn't put a lion in jail for killing an antelope.

You seem to reject the Bible, yet you say we should look to science for truth. But, apart from the Bible, how could we trust in the methods of science? Science requires an orderly, logical universe that can be understood by our minds. This is exactly what a biblical creationist would expect; God made an orderly universe and has constructed our minds to be able to understand it. But apart from the Bible, how could we trust that our senses reliably inform us about the universe? Apart from the biblical God, what basis would we have for expecting that the universe is orderly and understandable? Your acceptance of science seems rather arbitrary and inconsistent with your apparent rejection of the Bible.

— Dr. L.

3. "The world is senseless — deal with it!"

B. from Buffalo, New York, writes:

Get over your childish, self-pacifying beliefs and deal with the fact that the world is senseless. If perchance there is a god and a reason behind this madness, they certainly will not be found in a book as flawed and disgusting as the bible (unless you promote slavery, misogyny, and the condemnation of billions of people to eternal torment). The claim that T. rex was a vegetarian prior to the fall is so absurd that it scarcely deserves commentary.

Analysis:

This person tells us that the world is senseless — in which case it would have no moral code. But he or she also tells us what we *should* do, and judges the Bible as "disgusting," thereby indicating that there *is* a moral code — a standard of goodness. This person is inconsistent; he has a behavioral inconsistency.

We must avoid the temptation to "answer the fool according to his folly" in the sense of embracing his arbitrary standard and thereby becoming like him. So we should *not* try to show that the Bible is "good" according to the critic's arbitrary standard (which is an example of "mere opinion"). Rather, we point out that apart from the Bible he can have no fundamental standard of goodness at all. We thus "answer the fool according to his folly" in the sense of showing how his presuppositions do not comport with each other and fail to provide the preconditions of intelligibility.

Possible Response:

Dear B.,

If the world were really senseless as you claim, then why would it matter what we believe or do? Why bother to write and correct us? For that matter, why do anything at all? You reject the Bible as "flawed and disgusting," but I have to ask by what standard do you make this assessment? Is it just an arbitrary opinion, or do you have a *rational* basis for measuring — and if so what is it?

As a Christian, the biblical God is my foundation for judging whether something is good or bad, rational or senseless. But apart from Scripture, what would be the absolute basis for making a (non-arbitrary) judgment about what is "disgusting" and what is good? In fact, if the world were really senseless, then how could you have an absolute standard for judging anything at all? By the way, do you have any *rational* reasons to believe that *T. rex* was not vegetarian before the Fall, or is it simply an arbitrary conjecture?

— Dr. L.

4. "The Bible is just a story."

S. from Rome, Italy, writes:

> *This has to stop, the bible is just a rework of other stories and religions around at the time in question. It is insane to keep saying it is the word of god. Jesus was no more a god than Krishna was or Horus. It is not good for humanity to continue being so supersticious [sic] and ignorant of fact. You have no proof that the bible is divine just like there is no proof that Sai Baba is divine yet he has follow-ers in the millions. The bible is a forgey [sic] just like the Talmud is a forgery.*

Analysis:

This critic demonstrates the type of arbitrariness we previously described as "prejudicial conjecture." She opens and closes with claims that are totally unsupportable: that the Bible is a forgery and just a re-work of other stories. If she had bothered to consult a local library, she would have found that archaeological findings coincide with many of the historical accounts of the Bible.

This critic invokes both a rational standard ("It is insane to") and a moral standard ("It is not good for"). Yet, apart from the literal history of the Bible (which she rejects), there is no basis for these things. She asserts that Jesus is not God but provides no evidence for this claim. Her rejection of all things biblical appears to be nothing more than ar-bitrary: an unargued philosophical bias. She believes that it is not good for humanity to be "superstitious and ignorant of fact," which ironically best describes her position since she clearly has not researched these issues.

Possible Response:

Dear S.,

Since you have not provided any evidence at all to support your claim that the Bible is a forgery or a rework of religious stories, I'm very curious how you came to believe such things. After all, even secular historians will admit that there is a great deal of archaeological support for the accounts in Scripture. So I must ask, do you have a good, logical reason to dismiss the consensus of biblical scholars, or is it simply an uneducated opinion?

Perhaps most significantly, if the Bible were not the Word of God, what would be the foundation for morality, or rational reasoning? These things make sense if there is a God who is sovereign over the entire universe, and who has revealed His standards in His Word. But without the Bible, moral and rational standards are reduced to mere subjective opinions with no binding power whatsoever. I certainly agree that "it is not good for humanity" to be "superstitious and ignorant of fact" since God has told us that we should study and gain knowledge (Prov. 4:5, 7; 16:16). But apart from literal truth of Scripture (which you reject), what would be the foundation for such a conclusion?

— Dr. L.

5. "Morality is just common sense!"

D. of South Dakota, writes:

> After all the atrocites [sic] god has committeed [sic], why should he expect his "creation" to be any different! Do you really expect rational beings to accept the word of bronze age mythologies over modern scientific evidence? I'm sorry, but I need proof or a reasonable explation [sic] that can be substatiated [sic] before I believe anything. If you provide me with any proof or reasonable explanation for anything in your fable, I will recant every statement I ever made about the god myth!
>
> Why do atheist [sic] statistically lead just as or more moral lives than theists? Morality is common sense! I know that it's wrong to kill because I wouldn't want to be killed. The same could be said for all your so called commandments! Sorry if I've been a little harsh, but the stupidity/gullibilty [sic] of mankind is a little troubling to me. I think that anyone can believe what they want. But don't force feed theistic superstitions on me, innocent kids or anyone else. That's my main problem with religion!

Analysis:

This critic has quite a lot to say against the Bible. But notice the inconsistencies in his thinking. He believes in scientific evidence while rejecting the foundation for science: the Bible, which he dismisses as bronze age mythology. Such inconsistency is a presuppositional tension. He states that he needs proof before he will believe anything; this indicates that he does not understand the nature of logic and presuppositions. Presuppositions must be assumed before they are proved. His inconsistency here will lead to the conclusion that he cannot believe in laws of logic — a *reductio ad absurdum*.

Also, D. claims that morality is common sense. But this claim does not provide a basis for morality. He claims that atheists are more moral than theists. This is dubious but is not relevant to the question of how there could possibly be absolute morality in an atheistic universe. Since D. has covered many different topics, we will use a point-by-point rebuttal style: my comments will be prefixed by "Dr. L:" and interspersed between D's letter.

Possible Response:

Dr. L: Dear D., Thank you for your e-mail. I will now respond to your comments in a point-by-point fashion. I hope my reply is helpful.

D: *After all the atrocites [sic] god has committeed, why should he expect his "creation" to be any different!*

Dr. L: One of the problems you are going to find when you examine atheism (or any non-biblical worldview) from a *rational* perspective is that there is no foundation for making any moral claims whatsoever. That is, as a non-Christian, you cannot rationally claim that anything is an *atrocity*, or that anyone has ever done anything *wrong*. You can certainly say that the biblical God has done things that *displease* you, but the concepts of "right" and "wrong" are meaningless in an atheistic universe because there can be no objective universal standard — only personal, subjective opinions.

D: *Do you really expect rational beings to accept the word of bronze age mythologies over modern scientific evidence?*

Dr. L: No, but we do expect rational people to accept *recorded history* (i.e., the Bible) and not arbitrarily reject it simply because it is not what they want to believe. The Bible is not mythology but a history book that has been confirmed time and again. Moreover, it is not just any history book, but claims to be the very Word of God. This claim can be demonstrated to be true by considering that the alternative leads to the absurd conclusion that it would not be possible to know anything.

D: *I'm sorry, but I need proof or a reasonable explation [sic] that can be substatiated [sic] before I believe anything.*

Dr. L: What about laws of logic? Did you have a (logical) proof that there are laws of logic before you accepted them? Clearly this cannot be done; you would need to first accept laws of logic in order to prove them. Some things must be accepted before they are proved; these are called "presuppositions." We all have presuppositions that control our understanding of the world. But not everyone has rational presuppositions. If you study this topic, you will find that atheistic presuppositions lead to the strange conclusion that it is not possible to know anything at all (because there will be no justification for laws of logic or for science).

D: *If you provide me with any proof or reasonable explanation for anything in your fable, I will recant every statement I ever made about the god myth!*

Dr. L: It is easy enough to show that my worldview is the correct one. I have a rational foundation for the things that are necessary for knowledge: laws of logic, uniformity of nature, and morality. But these things make no sense in an atheistic universe. Take morality, for example. Why is it that everyone should behave in a certain way? If we are just rearranged pond scum, then such a notion makes no sense. But if there is a God who has created us, then we are responsible to Him for our actions.

D: *Why do atheist [sic] statistically lead just as or more moral lives than theists?*

Dr. L: I'm not sure that is so. But even if it were, it misses the point. The question is: "How can there be such a thing as morality in an atheistic universe?" I've never claimed that all atheists are "bad guys." But the fact that atheists attempt to be moral shows that they, too, know in their heart of hearts the biblical God.

D: *Morality is common sense!*

Dr. L: In a Christian universe it is! In the biblical worldview, there is a universal standard for behavior because there is a God who is sovereign over all creation. Moreover, God has "hardwired" His Law into our mind because He knew we would need it. So, the Christian worldview can explain why (1) there is an absolute moral code, and why (2) everyone knows about it (it's "common sense"). The atheistic worldview cannot explain either of these things. Therefore, atheists must "steal" morality from the Christian worldview. (And isn't it *wrong* to steal? ☺)

D: *I know that it's wrong to kill because I wouldn't want to be killed.*

Dr. L: That's the golden rule — right from Scripture (Matt. 7:12). The golden rule makes sense in a Christian worldview. We are all made in God's image, and thus should treat one another with respect and dignity. But if we are just evolved chemicals, why should we care about others? Why not hurt people if it improves our chances of survival in this dog-eat-dog world?

D: *The same could be said for all your so called commandments!*

Dr. L: All of the biblical commandments only make sense if people are made in God's image and responsible to Him for their actions. Otherwise, why not do whatever we feel like doing?

D: *Sorry if I've been a little harsh, but the stupidity/gullibilty [sic] of mankind is a little troubling to me.*

Dr. L: I would encourage you to think through these kinds of issues. Read some of the articles on morality on the Answers in Genesis website.

D: *I think that anyone can believe what they want.*

Dr. L: Ironically, if atheism were true, then people *cannot* think what they want; their thoughts are merely the necessary result of chemical reactions in the brain. Only in a Christian worldview can we account for human freedom and rationality.

In a Christian worldview, people are more than just an assemblage of atoms.

D: *But don't force feed theistic superstitions on me, innocent kids or anyone else. That's my main problem with religion!*

Dr. L: Everyone has a "religious" view — even if it is the religious opinion that "there is no God." Ironically, you, too, are "force feeding" your position on us. I have found that non-Christian worldviews (including atheism) are very superstitious; they cannot be rationally justified. Such worldviews cannot account for the things we take for granted, such as laws of logic or morality. I hope you have found these comments helpful, and I would encourage you to study this topic. I think you will find it very enlightening.

6. "Did God create logic?"

J. from Germany writes:

I have a question about "Atheism: An Irrational Worldview" by Dr. Lisle, which seems a quite strange article and not up to the usual quality of your website — but maybe that's just me.

Dr. Lisle posits that the laws of logic are created by God, thus disbelief in God is irrational. He didn't provide a rationale for his belief, and he obviously confuses atheism, materialism and naturalism in his article, but that's another story.

My question just is: If God created the laws of logics as Dr. Lisle believes, did He behave illogical before he created them?

Analysis:

In this letter, J. criticizes an article I wrote some time ago that is posted on the Answers in Genesis website. The article is similar to logic illustration #2 in chapter 3 of this book, except the web article is specifically refuting atheism rather than evolutionism (both worldviews have essentially the same defects — they cannot account for logic). The critic seems to think that we are arguing that God created logic, but this is not exactly true. The response I gave to him is posted below and is also posted on the Answers in Genesis website. I have responded in a point-by-point rebuttal style.

Response:

J: *I have a question about "Atheism: An Irrational Worldview" by Dr. Lisle, which seems a quite strange article and not up to the usual quality of your website — but maybe that's just me.*

Dr. L: People often take biblical truths for granted (like laws of logic). We are not used to thinking through these kinds of issues: why are there laws of logic, and what worldview can account for the laws of logic? The article may have seemed unusual to you because it deals with these foundational questions.

J: *Dr. Lisle posits that the laws of logic are created by God,*

Dr. L: This isn't quite correct. The article doesn't state that laws of logic were *created* by God, as though they were independent entities that came into existence at some point in time. Rather, the article teaches that laws of logic are contingent on God. They are a reflection of the way God thinks. Thus, they cannot exist without Him any more than your reflection in a mirror can exist without you. Since God is a thinking being and since He has always existed, laws of logic have always reflected His thinking.

J: *thus disbelief in God is irrational.*

Dr. L: I'm not sure you've quite grasped the argument. Laws of logic cannot exist in a materialistic, atheistic universe because laws of logic are not material. The laws of logic are a universal standard for reasoning, but how can an atheist have a (non-arbitrary) universal standard for anything? Atheists do believe in laws of logic, but they cannot justify the existence of universal, abstract, invariant laws within their worldview. An unjustified belief is arbitrary, which is one form of irrationality.

J: *He didn't provide a rationale for his belief,*

Dr. L: The rationale is there though perhaps you didn't see it. I'm happy to elaborate: first, the Christian worldview can make sense of laws of logic. The Christian believes in universal, immaterial, invariant entities because God Himself is omnipresent, immaterial, and invariant. Moreover, God has thoughts, and these thoughts are reflected in the way God upholds the universe. As one example, we saw how the law of non-contradiction reflects God's internal consistency: all truth is in God (Col. 2:3), and God cannot deny himself (2 Tim. 2:13); therefore, truth cannot be contradictory. The Christian worldview makes sense of the law of non-contradiction.

Second, the atheist *cannot* make sense of the laws of logic because there is no rational justification for universal, immaterial, invariant entities in an atheistic universe. In particular, those atheists who hold to a materialistic philosophy cannot make sense of laws of logic because laws of logic are not material.

J: *and he obviously confuses atheism, materialism and naturalism in his article, but that's another story.*

Dr. L: Actually the usage of these terms is quite correct and consistent with the way they are used in philosophy.

J: *My question just is: If God created the laws of logics as Dr. Lisle believes,*

Dr. L: This is a straw-man argument; our position has been misrepresented (perhaps unintentionally), since I did not state that laws of logic were created by God. Laws of logic reflect God's thinking; God has always existed (and has always had thoughts); therefore, laws of logic have always existed. They are eternal, but nonetheless contingent upon God (i.e., if God did not exist, there would be no thoughts to reflect).

J: *did He behave illogical before he created them?*

Dr. L: Since laws of logic were not "created" by God, the question isn't meaningful. But perhaps I can help clarify anyway. God could never behave illogically because He doesn't think illogically. It is impossible for God to think illogically because in the Christian worldview, logic is a description of the way God thinks. The believer has a universal standard of reasoning that makes sense within his own worldview. The atheist does not.

I hope this helps.

— Dr. L.

7. "Uniformity of nature doesn't need to be justified!"

L. from (unnamed city) writes:

> *First: Uniformity and Uniformitarianism are the same thing. Invariance (backwards and forwards) over time (Uniformity) of natural laws gives both: the future reflects the past and the present is the key to the past. If natural laws are invariant, then processes, which are the implementation of natural laws must also be invariant: a chemical reaction at STP done at T1 will be the same reaction at STP done at T2 regardless of T1 and T2.*
>
> *Second: why do you insist the evolutionist justify Uniformitarianism? It is an axiom! A scientist (evolutionist or creationist) deals with the way the universe operates; he is not concerned with why it is the way it is. This does not make him inconsistent.*
>
> *Third: Are you saying that Genesis 8:22 is the only rationale for Uniformity. One can infer Uniformity based on the nature of God who is beyond time, consistent, faithful, all powerful, omnipresent without invoking Gen 1-11.*

Analysis:

This critic is responding to one of my articles ("Evolution: The Anti-Science") in which I have demonstrated that science requires uniformity of nature, and therefore cannot be justified apart from the biblical worldview (as in illustration #3 of chapter 3). Based on the critic's third paragraph, he seems to be a theistic evolutionist, or possibly an old-earth creationist. He believes in God but apparently rejects Genesis 1–11.

The critic confuses uniformity and uniformitarianism, and so it will be necessary to educate him on the difference. Notice that this critic contradicts himself: he first states that uniformity and uniformitarianism are the *same* thing, then he argues that uniformity will necessarily lead to uniformitarianism — indicating that they are *not the same* but causally connected. I chose not to address this in my response, but to hit only the main points instead.

Perhaps most significantly, this critic feels that he does not need to justify his beliefs; this is an open admission of arbitrariness — one of the forms of irrationality. This letter and my response are posted on the Answers in Genesis website under the title: "Feedback: Is the Present the Key to the Past?" My point-by-point rebuttal was as follows:

Response:

L: *First: Uniformity and Uniformitarianism are the same thing. Invariance (backwards and forwards) over time (Uniformity) of natural laws gives both: the future reflects the past and the present is the key to the past.*

Dr L: Uniformity is distinct from uniformitarianism. The former asserts a consistency in the way the universe operates (*if* conditions are the same, one can expect the same outcome). In other words, the laws of nature are constant, but conditions and specific processes may be quite different in time or space. Conversely, uniformitarianism asserts that there is a consistency of *conditions* and *processes*. Uniformitarianism, as it pertains to geology, asserts that the geological past must be understood in light of present conditions and processes.

As an example, consider canyon formation. Today, canyons are gradually deepening as water slowly erodes the surrounding rock layers. A person holding to uniformitarianism would assume that this has always been the case; he would believe that a canyon has formed by water slowly eroding the surrounding rock layers since "the present is the key to the past."

However, this need not be so. A number of geologists believe that many canyons (such as the Grand Canyon) were not formed (entirely) by the slow and gradual erosion from the river they now contain. Rather, some canyons were formed quickly under catastrophic conditions. So the present is *not* the key to the past in these cases. Yet the laws of nature presumably have been the same. Therefore, this is an example of uniformity, but not uniformitarianism.

L: *If natural laws are invariant, then processes, which are the implementation of natural laws must also be invariant:*

Dr. L: No, this doesn't follow logically. Many processes (such as erosion) are not only dependent on the laws of nature, but also on *conditions*. For example, during flood conditions, erosion happens much more quickly than at other times, even though natural laws remain constant.

L: *a chemical reaction at STP done at T1 will be the same reaction at STP done at T2 regardless of T1 and T2.*

Dr. L: Your analogy above is an example of uniformity — not uniformitarianism. If the conditions are the same, then the same result happens. But there is no guarantee that conditions have always been constant. Chemical reactions in nature, for example, may have happened at different temperatures and pressures than today, leading to different results. So we have uniformity, but not uniformitarianism. Hopefully, the difference is now clear.

L: *Second: why do you insist the evolutionist justify Uniformitarianism?*

Dr. L: A belief must be justified if it is to be considered rational. Otherwise it is merely an arbitrary "blind" assumption. Children believe things without good reasons; they are convinced that there is a monster in the closet. And they feel no need to justify their belief; it is enough that they act on it (by pulling the sheets over their head). But more should be expected from adults. The rational person has a reason (or reasons) for the things he or she believes.

L: *It is an axiom!*

Dr. L: Even if we accept it as an axiom, a belief still requires some sort of justification if it is to be considered rational, and not arbitrary. If it is arbitrary, then why not assume the exact opposite? Uniformity makes sense in my worldview: uniformity is what I would expect based on the Bible. I have a reason to believe in uniformity and thus I have justification for science. The evolutionist does not. He or she must either accept uniformity without reasons (on "blind faith") or justify it by the Bible, which is contrary to evolution. The evolutionist cannot escape the irrationality of his or her position.

Incidentally, I reject uniformitarianism because the Bible indicates that past conditions (such as during the Flood year) were quite different than today's conditions.

L: *A scientist (evolutionist or creationist) deals with the way the universe operates; he is not concerned with why it is the way it is.*

Dr. L: In order to study how the universe operates, we need to know something about why it is the way it is. The two are different, but not totally unrelated. If the universe is merely a mindless accident, why would we expect it to be orderly, or obey mathematical laws? Why should I expect my senses to reliably inform my mind, if both are simply the results of mutations that conveyed some sort of survival value in the past? There would be no reason to think that science is even possible in such a universe. On the other hand, the biblical worldview makes sense of science. So the way in which we do science (and even the possibility of doing science at all) requires us to know something about how the universe came to be.

L: *This does not make him inconsistent.*
Third: Are you saying that Genesis 8:22 is the only rationale for Uniformity. One can infer Uniformity based on the nature of God who is beyond time, consistent, faithful, all powerful, omnipresent without invoking Gen 1-11.

Dr. L: Uniformity cannot be justified without the Bible. The divine qualities you listed are necessary but not sufficient to warrant uniformity. The reason is that although such a God has the power to uphold the universe in a uniform fashion, He might not choose to do so. A God who has revealed Himself to mankind is required. Without the Bible we would have no guarantee that God has indeed chosen to uphold things uniformly in the future. Nor could we know that God is indeed all-powerful, beyond time, faithful, and so on, unless He has told us so.

Although there are verses beyond Genesis 8:22 by which one might infer uniformity, a biblical worldview is required nonetheless. And since all the other books of the Bible depend on a literal Genesis in order to be meaningful, Genesis is required to justify uniformity.

Thank you for your message. I hope my response has been helpful to you.

— Dr. L.

8. "I'm an atheist, and I'm moral!"

D. from St. Cloud, Florida, writes:

> *I just happened across the article on how to build a bomb in the public school system, by David Catchpoole. I would just like to know if this article is being absolutely serious? I mean, I just recently graduated.... Without a God. With a love of violence. And an understanding and agreement on evolution. Yet ... where I'm confused at, is.... Why didn't I shoot all the kids at school? Or, I guess, "blow up"?*
>
> *I mean, I am a sinner after all, damned to hell for eternity. One of my favorite bands even has a song titled "Shoot the kids at school."*
>
> *Now, I'm just going to assume you can't answer me as to why I haven't killed anyone and even graduated school with many friends, a good social life, and a decent education.... seeing that I'm an Atheist after all.*
>
> *The answer is simple. God is not real. He never was. Me not believing in your imaginary friend would have never led to me killing anyone. A life without God does -not- mean a life of moronic decisions. Quite the opposite.*

Analysis:

We have often pointed out that people have a tendency to act on what they believe. Therefore, as more kids are taught that they are nothing but rearranged pond scum, we expect to see more school violence. This doesn't mean that they have no choice of course. But it's not surprising that those children who are taught that life is a meaningless accident will sometimes act on that belief. D. takes issue with this principle. However, it is clear that he has not fully understood the argument.

Fortunately, this critic is upfront about his worldview — he is an atheist. This helps us to know how to best respond because we understand "where he's coming from." D. seems to think that he can be perfectly moral as an atheist. So we need to show him that morality does not make any sense in an atheistic universe. He can deny God (just as the critic of air denies air), but God must exist in order for anyone to be moral (just as air must exist for anyone to breathe). I discerned that this e-mail deserved a more detailed response than the others, so my point-by-point reply to D. was rather lengthy. I really wanted D. to understand the issues involved; ultimately, I would like to see him come to know Jesus as Savior and Lord.

Response:

D: *I just happened across the article on how to build a bomb in the public school system, by David Catchpoole. I would just like to know if this article is being absolutely serious?*

Dr. L: Yes, though you seem to have misunderstood the article. No one is arguing that evolutionists are always immoral in everything they do. Rather, we argue that only the Christian worldview provides a rational, logical basis for an absolute and authoritative moral code. So when an evolutionist behaves as if he is following a moral code, he's actually being *irrational*. Moreover, when an evolutionist behaves as if he is merely an animal (for example, by murdering people he doesn't like), he is actually starting to be *consistent* with his worldview.

D: *I mean, I just recently graduated. . . . Without a God.*

Dr. L: Actually, without God you could not do anything. Certainly you could not have graduated school — for this requires that you know some things. But all knowledge is in God (Col. 2:3; Prov. 1:7). Without the biblical God there would be no basis for laws of logic, the reliability of senses, the reliability of memory, the uniformity of nature, or rational analysis (as we've demonstrated on this [the Answers in Genesis] website), all of which you use when learning things. In fact, the only reason you even continue to exist is because God upholds your existence (Heb. 1:3). So you may not *profess* God or be thankful to Him, but you do rely on Him.

As Dr. Cornelius VanTil put it: The atheist is like a child sitting on his father's lap and slapping and insulting his father. The child is only able to do this because his father is supporting him. Likewise, the atheist is only able to rant against God because God is supporting him.

If you disagree, then please tell me: what is the basis for uniformity of nature without God? This will be hard to do, as shown here [Evolution: the Anti-Science — see illustration #3 in chapter 3]. For that matter, how could you really know that your senses and memory are reliable? Can you rationally (without "begging the question") justify any of these assumptions without the biblical God?

D: *With a love of violence.*

Dr. L: Psalm 11:5 teaches that the one who loves violence hates his own soul. I have to wonder if you would love violence if it were visited upon you.

D: *And an understanding and agreement on evolution.*

Dr. L: Ironically, if evolution were true, it wouldn't be reasonable for you to understand it. "Understanding" implies that we have a mind and freedom of thought to consider alternatives and choose the best. But if evolution is true, then our brain is simply the result of mindless chemistry that happened to convey survival value in the past. So there would be fundamentally no reason to think that we can reason in an evolutionary worldview. If evolution were true, then what you think and say could not be rational, but would merely be the inevitable result of chemistry over time.

D: *Yet. . . . Where I'm confused at, is. . . . Why didn't I shoot all the kids at school? Or, I guess, "blow up"?*

Dr. L: Because the atheist position is *inconsistent*. On the one hand, the atheist teaches that people are simply chemical accidents. On the other hand, the atheist treats people (to some extent) respectfully, as if they were *not* just chemical accidents. So, with respect, your position is intellectually schizophrenic. The Bible explains why the atheist behaves this way. It tells us that everyone knows in his heart of hearts the biblical God (Rom. 1:19–20). (This is why we all know that it's wrong to murder.) But people suppress that truth (Rom. 1:18). They reject the light of knowledge that is only found in Christ (Col. 2:3) because they prefer darkness (John 3:19) and ignorance (Prov. 1:7, 1:29). D., I do not doubt that you are moral, and that you know it is wrong to murder. My point is that on *your professed beliefs as stated*, such morality would not make sense.

D: *I mean, I am a sinner after all, damned to hell for eternity.*

Dr. L: In terms of *rationality*, you're already there. An atheist lives in an irrational, intellectual "hell" — believing contrary things at the same time. On the one hand, people have intrinsic value; on the other hand, they are said to be simply chemical accidents. Do you see the inconsistency?

The only way to escape your "intellectual hell" (that is, having an inconsistent/irrational worldview) is to repent and ask God to give you a renewed mind, just as I and all other Christians have had to do. Only then will you be able to have a worldview that is rationally consistent and makes sense of human reasoning and experience. I know you don't want to hear that. But you see, that's part of the problem.

D: *One of my favorite bands even has a song titled "Shoot the Kids at School."*

Dr. L: From a purely atheistic standpoint that does not promote the inherent value of human life, can you explain to me why you would consider it be wrong to act out that title?

D: *Now, I'm just going to assume you can't answer me as to why I haven't killed anyone and even graduated school with many friends, a good social life, and a decent education . . . seeing that I'm an Atheist after all.*

Dr. L: This is a bad assumption. Not only can I answer your question, but I can even explain why you cannot (cogently) answer your own question from your own perspective.

You haven't killed people because in your heart of hearts you really do believe in God (Rom. 1:21), and therefore you know that it would be wrong to kill people. You have friends and a good social life because you know that people are not really just random chemical byproducts of evolution. Yet you claim to be an atheist, and so your behavior just isn't consistent and logically rational. Please don't misunderstand; this doesn't mean that I think you are unintelligent or uneducated. It simply means that you haven't really thought through this issue. On the one hand, you say there is no God. Yet you know in your heart of hearts the biblical God and that people are made in His image and are responsible for their behavior. It is obvious by your actions that you don't really believe what you profess. This is a *behavioral inconsistency* — [one of the forms of irrationality listed in chapter 5].

Ironically, you cannot answer your own question from within your own professed worldview. As an atheist, why did you not kill those people who annoyed you? If you are simply rearranged pond scum, and if other people are too, then why not rearrange them a bit more? I'll put it to you simply: "In an atheistic universe, why would it be *wrong* to kill someone?"

The reason this question is unanswerable in the atheist worldview is that you would need to appeal to an absolute universal moral code in order to say that murder is wrong. But in an atheistic universe, "morality" can only be subjective and local.

D: *The answer is simple. God is not real.*

Dr. L: Do you have evidence for this claim (that "God is not real"), or is it simply a blind faith? In order to know for certain that God does not exist, you would have to know everything about the universe; otherwise, how could you be sure that God is not found in some area of the universe that you have not explored? And you'd also have to know about everything that is potentially beyond the universe — otherwise, how could you know that God is not found "outside" the physical universe?

You'd have to know absolutely everything about everything in order to know that there is no God: in which case you would be omniscient — one of the aspects of deity. So you would essentially have to be God in order to know that there is no God — in which case God does exist. This is yet one more example of the fact that atheists are irrational; they just don't think things through. Their beliefs are arbitrary (without logical justification).

D: *He never was. Me not believing in your imaginary friend would have never led to me killing anyone. A life without God does not mean a life of moronic decisions.*

Dr. L: Actually, that's exactly what it means. All decisions would have an arbitrary (and thus irrational) foundation without the biblical God. There would be no basis for the laws of logic which govern correct thinking, as shown here: ["Atheism: an Irrational Worldview" — available on the Answers in Genesis website]. All knowledge starts with God (Prov. 1:7).

D: *Quite the opposite.*

Dr. L: D., I want to encourage you to actually think through these issues. We have a number of articles that show how an atheistic evolutionist really cannot make sense of human experience and reasoning, but that the Christian can. Please read the article referenced above and carefully reflect on it (rather than simply giving an emotional "knee-jerk" reaction as some of our readers do). Have the intellectual honesty to consider the alternative to your worldview; think about how the Christian worldview would answer the questions of uniformity, laws of logic, morality, etc., and compare this to the atheistic (non-) answers to these crucial issues.

In particular, the famous debate between Dr. Greg Bahnsen and Dr. Gordon Stein would be very helpful to you. The existence of God, morality, and evolution are more than simply interesting academic issues. I encourage you to study these issues carefully, rather than just arbitrarily assuming an atheistic worldview.

— Dr. L.

9. "Atheists can indeed explain laws of logic!"

M. from Newcastle, NSW, Australia, writes this (fairly lengthy) letter:

In reference to the article by Dr. Jason Lisle titled "Atheism: An Irrational Worldview," I wanted to provide some feedback as I found the argument interesting, but to me it appeared flawed, although to be honest it did take some time to spot the inconsistencies.

To be clear up front as well (as I know AiG views the worldview as everything), I would call myself agnostic, but for purposes of this discussion I would have to say I am an Atheist (I don't believe in any Gods as preference to any other, and agnosticism is not a practical basis to any decisions or morality).

The first item that caught my attention was "The laws of logic are a reflection of the way God thinks." — how can we reconcile this with Isaiah 55:8–9 which reads:

For my thoughts are not your thoughts, neither are your ways my ways, saith the LORD. For as the heavens are higher than the earth, so are my ways higher than your ways, and my thoughts than your thoughts [KJV].

That would seem to me that we can't claim our understanding of logic mimics the same logic that God. This quote from the bible also casts doubt on the idea that "we are to pattern our thoughts after Gods. [sic]"

But, putting that issue aside for the moment, the main thrust of your argument appears to be that an Atheist can't explain logic — therefore using it they undermine any argument they seek to make. Which makes it an interesting proposition to refute, given logic is a tool you argue can't be used. But, I hope you'll grant that liberty for the moment.

I'd like to draw attention to a sleight of hand played in defining the problem — a "materialistic atheist" is distinct from an "atheist." An atheist simply denies the existence of any God's [sic] — it doesn't immediately imply all Atheists deny anything that isn't material which a material Atheist does. So while yes — your argument holds for a material atheist, the generic case for atheists still needs to be made.

There are many Atheists that accept the existence of non-material things — I am careful here to keep it distinct from supernatural or spiritual as they have other implications. A non-material entity that has effects in the real world that can be observed is perfectly acceptable to most forms of Atheism — the important part of it though is that we can observe some interaction with the real world (this is why I left out supernatural and spiritual entities) — and logic I would put in this category, alongside other concepts such as consciousness, free will, etc.

This doesn't explain the origin, but I believe it does undercut the first assumption made in the article that the laws of logic can't exist in the Atheist's world view.

As to the origin — I would personally argue that they are a reflection of the world we live in and as such can't be different given the world we have. That is, I can't park my car at home and not park my car at home at the same time — if we lived in a world that permitted that then yes, our notion of logic would be inherently different though.

This reasoning I see as no weaker to a Christians [sic] response though, as they would claim logic is due to God — hence the Christian shifts the origin of Logic to become the origin of God — which is then claimed to be eternal — side stepping explaining the origin. An Atheist could make a similar series of claims saying the Universe is eternal and the laws of logic are tied to it — hence avoiding the question the same way.

I appreciate the fact that many Christians would disagree with my fairly short critique of their origin of Logic, but I only mean to show it is of the same quality as an Atheists [sic] — neither is necessarily better than the other I feel.

One other point though . . . "Only the God of the Bible can be the foundation for knowledge" — I don't believe this is the case, this argument could really be used by any God that was eternal, absolute and unchanging. I understand you are a Christian apologist, so you may be taking a liberty there, but I can't see anything in the argument (other than the use of Bible quotes), that limit this argument to the Christian God.

I'll bite my tongue on your parting shots about Atheist morality, as you chose not to base that claim on anything — and I acknowledge that would be a lengthy discussion.

Anyway, I hope the points I provided were atleast [sic] interesting to you — the argument you provided was thought-provoking, but I hope as I showed limited to materialist Atheists and also perhaps not strictly biblical from plain reading.

Cheers,

M.

Analysis:

The examples we've had so far have been fairly short, and the critics have been rather uneducated on what creationists actually teach. This is very realistic since in my experience 99 times out of 100, the critic will not understand the position he's criticizing, or for that matter, his own position (in terms of its presuppositions). However, this letter is different. Rather than giving the usual emotional "knee-jerk" reaction, this critic has actually given some thought to the article in question, and has replied in a polite and thoughtful fashion. I appreciate cordial dialogue like this, and have replied in kind.

I wanted to include this example (even though it is quite long) because it is one of the best responses I've seen from the atheist camp. Yet it still fails. I believe it is worthwhile to show that even the best, most thought-out atheistic position simply *cannot* account for the laws of logic or other preconditions of intelligibility. Only Christianity can.

Notice that this critic does concede that the materialist atheist cannot account for the laws of logic. But he thinks that a dualistic position can "save the day." On the following page appears my point-by-point rebuttal to the critic's message as I sent it to him.

Response:

> M: *In reference to the article by Dr Jason Lisle titled "Atheism: An Irrational Worldview," I wanted to provide some feedback as I found the argument interesting, but to me it appeared flawed, although to be honest it did take some time to spot the inconsistencies.*
>
> *To be clear up front as well (as I know AiG views the worldview as everything), I would call myself agnostic, but for purposes of this discussion I would have to say I am an Atheist (I don't believe in any Gods as preference to any other, and agnosticism is not a practical basis to any decisions or morality).*

Dr. L: Thank you for being up front about your worldview. It helps us to understand where you're coming from and how to best respond.

> M: *The first item that caught my attention was "The laws of logic are a reflection of the way God thinks." — how can we reconcile this with Isaiah 55:8–9 which reads:*
>
> *For my thoughts are not your thoughts, neither are your ways my ways, saith the Lord. For as the heavens are higher than the earth, so are my ways higher than your ways, and my thoughts than your thoughts.*
>
> *That would seem to me that we can't claim our understanding of logic mimics the same logic that God. This quote from the bible also casts doubt on the idea that "we are to pattern our thoughts after Gods. [sic]"*

Dr. L: Notice that the biblical passage does *not* say that "my thoughts are of an entirely different nature than yours." It tells us that God's thoughts are *higher* than ours. This actually implies that they are similar in at least some respects (otherwise, higher/ lower wouldn't be meaningful), but that God's thinking is superior in some ways — and infinitely so ("as the heavens are higher than the earth"). This makes sense since God's knowledge is infinite, but ours is finite. Nonetheless, God's thinking is rational, and we who are made in God's image have the ability to be rational as well. Although we will never have God's infinite knowledge, He expects us to base our thinking on His standards, because there is no foundation for knowledge/truth apart from the biblical God (Prov. 1:7; Col. 2:3).

M: *But, putting that issue aside for the moment, the main thrust of your argument appears to be that an Atheist can't explain logic — therefore using it they undermine any argument they seek to make. Which makes it an interesting proposition to refute, given logic is a tool you argue can't be used. But, I hope you'll grant that liberty for the moment.*

I'd like to draw attention to a sleight of hand played in defining the problem — a "materialistic atheist" is distinct from an "atheist." An atheist simply denies the existence of any God's [sic] — it doesn't immediately imply all Atheists deny anything that isn't material which a material Atheist does. So while yes — your argument holds for a material atheist, the generic case for atheists still needs to be made.

Dr L: Both materialistic and non-materialistic atheism were addressed in the article. Since materialistic atheism is the more consistent of the two (in the sense that the materialist consistently rejects all immaterial entities, whereas the other arbitrarily rejects some, while accepting others), that was the main thrust of the article. However, an atheist might hold to a form of dualism; and this seems to be the position that you are advocating. In this view, there is both a material world (containing things like ducks, wrenches, and rocks) and an immaterial world (containing things like laws of logic, conceptual relationships — "duckness," mathematical relationships, and so on). But then the problem is this: how do we bring these two worlds together? What is their point of contact? Putting it another way: why does the material world feel compelled to obey immaterial laws? Moreover, what enables the material world to change, while the immaterial world apparently does not? These questions are easily answered in the Christian worldview, but I've not heard a cogent response from the atheist camp.

M: *There are many Atheists that accept the existence of non-material things — I am careful here to keep it distinct from supernatural or spiritual as they have other implications. A non-material entity that has effects in the real world that can be observed is perfectly acceptable to most forms of Atheism — the important part of it though is that we can observe some interaction with the real world (this is why I left out supernatural and spiritual entities) — and Logic I would put in this category, alongside other concepts such as consciousness, free will, etc.*

Dr L: If you think about it, we don't actually observe causation. At best, we observe succession. Causation can only be inferred. (Causation is "necessary succession" — but it is hard to prove that any given succession is ever necessary.) We don't actually observe the interaction between immaterial entities and the physical world. One cannot "see" the laws of logic (nor consciousness, nor free will) acting on the physical universe. Rather, we see a succession of events, and the immaterial things (sometimes) are inferred to be the cause.

Such an assumption makes sense in a Christian worldview that has all these immaterial entities. I don't want to get too far off topic, but it was important to hit this, if only briefly. Laws of logic are necessary in order to make sense of the world, even though we don't actually observe these laws. And the biblical God is necessary to make sense of the laws of logic, even though we don't directly observe Him with our senses.

M: *This doesn't explain the origin, but I believe it does undercut the first assumption made in the article that the law's of logic can't exist in the Atheist's world view.*

Dr L: The argument against atheism in general would be that the atheist cannot *justify* the existence and properties of the laws of logic within his own worldview. Namely, why should laws of logic exist, and why are they universal, abstract, and invariant? The Christian worldview can answer these questions. I

contend that the atheist worldview cannot. Yet the atheist believes in and uses laws of logic. But to believe in (and act upon)
something that cannot be justified is to be arbitrary — which is
one form of irrationality.

M: *As to the origin — I would personally argue that they are a
reflection of the world we live in and as such can't be different given
the world we have. Ie I can't park my car at home and not park my car
at home at the same time — if we lived in a world that permitted that
then yes, our notion of logic would be inherently different though.*

Dr L: If laws of logic are a reflection of the world we live
in, then they actually become *contingent* on the world. And this
leads to consequences that you probably won't want to accept.
We wouldn't be able to say anything about the universality or
invariance of the laws of logic if they were contingent on the
universe. For example, we couldn't argue that laws of logic apply
in the core of Alpha Centauri, because no one has experienced
that part of the universe. Nor could we argue that laws of logic
will work tomorrow, since no one has experienced the future.
We take it for granted that the laws of logic are invariant and
universal, yet that assumption wouldn't make sense if the laws
of logic were contingent upon the physical world.

Different areas of the universe are just that: different. Why
then do they adhere to the same laws of logic? If laws of logic
were a reflection of the physical world, then we'd expect that
different regions of the universe that are physically different
would have different laws of logic. Moreover, the physical world
is constantly changing, yet the laws of logic do not. So, clearly
laws of logic cannot be simply a reflection of the world.

M: *This reasoning I see as no weaker to a Christians [sic] response
though, as they would claim logic is due to God — hence the Christian shifts the origin of Logic to become the origin of God — which
is then claimed to be eternal — side stepping explaining the origin.*

Dr. L: Just in case there was any misunderstanding, the argument presented in the article wasn't really about origins/first
cause. It was a question of justification. Which worldview can
justify (make sense of) the laws of logic?

M: *An Atheist could make a similar series of claims saying the Universe is eternal and the laws of logic are tied to it — hence avoiding the question the same way.*

Dr L: Again, the argument is really about justification rather than origin. I do believe the laws of logic are eternal because they reflect the thinking of the eternal God. But the laws still require justification if we are going to use them. Bottom line: how can one have abstract, universal, invariant laws in an atheistic universe?

M: *I appreciate the fact that many Christians would disagree with my fairly short critique of their origin of Logic, but I only mean to show it is of the same quality as an Atheists [sic] — neither is necessarily better than the other I feel.*

One other point though . . . "Only the God of the Bible can be the foundation for knowledge" — I don't believe this is the case, this argument could really be used by any God that was eternal, absolute and unchanging. I understand you are a Christian apologist, so you may be taking a liberty there, but I can't see anything in the argument (other than the use of Bible quotes), that limit this argument to the Christian God.

Dr. L: This concern is very worthy of discussion. There wasn't space in a brief article to elaborate on all the reasons why only the biblical God can account for the preconditions of intelligibility (such as the laws of logic). Nor will I have time to fully justify the statement here, but let me at least give you the flavor of the argument. The laws of logic as we understand them require more than the existence of simply *a* god. Not just any old god will do. God must have certain characteristics in order for laws of logic (and other preconditions of intelligibility) to make sense.

You've mentioned a few of these: eternal, absolute, and unchanging. This must be the case so that the laws of logic that reflect God's thinking are also absolute and invariant. Another to add would be omnipresence, so that the laws of logic apply everywhere. Omniscience is required, otherwise there might be true things that even God doesn't know (and thus do not necessarily conform to the laws of logic). A God who cannot deny Himself is necessary to justify the law of non-contradiction (this one was mentioned in the article).

A God who reveals Himself to man is also required; we wouldn't be able to know the laws of logic unless God revealed some of His thoughts to us. One could even argue that a triune God is required to explain a universe that has both universals and particulars (i.e., the fact that the universe is one [in one sense] and many [in another] is a reflection of its Creator). A complete justification would be lengthy, but I think you get the idea. Suffice it to say that I have not found any of the non-Christian conceptions of God to adequately provide the preconditions of intelligibility for human experience and reasoning, including (but not limited to) the laws of logic.

Also, the "use of Bible quotes" is very relevant to this issue. The claim made in Scripture is that knowledge starts with God (Prov. 1:7). So the Bible is our ultimate source of knowledge. I understand that not everyone accepts the claim. But we can't just arbitrarily dismiss what the Bible says, since this biblical claim is the very issue being debated.

M: *I'll bite my tongue on your parting shots about Atheist morality, as you chose not to base that claim on anything — and I acknowledge that would be a lengthy discussion.*

Dr. L: Just to be clear, this wasn't a dig at atheists' morality; no one is saying that atheists are just "big meanies." Rather, it again concerns the preconditions of intelligibility. Which worldview can make sense of morality? Which worldview can make intelligible the notion that all human beings ought to adhere to some universal code of behavior?

The kind of reasoning presented in the article is called the "transcendental argument" for God's existence. This type of argument asks about the preconditions of intelligibility — what things would have to be true in order for human reasoning and experience to make sense. Three of the big issues surrounding this are (1) laws of logic, (2) uniformity of nature (or induction), and (3) morality. Dr. Greg Bahnsen used this kind of argumentation very effectively. So, if you want to pursue this topic further, Dr.

Bahnsen's articles/lectures/books would be a great place to start. Many of these are available on the web. I highly recommend the "Great Debate: Does God Exist?" between Bahnsen and Stein available on the Answers in Genesis online bookstore.

M: *Anyway, I hope the points I provided were at least interesting to you —*

Dr. L: They were very interesting. I'm glad you wrote in and I enjoyed reading and responding to your email.

M: *The argument you provided was thought-provoking, but I hope as I showed limited to materialist Atheists and also perhaps not strictly biblical from plain reading.*

Thanks for writing us. I hope my comments are helpful to you and give you further food for thought.

— Dr. L.

Answering the Critics — Part II

We will now again look at actual letters written by those who oppose our position and think about how we might respond. As before, these are all real e-mails that have been submitted to Answers in Genesis. We will follow our apologetic procedure of (1) presenting the Christian worldview while (2) performing an internal critique of the non-Christian worldview. We will again apply the "AIP" test during our internal critique, looking for arbitrariness, inconsistency, and the (failure to provide the) preconditions of intelligibility in the critic's worldview.

But in this appendix we will also use the additional tools developed in chapters 6–10. For example, we now have some instruction on detecting formal and informal logical fallacies. And we are now in a position to answer some of the more advanced questions that come up in apologetics. As before, I will provide the e-mail message of the critic, using only their first initial and city, and then will provide an analysis and a possible response. I again suggest that you think about how you would respond to these claims before reading my response. It may be helpful to actually write a short response.

10. *"How can you be so misinformed?"*

J. (who supplied a false address) writes:

> *How can a group of individuals be so misinformed and idiot-ic??? How did you get the money to build this drivel and nonsense? My goodness, it is amazing that people can be so uneducated in this day and age. Incest was OK, you guys are obviously still practicing it. . . . Very funny stuff. Some day, when you grow up, you will look back at this and laugh at yourselves.*

Analysis:

This message begins with the fallacy of the complex question. Overall, the message is simply one giant example of the fallacy of the question-begging epithet. No argument whatsoever is presented. The author simply uses emotional and derisive language rather than making a logical case. It is the form of arbitrariness we called "mere opinion."

With messages like this, it is very important to remember Proverbs 26:4 — we should not answer the fool according to his folly. We must avoid the temptation to reason with the critic on his erroneous, arbitrary, and emotional standard. We should instead point out that the critic really has not made a logical case. My response would be very short.

Possible Response:

> Dear J.,
>
> Did you have any *logical* arguments or actual evidence that you believe challenges our position? With all respect, your message contained a lot of emotional opinions, but I couldn't find any logical arguments within it. If you are able to come up with a rational objection to our position, I would be happy to respond to it.
>
> — Dr. L.

11. *"I'm a pre-med major"*

C. from Brighton, Massachusetts, writes:

> *I am a 3rd year, pre-med Biochemistry major at Boston College. I have extensive background in biology, evolution, genetics, and chemistry. The so-called "study-guides" that your site offers are truly*

absurd. You all should really be ashamed of yourselves for actually trying to convince children of this nonsense. There are so many simply false statements in the one study guide I read, a guide to human origins, I really would have laughed if it wasn't so disturbingly clear that you all actually MEAN what it is that you're saying. . . .

Analysis:

It's perfectly legitimate to try and correct errors in the opponent's position. But notice how C. attempts to do his. He begins with a faulty appeal to authority; he seems to want to intimidate us by implying that his background as a pre-med student makes him an expert on evolution, genetics, and so on. Far from it. If he had checked the Answers in Genesis website more thoroughly, he would know that we have a PhD biologist, a PhD geneticist, and a medical doctor on our full-time staff. Each is far more qualified on the topic in question than C. is. But ultimately, an argument should be evaluated on its own merit, not on the educational achievement of the one making it.

The other thing to notice is that C. attempts to use morality to argue against our position, by arguing that we should be ashamed for "trying to convince children of this nonsense." But on what basis does C. accept a moral code? Such a concept only makes sense in a biblical creation universe, which C. apparently rejects. The last statement in C's paragraph is nothing but a question-begging epithet.

Possible Response:

Dear C.,

We always welcome legitimate criticisms to our literature. We have a number of PhD scientists and even a medical doctor who would be happy to discuss such details with you. I'm glad you are concerned about the importance of truth and honesty in our study guides, and that you are particularly concerned about what is taught to children. But I just have to ask: why on your own worldview should you be concerned about such things?

Certainly, we as biblical creationists are very concerned that we should not lie — it's one of the Ten Commandments. Moreover, children (like adults) are special creations, and made in God's image. So it is important that they be treated with dignity and respect. But if evolution were true, why should we be concerned about what one chemical accident does to another chemical accident?

— Dr. L.

12. "When are you going to accept science?"

A. (who failed to provide an address) writes:

> When are you going to accept science and stop trying to create a new dark age for humanity? Your position is so stiff that if everyone were like you, we'd still be without cars, computers, mathematics, chemistry, geology, archaeology and any other science. . . . Hope you re-think your position and some day humanity can walk together towards progress and prosperity and knowledge.

Analysis:

This message begins with the fallacy of complex question. That is, A's opening question implies that we are against science and trying to create a dark age, which is clearly not our position. A. then proceeds with a fallacy called "elephant hurling" — listing a bunch of fields of science and technology, hoping that a long list will intimidate us to the point that we won't realize it is irrelevant. After all, none of the fields of science listed depend on evolution. This could provide a great opportunity to talk about the uniformity of nature.

The final sentence mentions "knowledge," which implies a system of rationality (laws of logic) and "progress and prosperity," which imply a system of goodness (morality).

This message is almost beautiful in its flaws; A. clearly assumes all three of the major preconditions of intelligibility, making this a very easy e-mail to answer. I chose to concentrate on uniformity and science.

Possible Response:

Dear A.,

It appears that you have not read much of our literature, for we are very pro-science. As creationists, we would expect that the universe would be logical and have an underlying uniformity, since God upholds all things by His consistent power. Furthermore, God designed the human mind, so it makes sense that we should be able to study and understand aspects of the universe. But in your worldview, how would science be possible? What is your reason for expecting that the universe should be understandable, or that the mind should have the ability to be rational?

How would any of the fields of science and technology you listed be possible if the universe were just a cosmic accident? All these fields of science require an orderly, rational universe — just what we creationists would expect. Moreover, if human beings were just rearranged pond scum, why should we care about "progress and prosperity"? Such things only make sense in a biblical worldview.

— Dr. L.

13. "Reliability of senses must come first."

K. (who asked that her location be withheld) writes:

> I read the article, "Feedback: Does Logic Supersede the Bible," and while I was reading it, I got a question of my own. This is the quote in particular I was thinking about:
> "In order for our observations of the world to be meaningful, the Bible would have to be true. Otherwise, we would have no reason to think that our senses and memory are reliable, or that there is uniformity in nature."
> Don't I already have to assume that my senses are reliable in order to read and understand the Bible? I have to either use my eyes to read it, my ears to hear it, or if I was blind I would use my fingers to read Braille. I'd have to use my brain to understand it and my memory to remember it. So wouldn't my senses have to be reliable in order to even know whether the Bible was right or wrong or even that it and its message existed?
> Thanks in advance for your reply,

Analysis:

K. is not necessarily a critic. She is polite and is just asking for clarification. But I thought her question was a really good one, and one that might be asked by a critic. I responded as follows:

Response:

Dear K.,

You are quite right that you must assume the reliability of your senses in order to read the Bible. The reliability of our senses and memory are *presuppositions* — things that are assumed at the outset before any investigation of evidence. But in order for those presuppositions to have any kind of foundation or justification, the Bible would have to be *true* (regardless of whether or not anyone had read it).

God knew that we would need to assume certain things right away in order to make sense of the world in which we live. So, God has "hardwired" certain presuppositions into our mind; we don't *learn* that our senses are reliable, we *presume* it. When we then read the Bible, we find that our presuppositions are *justified*: they are not merely "blind" assumptions. The Bible tells us that God designed our mind and body, and God also made the universe; so it makes sense that our mind would be able to understand aspects of the universe. However, if evolution were true, if our brain and sensory organs are simply accidents of nature, and if nature itself is merely an accident of a big bang, then there would be no reason to trust that our senses and memory are reliable, or that there should be any order in the universe to study.

So even though we first presume that our senses are reliable, and then read the Bible, the Bible is the foundation for the reliability of our senses. The same is true for essentially all the other presuppositions that we take for granted. The presuppositions that virtually all human beings have are justified in the Christian worldview, but are contrary to the evolutionary worldview.

— Dr. L

14. *"Supernovas prove that the universe is billions of years old."*

S. from Elk Grove, California, writes:

> *I have read your article "Where Are the Supernova Remnants?" in which you claim that there are not enough supernova remnants to support the Big Bang cosmology. Has it occurred to you that the existence of even one supernova remnant makes your 6,000 year old Universe cosmology untenable? Even the most massive OB supergiants require at least a million years to exhaust their supplies of nuclear fuel before they explode. Therefore, no matter what state of expansion they are in, finding any supernova remnants at all means the Universe is at least millions, and definitely not just thousands, of years old.*

Analysis:

S. (who has written us many times) seems to be either an old-earth creationist or a theistic evolutionist. Virtually all of his e-mails commit the same logical fallacy. In fact, almost all people who claim that they have scientific evidence that proves that the universe is billions of years old have committed this fallacy, and perhaps you caught it. S. has begged the question. His entire argument boils down to this: "The universe cannot be thousands of years old, because we know it is billions of years old."

S. has assumed that the secular theories of stellar evolution are all correct, and has then argued that this proves the biblical creation cannot be correct. But by assuming that the secular theories are correct, he has already arbitrarily dismissed biblical creation. The only logically cogent way to refute a competing worldview is with an *internal* critique — assuming the opposing worldview for the sake of argument and showing that it leads to an absurd or inconsistent result. It would also have been appropriate to point out that as a non-creationist, S. has no reason to trust in the methods of science anyway. But I decided to concentrate on S's fallacy of begging the question.

Response:

Dear S.,

Thank you for your e-mail. The argument you've offered here is actually circular. That is, you've assumed the secular interpretation of astronomical evidence in order to prove the secular interpretation of astronomical evidence. For example, how do you know that supergiants require at least a million years to exhaust their supply of nuclear fuel? Certainly no human being has observed this. Even assuming the rate is known, how could you possibly know the initial core conditions of such stars? Without the initial conditions, the time scale cannot be computed.

Granted, secular astronomers *assume* that all stars have formed spontaneously from collapsing hydrogen clouds, and this would give an estimate of the initial core conditions. But creationists do not assume this. So you are attempting to argue against the creationist position by simply assuming *a priori* that it is false, which is not rational.

A correct way to argue is to assume (for the sake of argument) the position of your opponent, and then show that it leads to an inconsistency. For example, assume the standard cosmology — that the universe is billions of years old, and that the rate of supernovae is about what it is today. Then there should be an enormous number of widely expanded supernova remnants. Yet we detect only a handful — an inconsistency. So the original article actually uses logic correctly to show an inconsistency in secular thinking. And the supernova remnants we do find are perfectly consistent with a "young" universe.

— Dr. L.

15. "Science doesn't have presuppositions. Facts speak for themselves!"
S. from San Jose, California, writes:

> In an article on your site, the author says, "The difference is in the way we all interpret the facts. And why do we interpret facts differently? Because we start with different presuppositions."
>
> This "author" continues to throw around the word presuppositions. Please, enlighten me, on what axioms does modern science exist upon? I'm aware of mathematical axioms, but never have I even heard anything resembling scientific axioms. What does science "assume" to be true?
>
> Any time I question a religious person about this, they fail to respond with a credible answer. Biologists do examine evidence, however there is no room for interpretation. You can NOT say that carbon dating is based on an axiom . . . it is not. Are you the same people who believe the earth is flat?
>
> Choke and die on your bibles already.

Analysis:
This critic clearly does not understand the foundational role of presuppositions in science. He thinks that "there is no room for interpretation" — an example of the pretended neutrality fallacy. Since this critic has asked us what the axioms (essentially the presuppositions) of science are, we need to educate him on that topic. Moreover, it would also be helpful to show him that only the biblical worldview can provide justification for the preconditions of science, such as the uniformity of nature.

Notice that S. has committed the common fallacy of false analogy, by implying that our position is like believing in a flat earth. His closing remark reveals an emotional, bigoted mindset, and this should be pointed out to him. After all, as a non-creationist, he really has no foundation for being rational anyway. I responded in the standard point-by-point style.

Response:

S: *In an article on your site, the author says, "The difference is in the way we all interpret the facts. And why do we interpret facts differently? Because we start with different presuppositions."*

Dr. L: The article is right. Presuppositions are our most basic assumptions about the world. Presuppositions are things you take for granted: like your own existence, the reliability of your memory, your continued personal identity, moral laws, laws of logic, induction, and many others. Most people assume all of these things, but they don't stop to think about *why* they assume these things. All the above presuppositions make sense in a Christian worldview, but are problematic in non-Christian worldviews. We'll see some examples of this below.

S: *This "author" continues to throw around the word presuppositions. Please, enlighten me, on what axioms does modern science exist upon?*

Dr. L: Science actually rests on a large number of critical presuppositions (presuppositions are like axioms, except Christian presuppositions are provable after the fact). In addition to those listed above, one must assume that his or her senses are reliable. What good would it be to do an experiment, if my eyes do not accurately relate to me the results of that experiment? And what good would it be to have accurate eyes if light traveled erratically? We presuppose that light travels in an orderly way. What good would it be to do any experiment if the universe did not behave in an organized, logical fashion? We presuppose the universe continually behaves in an orderly, logical way. Hopefully, you're now beginning to see just a few of the presuppositions that are rationally necessary for science to be possible.

S: *I'm aware of mathematical axioms, but never have I even heard anything resembling scientific axioms. What does science "assume" to be true?*

Dr. L: You've found one example yourself. Many areas of science are mathematical in nature, and thus rely on mathematical presuppositions. But let me give another example: science requires *induction*. Suppose I set up an experiment and get a certain result. I expect that if I set up an identical experiment under identical conditions *in the future* I will get an identical result. But why should that be? Most people don't stop to think about this; they just take it for granted. Why should it be that the future reflects the past in this way? In the Christian worldview, induction makes sense. God (who is beyond time) upholds the universe in a uniform way, and has told us that we can count on certain things in the future (Gen. 8:22). So I'd expect to get an identical result to an identical future experiment since God upholds the future universe in the same way He upheld the past universe.

But apart from the Bible, why should we assume that the future reflects the past? Since we're all made in God's image, we instinctively rely on induction. But how can a non-Christian assume that the future will reflect the past *in his worldview*? He might say, "Well, it always has" — but this doesn't in any way mean that it likely will continue to be that way *in the future* unless we already knew that the future reflects the past. In other words, when a person says, "Well, in the past the future has reflected the past, so I'd expect that in the future the future would reflect the past," he's using a circular argument. (Think about it.) He's assumed induction to prove induction. This is "begging the question" and isn't rational.

S: *Any time I question a religious person about this, they fail to respond with a credible answer.*

Dr. L: Ironically, *only* the Christian can provide a rational explanation for the presuppositions necessary for science. A logical, orderly universe, a rational mind, reliable senses, mathematical axioms, induction, and logical laws are just a few of the presuppositions required by science that are provided by the Christian worldview but which do not make sense in an evolutionary worldview.

S: *Biologists do examine evidence, however there is no room for interpretation.*

Dr. L: This isn't realistic; and it's just not how science is done. By examining evidence, the biologist has already presupposed that his senses are reliable. This presupposition would be held by essentially all scientists, otherwise they wouldn't be able to do science. The evolutionary biologist and creation biologist have *different* presuppositions regarding earth's history. Therefore, they draw different conclusions when examining the same evidence.

S: *You can NOT say that carbon dating is based on an axiom . . . it is not.*

Dr. L: Carbon dating is based on all the above presuppositions and many others. It presupposes that C-14 decayed in the past as it does today, that the C-14 in the atmosphere of the past was the same as today, that the system is uncontaminated, the laws of probability, and the equivalence of C-14 atoms, as well as the more abstract presuppositions listed above — induction, reliability of the sense, and so on.

By the way, carbon dating provides powerful confirmation of the biblical time scale. Scientists have found C-14 in coal and diamonds that are supposedly millions of years old (or over a billion years old for the diamonds) in the evolutionary view. But C-14 has a half life of around 5,700 years — it can't last even one million years. Do you suppose that evolutionists are convinced by such evidence that the earth really is just a few thousand years old as the Bible teaches? Or do they simply dismiss such evidence and assume that there must be some sort of contamination (regardless of any evidence of contamination) simply because of their presupposition that the earth is billions of years old?

Clearly, presuppositions vastly affect our interpretation of evidence. The problem (for the secular scientist) is that science itself is based on Christian presuppositions. Science is possible because God upholds the universe in a logical, orderly way and because God made our minds able to think and reason logically and made our senses able to perceive the universe.

S: *Are you the same people who believe the earth is flat?*

Dr. L: No, we believe the Bible which indicates that the earth is round in passages like Isaiah 40:22 and Job 26:10. Have you actually read the Bible?

S: *Choke and die on your bibles already.*

Dr. L: The above statement is a great example of how objections to biblical creation are ultimately subjective and emotional in nature — not logically rational.

— Dr. L.

16. *"How do we know that the Bible really is the Word of God?"*
R. of Edmonton, Alberta, Canada, writes:

> *I have read your article on "Is There Really A God?" I absolutely have to agree with you on your logic about inteligent [sic] design and the existence of God. However, I must admit, I do have a point of contention near the end. You wrote, ". . . it makes sense to base our worldview on what God has written in His Word." Now, of course, by His Word you mean the Bible. So, now I would like to ask you this: By what logic do [sic] infer that the Bible is God's word? If it's because, as you say, what we read in the Bible agrees with what we see in the World, than [sic] wouldn't that mean that what we see in the World supercede's [sic] what we read in the Bible? If what we saw in the world ever contridicted [sic] what we read in the Bible, than [sic] what are we to believe? And if the Bible were ever to be proven wrong, would that mean that God does not exist, or does the logic you spoke of earlier still prove His existence? And if it does, wouldn't that mean the logic supercedes the Bible. Just some food for thought.*

Analysis:
The author of this letter seems to be sympathetic to our position, but wants some clarification: how do we really know that the Bible is the Word of God? I thought it would be good to include this

non-critical letter because many critics ask the same question. This let-ter underscores one of the reasons why we do not try to prove the Bible by using "unbiased" external evidence. Such a tactic would indeed make evidence appear to supersede the Bible, and we would be in the awk-ward position of accepting empiricism as our (self-refuting) ultimate standard. This e-mail also provides a great opportunity to talk about ultimate standards and the nature of circular reasoning.

Response:

R: *I have read your article on "Is There Really A God?" I ab-solutely have to agree with you on your logic about inteligent [sic] design and the existence of God. However, I must admit, I do have a point of contention near the end. You wrote, ". . . it makes sense to base our worldview on what God has written in His Word." Now, of course, by His Word you mean the Bible. So, now I would like to ask you this: By what logic do [sic] infer that the Bible is God's word?*

Dr. L: Thank you for contacting Answers in Genesis. You've asked some really good questions. Let me start by point-ing out that we do not simply *infer* that the Bible is God's Word. Rather we accept this presuppositionally, as our ultimate starting point. An argument cannot go on forever. Therefore, all chains of argumentation must end in an ultimate commit-ment — a standard that cannot be established from something more foundational than itself (otherwise it would not be *ulti-mate*). Since an ultimate standard cannot be proved from any-thing beyond itself, it must be self-attesting. And the Bible is. It claims to be God's Word and one either accepts that claim or does not. (However, as we'll see, not accepting that claim leads to irrationality.)

Some might object that accepting the Bible as God's Word simply because it says so is circular reasoning. And I have sev-eral things to say about this. First, this objection is something of a double standard. For example, consider this very article. It probably didn't occur to anyone reading this that it was written by anyone other than me. This article claims to be written by me, and most people would accept it as written by me on that very basis! People often apply a double standard when reading the Bible.

Second, it's important to point out that some degree of circular reasoning is inevitable when it comes to an ultimate standard. Since an ultimate standard cannot appeal to a greater standard for its authority, it must appeal to itself. This is true of any alleged ultimate standard — not just the Bible. When people accept the Bible as God's Word because it says it is, this is circular. But when people *reject* the Bible as God's Word, they too are reasoning in a circle; that is, they start with the assumption that they do not need to begin their thinking with God (and thus they are assuming that the Bible is wrong — Prov. 1:7), and then conclude that the Bible is wrong. Any ultimate standard involves some degree of circularity.

Third, although both Christians and non-Christians must use a degree of circularity when appealing to an ultimate standard, not all circles are equal. The Christian worldview can make sense of human reasoning and experience. In other words, if (and only if) we start from the Bible as our ultimate standard, it makes sense that there would be laws of logic, uniformity in nature, senses and memory that are basically reliable, a moral code, and many other things that we take for granted. But without the Bible as our ultimate standard, the foundation for these things is lost, and so there would be no possibility for true knowledge (Rom. 1:21). Apart from Scripture, why should we expect that the universe would be rationally understandable? The Christian worldview confirms itself, but non-Christian circles contradict themselves, as shown in section #3 of [chapter 3].

So we accept the Bible as the inerrant Word of God by faith, but it's not a "blind faith." Faith in the Bible leads to rationality and knowledge; the Christian worldview makes sense of human experience and reasoning. However, a rejection of the Bible as the ultimate standard leads to irrationality; any other standard cannot make sense of human experience and reasoning. Apart from God's Word, why would we expect to be able to understand the universe?

This is the "proof" of the Bible as God's Word; without God as revealed in His Word, it would be impossible to prove anything (Prov. 1:7). So I have a very good reason for my faith.

Without the Christian worldview, I would not be able to account for reasoning. I believe so that I may understand.

R: *If it's because, as you say, what we read in the Bible agrees with what we see in the World, than [sic] wouldn't that mean that what we see in the World supercede's what we read in the Bible?*

Dr. L: If we thought we could conclude that the Bible is God's Word by observing the world alone, we would have it backward. In order for our observations of the world to be meaningful, the Bible would have to be true. Otherwise, we would have no reason to think that our senses and memory are reliable, or that there is uniformity in nature. That being said, what we do see in the world confirms what we read in God's Word. We see evidence of design in nature, order and regularity in the universe, and so on. We also see evidence of the Curse. These all confirm (but do not prove) the Bible. The Bible must be presupposed in order to make sense of anything else.

R: *If what we saw in the world ever contridicted [sic] what we read in the Bible, than [sic] what are we to believe?*

Dr. L: Since the universe is upheld by God's power (Heb. 1:3) it necessarily will be consistent with what God has said in His Word. However, there are instances where our interpretation of what we observe with our senses does not match our understanding of Scripture. When this happens, we should cautiously double-check to make certain we have done proper exegesis of the biblical text, and then use the clear propositional truth of the Bible to help correct our understanding of nature. After all, nature is not propositional truth and would be meaningless without presupposing the truths of Scripture. Without the Bible, there would be no reason to trust our senses in the first place, or to suppose that nature would be understandable in any fashion.

R: *And if the Bible were ever to be proven wrong, would that mean that God does not exist, or does the logic you spoke of earlier still prove His existence? And if it does, wouldn't that mean the logic supercedes the Bible. Just some food for thought.*

Dr. L: Upon careful reflection, it is clear that the Bible cannot be proved wrong. In order to prove something, you'd need laws of logic. But laws of logic presuppose the biblical God (see Atheism: An Irrational Worldview[1]). So without God as revealed in the Bible, there would be no foundation for the laws of logic, by which we prove other things. Logic is contingent upon the biblical God.

You asked some good questions. I hope my response and the referenced articles are helpful to you.

— Dr. L.

17. "Either the earth is old, or it looks old."

K. from Tulsa, Oklahoma, writes:

> *Message specifically for Dr. Jason Lyle [sic].*
>
> *I appreciated your reply about God creating illusions of movies of exploding stars more than 6,000 years ago. I completely agree with you that "Biblically, we can assume the [sic] our senses are basically reliable, even though we sometimes misunderstand what we observe."*
>
> *I recently sent a letter and printout of the PowerPoint file to Terry Mortenson which presents an argument that geological data abundantly demonstrates evidence for an old earth, OR that God created the earth to appear old. And science does not have the tools to distinguish between these two.*
>
> *I am inviting you to give your own eyes the opportunity to see ice cores from mountains in the Andes that have annual layers that extend well past 6,000 years. I also sent a letter to Ken Ham with this invitation.*
>
> *So please come and use your own senses to see some of God's Creation.*
>
> *Blessings,*

Analysis:

K. seems to be a Christian but has rejected the straightforward reading of Genesis in favor of an old-earth view. He presents us with two options: either the earth is old, or God created it with an appearance of age. This is fallacy of bifurcation — a false dilemma. The earth is neither old, nor does it "look" old (since age is not something that can be seen). When someone says that he thinks the earth "looks" old, this tells us much more about his biases than anything about the earth.

The fact that K. thinks that scientific evidence can prove that the earth is old (or at least "looks" old) indicates that he does not understand the nature of worldviews, presuppositions, and their relationship to evidence. Notice also that K. has begged the question when he refers to "annual layers" — how can he know that they are all *annual*? The fact that K. didn't even spell my name correctly suggests that his research of our literature may be less than thorough.

This e-mail gives us a great opportunity to refute old-earth creationism, which has the same defects as all the other non-biblical worldviews. Once someone gives up the straightforward reading of Scripture as his ultimate standard, he cannot maintain a rational worldview.[2]

Response:

Dear K.,

Thank you for your kind invitation. We actually are already familiar with ice cores, and many of the age claims that are based on them. In fact, Dr. Larry Vardiman has written a fine work on this topic, *Ice Cores and the Age of the Earth*, which is available at www.answersingenesis.org/PublicStore.

We also have a number of web articles on the topic. Briefly, I should just mention that we cannot actually observe *annual* layers (for more than a few years anyway). We can observe layers — but the idea that all of them are *annual* is an (unbiblical) uniformitarian assumption.

I'm glad you agree with me that our senses are basically reliable. Of course, almost everyone believes this. But interestingly, only a Christian can give a good reason for why this must be so. The basic reliability of our senses is a Christian presupposition. Since God made our senses (Prov. 20:12), we can expect them to work properly most of the time (though because of sin and the Curse, not all of the time). Furthermore, since God made both our mind and the universe (John 1:3), we can expect that these things "go together." That is, the Christian has the right to expect that the mind has the capacity to understand aspects of the universe. There would be no reason to expect any of these things if the eyes, the mind, and the universe were merely accidents of a big bang and evolution.

The Bible gives us a reason for why we should be able to reason. However, God also tells us that we need to start with Him in our reasoning. We must build our thinking on what God has revealed in His Word (Luke 6:47–49); otherwise, we will draw the wrong conclusions and will be reduced to foolishness (Prov. 1:7). Therefore, we must interpret what we observe in the world in light of what God has said in His Word.

The ideas that God created the earth with appearance of age or that the earth actually is old are both easy to refute. "Appearance of age" is refuted because it is an oxymoron; age cannot be seen. Therefore, something cannot really "appear" old or young. Age is a question of history, not a matter of present observation. We sometimes use the phrase loosely (and technically incorrectly) when we say that a person "looks" a particular age. But what we really mean is that the person resembles (in some ways) other people who are known to have a particular age. Formally speaking, there is no such thing as an "appearance of age." The universe was created *mature*, in the sense that it was complete and functional by the end of the sixth day; but this is not the same as "age."

It's also easy to refute the idea that the earth is actually old. The Bible tells us that God made the earth in six days. It's clear from context (the days are bounded by an evening and morning) that these are days in the ordinary sense — the same as our work week (see Exod. 20:8–11). And it's clear from the genealogies that this happened thousands of years ago. Those who argue against this must either assume that (A) the Bible is wrong, or (B) the Bible does not mean what it says.

(A) If the Bible is wrong, then we have no reason to think that our senses are basically reliable. If our brain and eyes are merely the result of molecules in motion, then why should we think that what we see and what we think are actually *true*? Only if God created the universe and our senses (as the Bible teaches) would we have the right to assume that our senses are basically reliable, and that the mind is capable of interpreting what the eyes sense.

(B) If the Bible doesn't mean what it says, then we have the same problem. How could we know that God really did create our senses, our mind, and the universe, and thus that our senses are basically reliable? Granted, the Bible *says* this, but how would we know that it *means* this if the Bible doesn't mean what it says? A straightforward reading of the Bible is necessary in order to make sense of anything else.

Your message implies that science cannot actually determine the age of the earth; this is true. Since science deals with predictability in the present, it cannot definitively answer history questions — such as age. Age is not a substance that can be measured by scientific means. Granted, there are many powerful examples of scientific evidences that are inconsistent with an old earth, such as C-14 in diamonds [see chapter 1]. But the *proof* that the earth is young is that this is the clear teaching of the Bible, which cannot be wrong since any alternative leads to irrationality (Prov. 1:7; Col. 2:2–4).

— Dr. L.

18. "Science doesn't require the Bible. Look at the ancient Greeks."
S. from Elk Grove, California, writes:

> *Jason Lisle wrote, "The secular astronomers before the time of Pythagoras must have thought the Bible was wrong about its teaching of a round earth, yet the Bible was exactly right." Even if the ancient Hebrews realized that the Earth was a sphere, which is not explicitly stated in the Bible, their achievements in Astronomy pale in comparison to those of the ancient Greeks. Not only did the Greeks clearly state that the Earth was a sphere, they also calculated its circumference to a high degree of accuracy. In addition, they also made surprisingly accurate calculations for the Moon's diameter and its distance from the Earth. They were also able to determine that the Sun was much larger than either the Earth or the Moon even though their attempt to measure its distance from the Earth was not completely successful. These amazing feats were accomplished through pure human reason and a naturalistic philosophy, and not through recourse to sacred texts or divine inspiration.*

Analysis:

S. (the same critic as in #14) is responding to a section in one of my books (*Taking Back Astronomy*[3]) where I have shown that many scientific "factual" claims in the Bible were once at odds with the generally believed "science" of the day, but are now essentially universally accepted. This critic's attempted rebuttal misses this point entirely. As such, his response is nothing but an example of the fallacy of irrelevant thesis.

Moreover, S. seems to think that the ancient Greeks were able to achieve scientific success without relying on biblical concepts. He thinks that "pure human reason and a naturalistic philosophy" are responsible for the scientific success of the ancient world. However, nothing could be further from the truth. Remember, the ultimate proof is *not* that people must read the Bible in order to know anything; but rather, the Bible *must be true* in order for us to know anything. Only biblical presuppositions can make sense of science and reasoning.

Response:

Dear S.,

With respect, you seem to have missed the point of the chapter. There has always been a conflict between the clear teachings of the Bible and the secular science of the day. Throughout history, the Bible has been continually vindicated. History has taught us that when a conflict between the Bible and secular science arises, the Bible is always correct. As the Word of God, how could it be anything else? Yet so many people today have not learned that lesson.

The text was not intended to trivialize the accomplishments of the Greek philosophers. I happen to think that many of their accomplishments and discoveries were truly brilliant. But were such discoveries made "through pure human reason and a naturalistic philosophy" without any "divine inspiration"? No.

The Greeks were successful because they were implicitly relying on a biblical worldview (without acknowledging this, of course). Science requires uniformity of nature — but uniformity requires a biblical worldview as shown here: [chapter 3, illustration #3].

Moreover, the Greeks used logical reasoning, but laws of logic only make sense in a biblical worldview. They are incompatible with naturalism as shown here: [chapter 3, illustration #2]. The Greeks were able to discover some amazing things — but only because the Bible is true.

—Dr. L.

19. *"Supernatural explanations must be excluded from science."*

S. from Elk Grove, California, (again) writes:

> *Jason Lisle wrote in regard to the distant starlight problem; "It is ridiculous to argue that a supernatural explanation is wrong because it cannot be explained by natural causes." For this to be true we would have to redefine Astronomy in a way that it would no longer be a natural science. The advantage of retaining it as a purely natural science is that there are observations we can make that allow us to choose between competing theories. When the CBR was discovered in 1965 it allowed astronomers to determine that the Big Bang was a better explanation for the Cosmos than the Steady State Theory. If supernatural explanations are allowed which would we use? There are Buddhist, Hindu and many other supernatural explanations, in addition to the one found in the Bible, for astronomical phenomenon [sic] and no observation we can make or experiment we can perform that would favor one over the other. Natural explanations may or may not represent reality but they are testable.*

Analysis:

In the original text to which S. is responding, I had pointed out the fallacy of begging the question — that we should not dismiss a supernatural claim simply because it is supernatural. S. disagrees. He believes that science should be approached from the perspective of methodological naturalism — that we must exclude the supernatural in our research. He gives us a very interesting reason for his position; excluding the supernatural makes science more testable. But this is the fallacy of irrelevant thesis (whether something is testable or not is totally irrelevant to whether or not it is *true*.) Rather than naming the fallacy, I chose to refute this claim using a logical analogy.

Many people want to dismiss the possibility of the supernatural from the start. But this is arbitrary — it is an unargued philosophical bias. Remember, atheism is also a religious view; atheists have a position on origins, metaphysics, and even ethics. So when people want to approach science from the perspective of atheism/naturalism, they are arbitrarily accepting one philosophical view, and arbitrarily dismissing others.

Response:

S: *Jason Lisle wrote in regard to the distant starlight problem; "It is ridiculous to argue that a supernatural explanation is wrong because it cannot be explained by natural causes." For this to be true. . . .*

Dr. L: All I'm pointing out is that a vicious circular argument is bad reasoning. I would hope that most people would immediately realize that is true.

Consider the argument I'm critiquing: "(A) A supernatural explanation is wrong because (B) It is not explained by natural causes." Since (B) is essentially synonymous with (A), the argument is circular. It concludes that all things must be explained by natural causes (A) by simply assuming that all things must be explained by natural causes (B). This is not a good argument. So my assertion that such an argument is ridiculous is a good point.

S: . . . *we would have to redefine Astronomy in a way that it would no longer be a natural science.*

Dr. L: Not at all. Astronomy is a natural science in the sense that astronomers study nature. However, there is nothing in the definition or methods of astronomy that requires it to be "naturalistic" (to exclude the supernatural). There is nothing in astronomy that precludes the possibility that God created the universe in six days as He said He did in Genesis. In fact, if God were not constantly upholding the universe in a consistent way, science would not be possible as shown here: [chapter 3, illustration #3].

Your letter implies that you believe that astronomy should be approached with the philosophy of methodological naturalism. Naturalism (metaphysical naturalism) is the belief that nature is all there is; it is the position that there is no God — at least not a transcendent Creator. Methodological naturalism is the belief that we should approach science from the perspective of naturalism — regardless of whether or not naturalism is actually true. In other words, a methodological naturalist might believe in God, but he or she believes that we should restrict our conclusions to natural explanations — we should essentially pretend that God does not exist when we approach science.

Such an approach is arbitrary and irrational. Why should we dismiss the possibility of creation before any investigation of evidence? The notion makes even less sense for those who are convinced that God does exist. Why would a theist assume to practice the exact opposite of his conviction? Unless it is possible to prove that God does not exist (which it isn't), to simply assume that He does not (if only in methodology) would be arbitrary — without justification. Methodological naturalism is irrational.

As an analogy, consider people studying the construction of a car. Can you imagine one of them arguing, "We must assume this car came about by the forces of nature acting over time with no designer as we study how it works, even though we know this isn't true." Such an approach would be absurd. Yet some people use effectively the same approach when studying God's creation.

S: *The advantage of retaining it as a purely natural science is that there are observations we can make that allow us to choose between competing theories.*

Dr. L: The advantage of assuming that the universe is completely empty is that it makes the math a lot easier. But it would be ridiculous to assume such a thing since we have evidence to the contrary!

Likewise, simply arbitrarily dismissing a supernatural explanation for the origin of the universe may make it easier to choose between the remaining ones. But it's not at all rational since we have evidence to the contrary.

S: *When the CBR was discovered in 1965 it allowed astronomers to determine that the Big Bang was a better explanation for the Cosmos than the Steady State Theory.*

Dr. L: This is the fallacy of bifurcation (false dilemma). Some secular astronomers argue that there are only two options: steady state and big bang. Steady state cannot justify the cosmic microwave background, so they conclude the big bang must be true. But of course, there is a third alternative: the Bible is true. Neither the big bang nor the steady state can account for the uniformity of nature upon which science depends, but the Bible can.

S: *If supernatural explanations are allowed which would we use?*

Dr. L: How about the one written by the God who actually created the universe, knows everything, never makes mistakes, and never lies? Only God's account of origins makes sense of scientific observations and provides rational justification for the methods of science and reasoning.

S: *There are Buddhist, Hindu and many other supernatural explanations, in addition to the one found in the Bible, for astronomical phenomenon [sic] and no observation we can make or experiment we can perform that would favor one over the other.*

Dr. L: Actually, *every* experiment we perform demonstrates the truth of the Christian worldview, and the falsehood of others, such as Buddhism and Hinduism. Scientific experimentation relies on the principle of uniformity — the notion that the future will resemble the past. However, only the biblical worldview can account for uniformity. That is, without the Bible, there would be no basis for uniformity, and hence no possibility of science. This is explained in my article: Evolution: The Anti-Science [as in illustration #3 of chapter 3 of this book].

Other worldviews cannot make sense of science. As one example, many of the Hindu faith teach that the universe is Maya — illusion. But science would be impossible if the universe were merely an illusion. How could we study something that does not actually exist? The Hindu teaches that there are no distinctions and that all is one. But science presupposes distinctions; if there is no difference between the stars, planets, galaxies, and quasars, then astronomy would be meaningless.

ANSWERING THE CRITICS — PART II

S: *Natural explanations may or may not represent reality but they are testable.*

Dr. L: Any philosophy that arbitrarily dismisses possibilities that are potentially true is a bad philosophy. Naturalism arbitrarily dismisses the possibility of a supernatural origin and is thus a bad philosophy.

The Bible teaches that in Christ are hidden all the treasures of wisdom and knowledge (Col. 2:3), and therefore we should not be robbed of such treasures by being taken in by secular philosophies like naturalism. Such philosophy is "after the tradition of men, after the rudiments of the world, and not after Christ." (Col. 2:8; KJV).

To be clear, we have nothing at all against the idea of natural law. Natural law is simply the name we give to the normal way God accomplishes His will and upholds the universe. One of the problems with the big bang is that it assumes that the origin of the universe can be explained by natural law. However, the Bible tells us implicitly that God created the universe by a different method than the way He currently upholds it (because Genesis 2:2 says that God finished His work of creation by the seventh day — so He is no longer doing what He was during the creation week). Therefore, it is anti-biblical to argue that the universe was created by the same laws of nature that it currently exhibits.

I hope this clears up the confusion.

— Dr. L

20. "We know that nature is uniform because it always has been."

J. from Parker, Colorado, writes:

Dr. Jason Lisle's article, "Evolution: The Anti-science," is not persuasive on any level, religious, philosophical, scientific, mathematical, or moral.

The regularity of the natural universe can be reasonably and logically accepted on the bases of observation, inference, and the collective empirical evidence and experience of humankind. Nature whispers its essence in a rainbow of patterns that, to date, have been consistent. Any type of understanding about the past, present, or future isn't possible without this expectation being met.

No evidence so far has falsified the concept that nature is knowable. Whether God or nature is the root cause of this regularity is immaterial. Doing and understanding science does not require a Biblical worldview. Lisle's assertion that you can't be a scientist and believe in evolution is, at best, ignorance on a grand scale or he is being disingenuous with the obvious. The need for an absolute authority is a religious one, not a scientific one.

The universe, to the vast majority of scientists, is naturally, not supernaturally, designed. Most scientists accept evolutionary theory based on the merits of the evidence, not as a belief in an absolutist ideology. Lisle shouldn't try to speak for other scientists or evolutionists. He is so biased in his literal creationist mindset that it clouds his ability to talk about the subject objectively.

You don't need to be a biblical creationist to accept the uniformity of nature or the value of science. The actual study of nature itself will do that. If Dr. Lisle understood evolution at even a basic level, he should know that while variation via mutation is random, at least to the extent that natural laws allow, natural selection is not random at all.

The Bible, while important and interesting, is not a scientific book. Nothing within its pages suggests an understanding of the natural world beyond what would be understood by man at the time the various books were written, including ideas that are just plain wrong by today's scientific understanding.

Analysis:

This is one of my favorite feedbacks because the author commits so many fallacies. His main argument is that we can expect that nature will be uniform because it always has been. But the idea that something will be in the future as it has been in the past is the very concept of uniformity. So this critic is simply begging the question — he's defending uniformity by assuming uniformity. Much of his message is simply the fallacy of irrelevant thesis; his statements have no bearing on the issue at hand. He also does not understand the necessity of an absolute authority. Since this message is such a splendid example of common evolutionary fallacies, I decided to respond in a third person point-by-point format in anticipation of having this reply posted on our website.

Response:

This feedback provides us with great material to brush up on our critical thinking skills. In his letter, J. references my article ("Evolution: The Anti-science") [illustration #3 in chapter 3 of this book] in which I show that science requires a biblical worldview since only the Bible can account for uniformity in nature.[4] Uniformity is the concept that there is a kind of regularity throughout time such that the future "reflects" the past.[5] For example, if we repeat an experiment from the past, we expect to get the same results in the future if the conditions of the experiment are sufficiently similar. We see here that J. has not really understood the argument that he is attempting to refute. As a consequence, his criticisms fail in multiple ways.

J: *Dr. Jason Lisle's article, "Evolution: The Anti-science," is not persuasive on any level, religious, philosophical, scientific, mathematical, or moral.*

Dr. L: An argument need not persuade everyone in order to be conclusive. Proof is not the same thing as persuasion. If someone can find a genuine problem with the argument presented, that's one thing. But the fact that it didn't persuade J. is completely irrelevant.

J: *The regularity of the natural universe can be reasonably and logically accepted on the bases of observation, inference, and the collective empirical evidence and experience of humankind.*

Dr. L: No, it cannot, for this rather obvious reason: the "observation, inference, and collective empirical evidence and experience of humankind" *presuppose* regularity! If nature were not uniform, if the laws of physics and chemistry were not constant, our memories and senses could not be considered dependable since they employ physics and chemistry. So by assuming that our memories and observations are reliable and meaningful, we have effectively already assumed uniformity. Therefore, we cannot then turn around and use observation, empirical evidence, and so on as a proof of uniformity. This would be the fallacy of begging the question — simply assuming what we are trying to prove.

More importantly, there would be no reason to believe that the future "reflects" the past apart from the Christian worldview.

One important aspect of uniformity is that the regularity of nature also extends into the future. But how could we know this apart from the biblical God? To say that there has been uniformity in the past is logically irrelevant to the future, unless we already knew that the future reflects the past. J.'s argument here is nothing but simple circular reasoning.

J: *Nature whispers . . .*

Dr. L: This is the fallacy of reification: attributing personal and concrete characteristics to conceptual constructs — in this case, nature. Reification is acceptable in poetry, but should be avoided in rational argumentation because it is ambiguous and can be misleading. Nature doesn't literally "tell us" anything; rather, we draw certain inferences from the natural world based on our worldview.

J: *. . . its essence in a rainbow of patterns that, to date, have been consistent.*

Dr. L: Here, J. argues that nature has been consistent *so far* ("to date"). But, recall that the question I posed in my article is: "Why will the future reflect the past?" The fact that nature has been consistent *so far* (in the past) is totally irrelevant to the *future* unless we already presumed that the future will be like the past (uniformity). Any time we use past experience as a basis for what is likely to happen in the future, we are assuming uniformity. But only the consistent Christian has a basis for such a claim. To assert that "since there has been uniformity in the past, there will likely be uniformity in the future" is a circular argument because it assumes uniformity (i.e., the future will be like the past).

Also (to be thorough), apart from the Bible we couldn't really know that nature has been consistent in the past either, since the sections of our brain responsible for memory depend upon uniformity. In other words, J. must already *assume* that nature is uniform in order to argue that he correctly remembers that nature has been uniform — a circular argument.

J: *Any type of understanding about the past, present, or future isn't possible without this expectation being met.*

Dr. L: Exactly! Science wouldn't be possible without uniformity. Yet only the Christian worldview can account for uniformity. Thus, only the Christian worldview can account for science.

J: *No evidence so far has falsified the concept that nature is knowable.*

Dr. L: Here we see where J. has misunderstood the argument. The argument is *not* that nature cannot be known. The argument is that *if evolution were true*, nature could not be known (because there would be no basis for uniformity). Nature can be known, therefore evolution is not true. This is a simple form of argument called *Modus Tollens*.[6]

J: *Whether God or nature is the root cause of this regularity is immaterial.*

Dr. L: Actually, it's crucially relevant. Apart from the biblical God who is beyond time, knows the future, and has told us that the future will reflect the past (Gen. 8:22), there would be no rational basis for uniformity. Apart from the biblical God, how could we possibly know anything about a future that no one has experienced?

J: *Doing and understanding science does not require a Biblical worldview.*

Dr. L: Then how would we account for uniformity? Science is all about making successful predictions about the future (outcomes of experiments, positions of the planets, etc.), which requires uniformity. Apart from the biblical worldview, how could anyone know that uniformity extends into the future?

J: *Lisle's assertion that you can't be a scientist and believe in evolution is, at best, ignorance on a grand scale or he is being disingenuous with the obvious.*

Dr. L: This fallacy is called a straw-man argument: misrepresenting the position of the opponent. Did I assert that one cannot be a scientist and believe in evolution? In the article I stated, "The answer is that *evolutionists are able to do science only because they are inconsistent*" [emphasis added]. Again, J.

seems to have missed the argument entirely. The principles of science (such as uniformity) do not require a *profession of belief* in the Bible; they simply require that the biblical worldview is true. Therefore, as I stated, "evolutionists can do science only if they rely on biblical creation assumptions (such as uniformity) that are contrary to their professed belief in evolution." The fact that evolutionists can be scientists (due to their inconsistency) is mentioned again at the end of the article, so it's hard to understand how J. could have missed it.

J: *The need for an absolute authority is a religious one, not a scientific one.*

Dr. L: With all respect, this is philosophically absurd. All arguments must terminate in an ultimate standard — an authority that is held to be unquestionable.[7] Otherwise, the argument would go on forever and could not be completed. Thus, everyone has an ultimate standard/authority. However, like J., most people have not given much thought to what their ultimate standard is, and whether or not it is really consistent.

J: *The universe, to the vast majority of scientists, is naturally, not supernaturally, designed.*

Dr. L: This is the fallacy of appeal to authority/majority and is rationally irrelevant. At one time, the majority of scientists believed the sun and planets revolved about the earth — but that didn't make it so.

J: *Most scientists accept evolutionary theory based on the merits of the evidence, not as a belief in an absolutist ideology.*

Dr. L: That's very unrealistic. Creationists and evolutionists have the same evidence, but we draw different conclusions from it due to our different worldviews. Evolutionism is driven by secular ideology — usually naturalism/materialism. Consider this statement by (evolutionist) Richard Lewontin:

> We take the side of science in spite of the patent absurdity of some of its constructs, in spite of its failure to fulfill many of its extravagant promises of health and

life, in spite of the tolerance of the scientific community for unsubstantiated just-so stories, because we have a prior commitment, a commitment to materialism.

It is not that the methods and institutions of science somehow compel us to accept a material explanation of the phenomenal world, but, on the contrary, that we are forced by our *a priori* adherence to material causes to create an apparatus of investigation and a set of concepts that produce material explanations, no matter how counter-intuitive, no matter how mystifying to the uninitiated. Moreover, that materialism is an absolute, for we cannot allow a Divine Foot in the door. [8]

Does this quote sound like conclusions reached by unbiased objective analysis of evidence, or is it more indicative of "an absolutist ideology" (materialism in this case)? *Everyone* has a worldview through which they interpret evidence. However, not everyone is aware of his or her own worldview.

J: *Lisle shouldn't try to speak for other scientists or evolutionists. He is so biased in his literal creationist mindset that it clouds his ability to talk about the subject objectively.*

Dr. L: Everyone is biased — everyone has a worldview. The question is: which bias/worldview is best? Which worldview can make sense of scientific reasoning, logical deduction, morality, and so on? The Christian worldview can account for science and technology since it can make sense of uniformity. Evolutionism cannot.

J: *You don't need to be a biblical creationist to accept the uniformity of nature or the value of science.*

Dr. L: That's not the argument. No one is arguing that evolutionists don't accept these things; they obviously do. I've simply pointed out that such things only make sense if the Christian worldview is *true*. Thus, evolutionists who accept uniformity and science are being irrational, since such beliefs are baseless within their own professed worldview. In the same way that children act upon beliefs they cannot justify (pulling the covers over their head to protect them from the monster in the closet), so evolutionists act on beliefs they cannot justify.

J: *The actual study of nature itself will do that.*

Dr. L: It won't. In order to study nature we must *presuppose* uniformity.

J: *If Dr. Lisle understood evolution at even a basic level, he should know that while variation vie mutation is random, at least to the extent that natural laws allow, natural selection is not random at all.*

Dr. L: Neither mutations nor natural selection can account for human freedom and rationality. Rational analysis presupposes that human beings are capable of consciously considering alternatives and choosing the best. Rationality makes sense in the biblical worldview, but does not comport with the evolutionary notion that human beings are merely the result of mutations and natural selection.

Though we've written on this a number of times, it's also worth repeating that neither natural selection nor mutations can generate the vast quantities of brand new information in the genome required for evolution to be possible. [See www.answersingenesis.org for more information on these topics.]

J: *The Bible, while important and interesting, is not a scientific book.*

Dr. L: On this we agree. After all, science books are not infallible. They require updates as older ideas are discarded in favor of newer ideas. But God got the Bible exactly right the first time!

J: *Nothing within its pages suggests an understanding of the natural world beyond what would be understood by man at the time the various books were written,*

Dr. L: This is the fallacy of irrelevant thesis. The claim has no bearing on the argument (that the Bible provides the preconditions for science, and that evolution does not). Since God intended the Bible to be understandable to a wide range of cultures and eras, it's hardly surprising that it doesn't contain a detailed schematic for a nuclear reactor, or a derivation of the Schwarzschild metric!

Nonetheless, the Bible does contain some examples of knowledge that was ahead of the secular science of the day. Chapter 2 of *Taking Back Astronomy*[9] mentions a number of these. More important to our current topic, the Bible contains information that we couldn't possibly know any other way than by God's revelation — such as the fact that the future (in certain respects) will be like the past (Gen. 8:22). I realize that virtually everyone assumes that the future reflects the past. The argument is that only the Christian has rational justification for this conviction.

J: . . . *including ideas that are just plain wrong by today's scientific understanding.*

Dr. L: This begs the question. We could equally well say that a number of modern ideas are just plain wrong based on what the Bible teaches.

Notice that J.'s main concerns are already answered in the article he is criticizing. In the section entitled "How Would an Evolutionist Respond?" we see the refutation of the ideas that uniformity can be inferred from past experience, or that uniformity is just a property of the universe itself. In the section sub-titled "Can Evolutionists Do Science?" we see the explanation of why evolutionists can do science despite their professed worldview.

21. A counter-response?

Most of the time, when I answer such e-mails, I never hear again from the critic. But J. (from the above letter) attempted a counter-response. Unfortunately, his letter was extremely long and not terribly relevant; too long to include here. But I thought it might be interesting to summarize the highlights: J. began by arguing that the more people persuaded by an argument, the more likely it is to be true (this is a faulty appeal to the majority). This view of epistemology is actually self-refuting: most people do not have J.'s view; thus he should not have much confidence in it by his own reasoning.

J. attempted a straw-man argument, claiming that I was attacking evolution by attacking those who believe in it. J. indicated that my argument was based on circular reasoning — assuming the Bible is true because it says it is. This shows that J. does not understand the nature of an ultimate standard, nor my argument (that the Bible must be true because without it we would have no basis for uniformity or any of the preconditions) — which is certainly not a vicious circle. J. argued that we don't need the Bible for uniformity because even plants grow in a uniform way. (Of course, they do this only because God sustains them in a uniform way.) So J.'s argument is utterly irrelevant (the fallacy of irrelevant thesis).

J. claimed that we can know nature apart from the biblical God. But he gave no reason as to how we can trust our senses, or the uniformity of nature. Like other evolutionists, he simply took these things for granted. It was an arbitrary, mere opinion. J. claimed, "Evolution is a fact by its scientific definition." But of course this is nothing more than the fallacy of begging the question. He argued that if the Bible were true, then really everyone ought to believe it. But the Bible says we have a sin nature, a tendency to rebel against our Creator.

There were a few other minor points, too, but the above is the essence of J.'s "rebuttal." But notice something about his counter-response: it is utterly irrelevant to the issue at hand. My argument was that apart from the Bible we would have no basis for believing that the future should reflect the past, and thus no foundation for science and technology. Therefore, J. should have attempted to show that we can indeed know that the future will be like the past apart from the Bible. But instead, his entire response was simply an example of the fallacy of *irrelevant thesis*.

This is actually pretty common. Evolutionists cannot answer the hard questions, and so they are always trying to change the subject. Don't let them. Of course, I could have responded to J.'s argument with a point-by-point rebuttal, showing all the fallacies and false assumptions. But when the evolutionist has strayed from the topic, it is often better simply to point out that they are not answering the question that has been asked. I decided to politely force J. to deal with the actual argument, and stop sidestepping the issue. Here is the actual response I sent to J:

Response:

Dear J.,

Thank you for your response. I respectfully suggest, however, that you still have not understood the argument that has been made, and thus you have not really rebutted anything. Let me put the argument in a very simple form and hopefully this will make things clear:

(1) A rational person must have *justification* for what he believes and acts upon; he has a *reason*. (In logic, no one is allowed to be arbitrary.)

(2) Only the Christian worldview provides a *reason* to believe that the future will be like the past. Only the Christian has justification for the uniformity of nature upon which all science depends.

(3) Therefore, when non-Christians do science, they are being irrational, since they are believing in something (uniformity) for which they have no justification.

Is this clear now? When non-Christians do science, they are assuming that the future will be like the past without having any logical justification for this principle. Thus, they are being irrational. The fact that non-Christians are able to do science is not in question. Clearly non-Christians do believe in uniformity and act upon it. But since they have no reason for it within their own professed worldview, they are being arbitrary — not rational. Children behave this way; they pull their bed sheets over their head because they believe there is a monster in the closet. But since they have no basis for their belief, they are being irrational.

I welcome challenges to my arguments and would like to help guide you in constructing one. Since my conclusion follows validly from the premises, any attempted refutation must challenge the truth of one or both of the premises. You must either argue that (1) it is perfectly rational to be arbitrary — to believe things with no logical reason whatsoever, or (2) that there is at least one self-consistent non-Christian worldview that has a basis for the future being like the past. I suggest you try to refute number 2. I don't think you will be able to (the philosopher David Hume was reduced to utter skepticism on this very issue), but I think the attempt would be a valuable exercise. Any response that does not include this has missed the point and is thus no refutation at all.

I hope this helps.

— Dr. L.

Pay special attention to the last sentence of my closing paragraph. With this sentence, I am attempting to force J. to actually deal with the argument itself, and not simply sidestep it again. I'm attempting to prevent him from doing what he did last time — simply writing a lengthy but irrelevant diatribe. I never heard back from J.

Endnotes

1. http://www.answersingenesis.org/articles/aid/v2/n1/atheism-irrational.
2. See appendix A for more information on various compromised views of Scripture.
3. Jason Lisle, *Taking Back Astronomy* (Green Forest, AR: Master Books, 2007).
4. We again remind the reader that uniformity should not be confused with uniformitarianism. The latter insists that present processes and rates are representative of past processes and rates — a constancy of conditions. Uniformity does not require any constancy of conditions; it is simply the idea that *if* conditions are the same, the same result will occur. See chapter 9 for elaboration on this concept.
5. If the conditions are the same, the same result happens. This is due to the fact that God (who is beyond time) has chosen to uphold the universe in a consistent fashion.
6. See chapter 8.
7. See chapter 9.
8. Richard Lewontin, "Billions and Billions of Demons, *The New York Review* (January 9, 1997): p. 31.
9. Lisle, *Taking Back Astronomy.*

INDEX

A Comprehensive Guide
to the Heavens

"This book is meant to be an introduction only — a starting point to a biblical view of the universe. . . . Who knows what amazing truths are waiting to be discovered if only the shackles of secular thinking are removed. Now is the time of discovery. . . ."

7 x 9 • Hardcover
128 pages • $16.99
Full color interior
ISBN: 978-089051-471-9

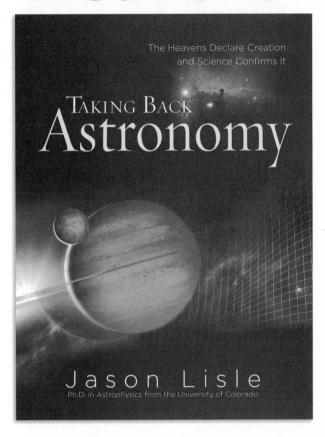

The Heavens Declare Creation
and Science Confirms It

TAKING BACK
Astronomy

JASON LISLE
Ph.D. in Astrophysics from the University of Colorado

With a doctorate in astrophysics from the University of Colorado, Dr. Jason Lisle is your guide to the universe beyond our world in this remarkable book.

Taking Back Astronomy is filled with facts that challenge secular theories and models of the universe — how it began and how it continues to amaze the scientific community. This book explores numerous evidences that point to a young universe: magnetic poles of planets, the spiral shape of galaxies, comets, and more. It explains the scale and size of the universe — something that is hard for our minds to imagine. With over 50 color photos of rarely seen stars, nebulas, and galaxies, Dr. Lisle guides you out among the stars to experience the awesome power of God's vast creation.

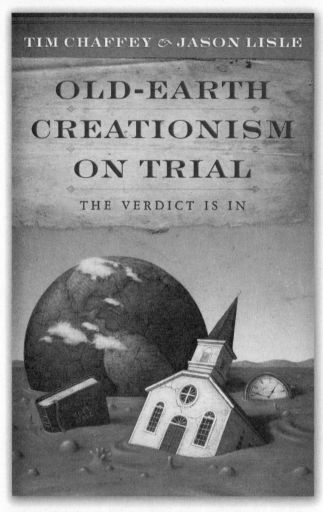